Clusters and Sustainable Regional Development

Clusters and Sustainable Regional Development conceptualises the role of managed or organised clusters in the transition towards sustainability. It introduces a novel perspective on these clusters, viewing them as deliberate collective actors within their environments that can become the driving force for transformation in their regions or nations.

The book draws upon the meta-organisational perspective in cluster studies, in contrast to traditional approaches. This view suggests that clusters are not merely territories or geographical areas, but organised entities. As such, they are defined as territorially anchored groups of independent organisations engaging in joint decision-making, pursuing system-level goals and capable of purposive collective action.

This text introduces a new set of ideas and questions at the intersection of economic geography, regional and cluster studies, organisation and management, and policy and governance research and will appeal to researchers from these diverse fields to address and further develop the meta-organisational view of clusters.

This book will also be a useful guide for policymakers who have an interest in the dynamics of economic development.

Evgeniya Lupova-Henry is Lecturer in Creative Business at the University of Applied Sciences Utrecht, the Netherlands. She holds a PhD in Management from the University of Neuchâtel in Switzerland. In her research, she explores topics at the intersection of management, organisation, and innovation studies with a particular focus on 'non-traditional' forms of organisations such as meta-organisations.

Nicola Francesco Dotti, independent scholar, Brussels, Belgium, was Senior Researcher in Regional Economics and Policy Studies at the Vrije Universiteit Brussel (VUB). Among his main research interests are knowledge for policymaking, science policy, and the EU Cohesion Policy. In 2021, he moved to Science Europe as Senior Policy Officer working on the Green and Digital Transitions.

Routledge Advances in Regional Economics, Science and Policy

Defining the Urban and Rural
Valentina Cattivelli

Designing Smart and Resilient Cities for a Post-Pandemic World
Metropandemic Revolution
Anthony Larsson and Andreas Hatzigeorgiou

Political Geography of Cities and Regions
Changing Legitimacy and Identity
Kees Terlouw

The Economic Geography of the Car Market
The Automobile Revolution in an Emerging Economy
Edited by Bartłomiej Kołsut and Tadeusz Stryjakiewicz

Worker Mobility and Urban Policy in Latin America
Policy Interactions and Urban Outcomes in Mexico City
David López-García

Cities Learning from a Pandemic
Towards Preparedness
Edited by Simonetta Armondi, Alessandro Balducci, Martina Bovo and Beatrice Galimberti

Urban Change in Central Europe
The Case of Kraków
Jacek Purchla

Clusters and Sustainable Regional Development
A Meta-Organisational Approach
Edited by Evgeniya Lupova-Henry and Nicola Francesco Dotti

The Economics of Affordable Housing
Alexander Styhre

For more information about this series, please visit: https://www.routledge.com/Routledge-Advances-in-Regional-Economics-Science-and-Policy/book-series/RAIRESP

Clusters and Sustainable Regional Development

A Meta-Organisational Approach

Edited by

Evgeniya Lupova-Henry and Nicola Francesco Dotti

Routledge
Taylor & Francis Group
LONDON AND NEW YORK

First published 2023
by Routledge
4 Park Square, Milton Park, Abingdon, Oxon OX14 4RN

and by Routledge
605 Third Avenue, New York, NY 10158

Routledge is an imprint of the Taylor & Francis Group, an informa business

British Library Cataloguing-in-Publication Data
A catalogue record for this book is available from the British Library

ISBN: 978-1-032-10383-9 (hbk)
ISBN: 978-1-032-10385-3 (pbk)
ISBN: 978-1-003-21506-6 (ebk)

DOI: 10.4324/9781003215066

Typeset in Bembo
by Apex CoVantage, LLC

For peace. Everywhere, always.

Contents

Figures

Tables

Foreword

The research presented in this volume is a valuable contribution to filling one of the most neglected areas of the social sciences: the understanding and knowledge of relations between and among organisations. There are many theories about society, but in no general social theory, neither organisations nor relations between them have any prominent place. There is talk of social systems and social structures or of such things as institutions and networks, but none of these seem to be connected to organisations. At the same time, most organisational theorists seem to be content with the fact that their study objects are assumed to have little significance for what happens in society and how it changes; they accept their hidden position and talk about how society affects organisations but not the other way around.

Organisational theory has been about what happens inside organisations, while what happens outside is perceived as something essentially separate and described with other concepts such as markets, politics, or civil society. And different kinds of collaborations between organisations are, according to this approach, not regarded as organised but things like partnerships or alliances.

The object of study in this book is clusters. They are traditionally in social science research regarded as spontaneous geographical agglomerations of firms and networks. But all the case studies in this volume clearly demonstrate how clusters can act as organised collective actors and cannot be understood as merely spontaneous agglomerations of firms. They are organised entities with attributes of formal organisations such as membership and rules; they are meta-organisations that may have agency and competencies to deliberately affect and change their environments.

In the case studies, variations in the internal dynamics of clusters as meta-organisations are investigated, and how agency is constructed through different forms of decision-making. Some key factors determining cluster agency are distinguished, such as legitimacy, levels of organisationality as well as their ability to mobilise visions and discourses for their members.

The case studies also illuminate how the agency of clusters can contribute to social change, not least in terms of a sustainability transition.

There is organisation outside organisations. This applies not only to the insight that the environment of organisations consists of organisations but also that organisations organise and make decisions for other organisations. The studies in this book clearly support the intuition that organisations are not actors completely exposed to pressure from their environments and controlled by institutions, but that organisations together can set rules for their own activities; they do not just create organisation, they simultaneously create society. Social change must be understood by looking at how organisations change and not the other way around. Organisation takes place through decisions for others and for the future. In decision-making processes, alternatives are formulated, and the future is not given. When we realise that organisation, to a large extent, is the stuff that society is made of, research on organisations and the relationships between them becomes increasingly important. Gaining knowledge about the conditions that enable organisation of organisations is one of the most urgent social science research tasks in the world today, and this book is a significant contribution towards this aim.

Göran Ahrne,
Professor Emeritus,
Stockholm University

Preface

The work on this book started in Spring 2020 when the first wave of the COVID-19 pandemic hit most countries, and we experienced lockdowns and isolation for the first time. It had its ups and downs as the pandemic has continuously disrupted our professional and personal plans. Nothing was certain, and our work's end sometimes seemed all too far and almost unachievable. We are finishing our work in Spring 2022 when the Russia – Ukraine crisis has been shuttering the world and directly affecting some of us. We have persisted throughout these challenges, and we believe that now, maybe more than ever, collaboration and joint action are necessary if we are to leave a liveable planet to our children.

This volume is the result of a fortunate meeting back in January 2017. We came from different countries, disciplines, and backgrounds but found a common interest in clusters and sustainability when we first met in Brussels. This joint reflection, carried out across time and space, has led to this book, bringing together many scholars sharing the interest in clusters as meta-organisations.

Previously, we analysed the role of governance in sustainable innovation (Lupova-Henry and Dotti, 2019) and conceptualised cluster development through an evolutionary framework (Dotti and Lupova-Henry, 2020). The present volume aims to provide a more comprehensive reflection on the role of clusters in sustainability transitions involving a broad range of scholars across Europe and beyond.

When researching the role of governance in sustainable innovation, we realised that state-driven approaches or market-based solutions might be too simplistic and insufficient for such an ambitious goal that requires the integration of environmental, social, economic, political, and cultural aspects. On the other hand, place-based approaches may naturally lend themselves to multi-disciplinarity. However, clusters – an essential tool for place-based innovation policies – are poorly adapted to cross-sectoral approaches being built on the premise of industrial specialisation. Thus, this volume was conceived based on the hypothesis that the meta-organisational approach can help combine all the relevant elements to conceptualise the role of clusters in sustainability transitions. The contributions to this volume thus sought to explore this assumption scientifically and argue for a new conceptualisation of clusters and their role in regional sustainability transitions supporting decision-makers engaged in such a crucial challenge for our societies.

This volume combines theoretical reflections and empirical analyses to provide insights and direction for scholars and policymakers who want to facilitate sustainability transitions. We hope that the new conceptualisation of clusters proposed in this book can help readers question their own assumptions, discuss their practices, and reflect on their experiences to facilitate the transition towards more sustainable development.

Acknowledgements

The editors are thankful to the publisher who supported the project during the difficult times of the COVID-19 pandemic. Special thanks go to all contributors to the volume for their efforts and contributions.

Our thoughts and gratitude go to Professor Bruno Dente, an inspiring master, who passed away while this book was being finalised.

Most importantly, we are grateful to our partners, children, and families who supported us in this adventure. Behind these pages, there are our daily lives, navigating through difficult times, and there is our willingness to contribute to solving the challenges we are facing collectively with the little we can do.

Contributors

BEAUCOURT Christel, LUMEN, University of Lille, France

Professor and Researcher in Human Resources and Innovation Management at IAE Lille (University of Lille – LUMEN Lab), her research themes are collective action dynamics, health at work, and management of social and health companies.

BERKOWITZ Héloïse, CNRS, LEST, Aix Marseille University, France

Héloïse Berkowitz works at CNRS (LEST, Aix Marseille University). Her research deals with transitions to sustainability, with a focus on collective action among organisations (meta-organisations) in various empirical settings from crowdfunding to oceans. She is coeditor-in-chief of *M@n@gement*, the first free and open access journal in management.

BOR Sanne, LUT-University, Finland

Sanne Bor is Postdoctoral Researcher and Project Manager at LUT-University, involved in a large multidisciplinary research project Package Heroes (2019–2023). Her current research focuses on topics related to collaboration among organisations, including meta-organisations, self-steering, horizontal organising, and collective decision-making in the context of sustainability transitions and environmental conflict.

CALAVITA Nico, San Diego State University, USA

Prof Nico Calavita is Emeritus Professor at San Diego State University with a key expertise in City Planning and is a recipient of the Marilyn J. Gittell Activist Scholar Award, sponsored by the Urban Affairs Association and SAGE Publishing.

CAPPELLANO Francesco, University of Eastern Finland

Dr Cappellano is Researcher at UEF, conducting research in North America and Europe in the field of Economic Geography with an interest in innovation-led transformative challenge-oriented policies. He has been publishing extensively on innovation systems with a spatial focus on border regions.

CHAUDHURY Abrar, Said Business School – University of Oxford, UK

Abrar Chaudhury is Research Fellow and British Academy Postdoctoral Fellow at Oxford Said Business School and Green Templeton College on Global Environmental Change, Climate Finance, and Organisational Purpose. He is investigating climate funding, such as the Green Climate Fund, and emerging technologies shaping climate actions in emerging economies.

DOBUSCH Leonhard, University of Innsbruck, Austria

Leonhard Dobusch is Professor of Business Administration specialised on organisation at the Innsbruck University, Austria. His main research interests include organisational openness and private regulation via standards. He is Cofounder and Academic Director of the Momentum Institute in Vienna and member of the ZDF television council and blogs at netzpolitik.org.

DOTTI Nicola Francesco, Independent Scholar, Brussels, Belgium.

He was Senior Researcher in Regional Economics and Policy Studies at the Vrije Universiteit Brussel (VUB). Among his main research interests are knowledge for policymaking, science policy, and the EU Cohesion Policy. In 2021, he moved to Science Europe as Senior Policy Officer working on the Green and Digital Transitions.

DUPRAT Lola, CNRS, LEST, Université Aix-Marseille, France

Lola Duprat, PhD, is Associate Researcher at LEST (Economics and Sociology of Labour Laboratory), specialised in Organisational Creativity. Her two lines of research include creativity management, creative organisations and environments, as well as inter-firm organisation forms (meta-organisations, clusters, cultural wastelands).

GADILLE Martine, CNRS, LEST, Université Aix-Marseille, France

Martine Gadille works at the CNRS (LEST, Aix Marseille University). Her research focuses on the theorisation of the role of meta-organisations and industrial clusters in regional economic development as well as on the actor–network theory to understand the transformation of actors' professionalities through the localised dynamics of technological innovation.

GEBHARDT Christiane, Drees & Sommer SE Switzerland

Dr Christiane Gebhardt holds a Master's degree in Public Administration from University of Konstanz and a PhD in Political Sciences from University of Giessen. The focus of her research and work is strategy, organisational development, and management of complex projects and stakeholder-driven innovation. She currently heads the regional division of Urban Integrated Solutions at Drees & Sommer in Switzerland.

ISMAGULOVA Saule, HSE University, Institute for Statistical Studies and Economics of Knowledge (ISSEK HSE), Russia

Saule Ismagulova works as Expert at Russian Cluster Observatory ISSEK HSE. Her main research interests include technological and creative urban development and cross-regional collaboration in the innovative sphere.

IVANOVA Ekaterina, HSE University, Faculty of Management (Nizhny Novgorod) and Institute for Statistical Studies and Economics of Knowledge (ISSEK HSE), Russia

Ekaterina Ivanova (PhD) is Associate Professor at Faculty of Management and Research Fellow at Russian Cluster Observatory ISSEK HSE. She conducts research and provides consultancy in cluster policy and internationalisation, smart specialisation, and living laboratories.

KUTSENKO Evgeniy, HSE University, Institute for Statistical Studies and Economics of Knowledge (ISSEK HSE), Russia

Evgeniy Kutsenko (PhD) is Head of Russian Cluster Observatory ISSEK HSE and Member of TCI Network Board of Directors. He has authored contributions on cluster policy, measuring and evaluating innovations in regions and cities, and developing creative industries.

LECOCQ Xavier, LUMEN, University of Lille, France

Professor in Strategic Management at IAE Lille (University of Lille – LUMEN Lab), his research themes include business models and collaborative forms of organisation, such as networks, open-source communities, and meta-organisations.

LUPOVA-HENRY Evgeniya, University of Applied Sciences Utrecht, the Netherlands

Evgeniya is Lecturer in Creative Business at the University of Applied Sciences Utrecht. She holds a PhD in Management from the University of Neuchâtel in Switzerland. In her research, she explores topics at the intersection of management, organisation, and innovation studies with a particular focus on 'non-traditional' forms of organisations such as meta-organisations.

NADEGGER Monica, University of Innsbruck, Austria

Monica Nadegger is PhD student at the University of Innsbruck (Department for Organisation & Learning) and the MCI – The Entrepreneurial School (Department for Tourism & Leisure Business). Her research focuses on materiality and communication in new forms of organising.

Her recent work has been published in the *Journal of Sustainable Tourism*.

O'SHEA Greg, LUT University, Finland, Mikkeli and Aalto University, Finland

Greg O'Shea is Researcher at LUT University and Executive-in-Residence at Aalto University, School of Business. He is currently also working on the Package Heroes project with Sanne Bor. His current research is around sustainability focused and regional entrepreneurial ecosystems and sustainability transitions.

SANIOSSIAN Jennifer, LUMEN, University of Lille, France

Jennifer has a PhD in Management and is currently Teacher and Researcher in Strategic Management and Organisations at IAE Lille (University of Lille – LUMEN Lab). Her research themes are based on collective and multi-stakeholder actions, meta-organisations, and collective and territorial actions for social and solidarity.

STECCA DOUEK Carolina, Lemann Fellow, Said Business School – University of Oxford, UK

Carolina Stecca Douek is Development Finance Professional and Research Associate at Said Business School. Previously, she was Analyst at the International Finance Corporation. She is currently working on the intersection of technology, policy, and finance to understand innovative ways of promoting coordination towards the Sustainable Development Goals.

VIACHKA Assia, Stockholm School of Economics, Sweden

Assia is PhD Candidate at the Department of Marketing and Strategy, Stockholm School of Economics. Her research considers issues in business strategy, economic geography, and economic psychology, connecting these subject areas to unifying themes and ideas. Assia's primary interests include inter-firm collaboration, competitiveness, innovation, business clusters, and regional development.

Introduction

Evgeniya LUPOVA-HENRY and
Nicola Francesco DOTTI

Objective

This volume develops a meta-organisational perspective on clusters, conceptualising them as drivers of sustainable development. Recent research has increasingly recognised the role of multi-actor approaches in solving today's societal and environmental challenges, enabling the transition towards more sustainable development (Lupova-Henry & Dotti, 2019). This volume sees clusters both as multi-actor settings and as collective agents capable of driving large-scale societal changes.

For a long time, ambiguity has existed in the theorisation of clusters: on the one hand, these have been seen as spontaneous geographical agglomerations of firms, while on the other, these have been conceptualised as 'organised' networks fostering regional economic competitiveness. Indeed, research initially was interested in uncovering the benefits provided by spatial agglomeration of firms, such as access to markets, better coordination with suppliers, common labour pools, improved innovation dynamics (Cooke et al., 1997; Doloreux & Porto Gomez, 2017; Moulaert & Sekia, 2003) as well as other elements 'in the air' (cf. Marshall, 1890). However, later, building on this evidence, clusters have been formalised and organised to purposefully promote these economic advantages, as proposed by Michael Porter (1990). This evolution resulted in clusters being seen simultaneously as spontaneous geographical agglomerations (Boschma & Frenken, 2009) and policy-driven organisations of networked firms fostering regional competitiveness (Baptista & Swann, 1998). Recently, the growing environmental concerns have been calling for urgent interventions, (re-)orienting regional economic development paths towards sustainable development, thus adding an extra layer of complexity to how clusters are, or should, be conceptualised (Tödtling & Trippl, 2018).

The meta-organisational approach embraces this dualism and allows to see clusters simultaneously as geographical agglomerations of firms and 'organised' collective actors leading to regional economic development. Specifically, the meta-organisational view suggests that an 'organised' cluster can be(come) a collective actor, coordinating joint actions of geographically agglomerated firms to (re-)shape its environment. Indeed, due to the collective power clusters wield,

DOI: 10.4324/9781003215066-1

the consequences of their collective actions for the regional economy can be more significant than those of individual companies. We assume that the meta-organisational approach allows to view 'organised' clusters as deliberate actors, holding them responsible for their action or non-action vis-à-vis the social and environmental challenges. This approach aims to make clusters more conscious of their choices, empowering them to become the drivers of collective change for sustainable regional development. At the same time, the meta-organisational perspective on clusters brings about a new set of questions at the intersection of the organisation and management fields, policy and governance research, economic geography, and regional and cluster studies. This volume aims to answer some of these questions and provide a novel way of looking at clusters and their role in sustainability transitions.

Structure

The volume is structured in four parts articulated in 13 chapters written by an international multidisciplinary collective of scholars. Part 1 lays out the theoretical foundations of clusters as meta-organisations combining organisation studies, evolutionary economic geography, and management. Chapters in Part 1 are mainly theoretical, with some empirical references to guide the reader towards the following parts, which are fundamentally empirical. In Part 2, four case studies 'zoom into' the internal dynamics of 'organised' clusters and discuss the role of meta-organising in cluster members' transitions towards sustainability. Part 3 presents a broader perspective, 'zooming out' to discuss the dynamic interactions between 'meta-organised clusters' and 'clustered meta-organisations' and their contexts. The final part, containing Chapter 13, summarises the main lessons learnt and key messages of this volume.

Part 1: the theoretical foundations of clusters as meta-organisations

In Chapter 1, Lupova-Henry and Dotti, as editors of the volume, conceptualise 'organised' clusters as collective actors and agents of change. Adopting the meta-organisational lens, this chapter sets the theoretical framework for understanding clusters' role in creating new paths towards sustainable regional economic development. It discusses the determinants of cluster agency, such as legitimacy, organisationality, decisionality, visions, and discourses. It also builds upon the evolutionary perspective and its fundamental concept of the 'survival of the fittest', discussing the importance of clusters' embeddedness in their ecosystems. It concludes by suggesting a dual role for clusters in new sustainable path development: as 'protective spaces' for sustainable innovations and as system-level actors capable of influencing their external environments. This theoretical framework provides links to the following chapters in the volume.

Berkowitz and Bor explore the variations in organisational structures of clusters seen as meta-organisations. Specifically, Chapter 2 proposes that such clusters may show variations in their degrees of organisationality and decisionality. The degree of structural organisationality is discussed along the dimensions of membership, hierarchy, rules, monitoring, and sanctioning. The degree of decisionality reflects the extent to which each of these organisational components is itself the object of decisions. Combining organisationality and decisionality, the authors identify four profiles of meta-organisations: thin partial meta-organisation, thin meta-organisation, thick partial meta-organisation, and thick meta-organisation. This theoretical contribution is supported by some empirical evidence exemplifying the role of clusters as social actors. The chapter provides a deeper understanding of the internal dynamics of meta-organisations and brings insight into the influence of organisationality and decisionality on clusters' collective agency.

Gebhardt discusses the challenges of governance of regional innovation clusters based on the experience of the German innovation cluster 'Physics for Food'. The chapter aims to contribute to the theoretical debate regarding the governance methods in regional innovation support programmes through this empirical case. It does so by bringing together organisation sciences and regional innovation studies. While place-based policies are expected to facilitate the transformation of regional economic development paths, their governance is often under-investigated. Chapter 3 argues for focusing on organisational components of governance, seeing clusters as meta-organisations for regional economic transformation and organisational sustainability.

In Chapter 4, Berkowitz and Gadille introduce the notion of 'responsible actorhood' to complete the theoretical framework on clusters as meta-organisations for sustainable development. Specifically, they discuss how to organise clusters as agents of transformative change, actively contributing to sustainable development. Looking at organised clusters through the meta-organisational lens, they suggest that some of the challenges clusters face in achieving transformative outcomes are their lack of answerability, their path dependency towards growth, and labour resistance to change. The concept of 'responsible actorhood' elaborated on in this chapter aims to address these challenges. Finally, this chapter completes the theoretical foundations of clusters as meta-organisations with policy implications.

Part 2: internal dynamics of clusters as meta-organisations

Viachka and Duprat present the case of La Friche la Belle de Mai in Marseille, France, discussing the role of meta-organising in the cultural field and its ability to address social sustainability issues. They analyse an empirical case of a community in the artistic and cultural sector located in a former urban wasteland. The case presented in Chapter 5 is an example of how meta-organisations establish their modus operandi, holding together a community seeking collaboration and trust instead of competition. Social and cognitive similarities allow the community to develop a strong shared identity, facilitating collective action. The combination of spatial localisation and an open organisation, able to welcome members and non-members, is a crucial element for the success of this meta-organisation. The chapter suggests that meta-organising could be a valuable strategy for supporting social sustainability by creating organised and territorially anchored cluster communities.

Saniossian, Beaucourt, and Lecocq examine meta-organisations as a cooperative form managed by members that remain independent. Multi-stakeholder meta-organisations analysed in Chapter 6 are a specific type of meta-organisation able to answer territorial social sustainability challenges. The meta-organisational lens is adopted to investigate the case of France's territorial poles for economic cooperation established in 2002. The specific processes adopted by this multi-stakeholder meta-organisation are presented and discussed in this chapter, focusing on the integration of activities, negotiation of common goals, and use of external communication to mobilise, engage, and involve a variety of stakeholders as members. The study suggests that the meta-organisational approach to clusters helps broaden the scope of actors involved, stepping away from a traditional understanding of an 'industrially specialised' cluster. This approach can be particularly relevant for addressing the issues of social sustainability that encompass a range of sectors and require collective action.

Cappellano and Calavita explore the transitions to clean technologies in North American clusters. Focusing on the United States and Canada, Chapter 7 discusses the role of cluster secretariats in orienting cluster members towards adopting clean technologies. In particular, the chapter focused on how they do it and why cluster members engage with greener technologies. Furthermore, the authors discussed the role of the policy landscape in North America and its influence on cluster orientation towards clean technologies. The key findings point to improving local labour conditions and helping businesses' reputations as some of the key motivations for a transition to clean technologies in North American clusters.

In Chapter 8, Viachka discusses the relationships between clustering and meta-organising in the context of 'clean technologies'. The so-called 'cleantechs' have potential for advancing sustainability transitions by developing products and services with low environmental impact. While cleantech actors tend to organise in clusters, which are believed to be able to drive regional transformations for sustainability, how these are organised and what role geographical proximity plays in such clusters are not yet well understood. This chapter analyses 34 cleantech clusters in Europe to investigate how the cluster concept is used in mobilising organisations to collectively seek a path to a greener economy. The chapter suggests that the studied cleantech clusters display the characteristics of meta-organisations, at the same time using the cluster concept to create an organisational space which is as much geographic as it is abstract, constructed of the different social, institutional, and cultural dimensions constraining and orienting economic action.

Part 3: clusters as meta-organisations in a broader context

Bor and O'Shea expand our understanding of the roles of clusters and meta-organisations in sustainability transitions. They suggest that these may range from roles focusing on harmonising internal relationships and protecting members from external pressures to change facilitation roles that aim to reshape the external environment. Chapter 9 also brings a different perspective on the relationships between the concepts of clusters and meta-organisations. Focusing on the food packaging industry in Finland, the authors see it as a cluster in its traditional sense – a geographic agglomeration of organisations – comprising multiple overlapping meta-organisations. This case shows that if clusters are not organised in a single meta-organisation, they may have limited ability to facilitate transitions at the industry level. The chapter concludes by arguing that the meta-organisational lenses might help solve this missed opportunity for sustainable development in an industry known for its environmental impacts.

Nadegger and Dobusch present the case of Alpine Pearls, a meta-organisation promoting green mobility and sustainable travel in Alpine regions and comprising several geographically dispersed tourism clusters. The tourism industry needs urgent changes to its business models to transition towards more sustainable development. However, tourism destinations, seen as geographical clusters, often lack the mechanisms and formal structures that would allow channelling collective action towards common goals. Chapter 10 demonstrates the dichotomy between internal, coopetitive dynamics within clusters and inter-cluster dynamics within the meta-organisational setting. This case shows how the Alpine Pearls as a meta-organisation fosters collective action among disjointed geographical clusters lacking internal organisation by adding an overarching goal to the localised ties. The chapter suggests that the meta-organisational framework can foster collective action and innovation through reflexivity, accountability, and responsiveness to grand challenges.

Kutsenko, Ismagulova, and Ivanova analyse the Moscow Innovation Cluster (MIC), explaining its rationale and evolution in the context of a large metropolitan area. The authors propose a framework of 'urban super-clusters' comprising smaller, more specialised clusters and other associational forms, single entities, and individuals that are locally anchored but not bound contractually. Chapter 11 thus analyses the MIC as an 'urban super-cluster' of a considerable size, which leverages digital technologies to bring together diverse actors from multiple industries. The chapter's findings show that the meta-organisational approach to designing urban clusters can allow leveraging some of the benefits of the urban settings while attenuating the adverse effects, such as congestion and increased transaction costs. However, while digitalisation allows for the involvement and engagement of a large number of members, it also weakens its members' mobilisation and commitment to sustainable-oriented transition.

Chaudhury and Stecca Douek widen the debate by looking at the Green Climate Fund (GCF) as a global meta-organisation comprising thematic, geographic, and strategic clusters. While the urgency of climate change has pushed many actors to work under a common umbrella, like the GCF, collective climate action is complex and requires significant coordination. At the same time, the ability of the meta-organisations to enable such coordination may be limited due to their loose structures and potentially competing interests of their constituent members. Chapter 12 proposes that these meta-organisational weaknesses can potentially be overcome by adding additional flexibility to the system. Member self-organisation into sub-clusters around their common goals and following their unique pathways can allow natural sub-networks to emerge. The chapter coins the 'cluster pathways' concept to reflect this differentiated approach. This latter may allow meta-organisational actors to build networks through interactions within and across clusters, thus opening the way to new sustainable development paths.

Conclusions

In the final part, Chapter 13, the editors summarise the main lessons learnt and identify new research avenues. First, the research presented in this volume shows that the conceptualisation of clusters as meta-organisations welcomes the ambiguity inherent to complex organisation forms. Indeed, 'organised' clusters are simultaneously networks of localised actors and organisations in their own right. The contributions to this volume demonstrate that the meta-organisational perspective on clusters allows embracing this ambiguity. They can provide niches or protective spaces for other organisations but can also act collectively to reshape their environment. Second, clusters are organisations of organisations embedded in their context. The contributions to this volume show that the relationships between clustering and meta-organising can vary significantly depending on the context clusters operate in and the goals they pursue. The meta-organisational perspective also allows incorporating this complexity inherent in multi-actor approaches to sustainability transitions. The perspectives presented in this volume invite the reader to move away from conceptualising clusters as 'simple' geographical agglomerations of firms towards seeing clusters as organised, deliberate collective actors that can drive sustainability transitions. Future research should develop a more comprehensive, large-scale analysis of how clusters as meta-organisations act worldwide to support policymakers engaged in the transition towards sustainable development.

References

Baptista, R., & Swann, P. (1998). Do firms in clusters innovate more? *Research Policy*, *27*(5), 525–540. https://doi.org/10.1016/S0048-7333(98)00065-1

Boschma, R., & Frenken, K. (2009). Some notes on institutions in evolutionary economic geography. *Economic Geography*, *85*(2), 151–158.

Cooke, P., Gomez Uranga, M., & Etxebarria, G. (1997). Regional innovation systems: Institutional and organisational dimensions. *Research Policy*, *26*(4–5), 475–491.

Doloreux, D., & Porto Gomez, I. (2017). A review of (almost) 20 years of regional innovation systems research. *European Planning Studies*, *25*(3), 371–387. https://doi.org/10.1080/09654313.2016.1244516

Lupova-Henry, E., & Dotti, N. F. (2019). Governance of sustainable innovation: Moving beyond the hierarchy-market-network trichotomy? A systematic literature review using the "who-how-what" framework. *Journal of Cleaner Production, 210*, 738–748. https://doi.org/10.1016/j.jclepro.2018.11.068

Marshall, A. (1890). *Principles of economics*. Macmillan and Co.

Moulaert, F., & Sekia, F. (2003). Territorial innovation models: A critical survey. *Regional Studies, 37*(3), 289–302. https://doi.org/10.1080/0034340032000065442

Porter, M. E. (1990). *The competitive advantage of nations*. Free Press.

Tödtling, F., & Trippl, M. (2018). Regional innovation policies for new path development: Beyond neo-liberal and traditional systemic views. *European Planning Studies, 26*(9), 1779–1795. https://doi.org/10.1080/09654313.2018.1457140

Part 1

The theoretical foundations of clusters as meta-organisations

1 Clusters as collective actors and agents of change for (new) sustainable path development

Evgeniya LUPOVA-HENRY and
Nicola Francesco DOTTI

Introduction

It is increasingly evident that technological innovation alone is not enough to tackle today's grand societal challenges, such as the climate crisis, growing social inequality, and the recent COVID-19 pandemic. Indeed, there is a growing realisation that a transition towards sustainability is necessary, and it should involve large-scale changes in socio-technical systems (cf. Köhler et al., 2019). The question is thus how we might collectively adopt new practices, co-create innovative solutions, and align the agendas of multiple stakeholders (Lupova-Henry & Dotti, 2019).

In this chapter, we theorise the role of clusters – geographic concentrations of organisations in a particular field (Porter, 1998a) – in addressing grand societal challenges and facilitating sustainability transitions. Previous research has recognised the importance of geographical clustering for promoting sustainable innovations due to the agglomeration economies (Hansen & Coenen, 2015). However, recent developments suggest that clusters may play a more significant role than previously believed. The conceptualisation of clusters has been evolving in the past decades from perspectives focusing on the benefits of spatial co-location to those emphasising 'immaterial' factors facilitating inter-firm interactions (Asheim et al., 2016; Moulaert & Sekia, 2003; Tödtling & Trippl, 2013). More recently, research into 'organised' clusters – that is formal organisations having features like membership and joint decision-making (Ahrne & Brunsson, 2005) – suggested that these can be seen as 'meta-organisations'. As such, they can act collectively to deliberately transform their environments, that is their regional economic ecosystems (Gadille et al., 2013; Lupova-Henry et al., 2021b; Viachka, 2013).

Several research streams – such as sustainability transitions (Loorbach et al., 2017), neo-institutional organisation theory (Battilana et al., 2009; Zietsma & Lawrence, 2010), and evolutionary economic geography (Hassink et al., 2019; Tödtling & Trippl, 2013) – have been looking at the role of geography and agency in transitioning towards sustainability (cf. Pflitsch, 2019). This literature has suggested that sustainability transitions are 'constituted spatially' as they are embedded in specific contexts (Hansen & Coenen, 2015) shaped by their

DOI: 10.4324/9781003215066-3

histories and evolving along specific 'paths' (Martin & Sunley, 2006). Finally, scholars have started to recognise the importance of organisational agency for institutionalising new development paths and de-institutionalising the existing ones to promote sustainability transitions (Strambach & Pflitsch, 2020).

This chapter proposes a three-step theoretical framework allowing to analyse clusters' role as drivers in sustainability transitions, building upon meta-organisational and the evolutionary frameworks. In what follows, we first discuss the evolution of the cluster concept from a 'geographic' to an organisational phenomenon. Second, we build upon the 'meta-organisational' view of clusters and discus the determinants of their capacity to drive sustainability transitions: legitimacy, organisationality and decisionality, and visions and discourses. We then propose an evolutionary perspective to frame the role of organised clusters in their regional ecosystems and elaborate on their dual role in driving regional development paths towards sustainability. This discussion provides a framework for the whole volume, including links to the other chapters where theoretical contributions and case studies are discussed.

Theoretical foundations of clusters as meta-organisations

In the conceptualisation of clusters, four fundamental phases can be distinguished based on the contributions of Marshall, the Italian Industrial Districts school, Porter, and, more recently, the transition-oriented perspective on clusters (Doloreux & Porto Gomez, 2017; Hassink et al., 2019; Iammarino, 2005; Moulaert & Sekia, 2003). The first conceptualisation comes from the early contributions of Alfred Marshall (1890). He proposed the well-known idea that firms benefit from 'something in the air', that is economic competitiveness of individual firms is affected (positively or negatively) by the place where they are located, not just by 'internal' firm features. This expression is often taken as the inception of regional economics, which identified two types of regional specialisation (Armstrong & Taylor, 2000; Capello, 2007; McCann, 2013). The first refers to firms clustering to facilitate intra-industrial interactions, the so-called Marshall–Arrow–Romer (MAR) specialisation. Specifically, firms benefit from being closer to their suppliers and consumers, facilitating interactions and informal exchanges. The alternative type is the 'Jacobsian specialisation' (cf. Florida et al., 2017): firms benefit also from being located close to other economic actors with whom they do not have direct economic interactions (see also Kemeny & Storper, 2015). Thus, regional economic literature has extensively demonstrated the importance of localisation for firms and their tendency to cluster.

The second conceptualisation has more heterogeneous origins coming from the Italian school of Industrial Districts (IID) (Brusco, 1986), developed mainly by Italian- and French-speaking scholars (Crevoisier & Camagni, 2000; Markusen, 1996; Storper, 1997; Trigilia, 1992). The notion of industrial districts is strongly related to Marshall's intuition but emphasises the social dimensions of economic competitiveness. Specifically, IIDs built their economic competitiveness on the social interactions among their members, the common cultural identity, and willingness to cooperate beyond market-like dynamics as the competition is mainly exogenous to the districts. These factors were first identified in small, spontaneous clusters of Italy's spatially concentrated and industrially specialised firms. However, the following literature found the same features characterising other types of economies across the world at various scales, including large metropolises (Camagni, 2004) and multi-specialised clusters (Katz & Wagner, 2014).

The third fundamental step is related to the works of Porter (1990, 1998a, 1998b), who adopted a more normative, policy-oriented approach. Specifically, Porter-like clusters acknowledge the benefits of firms' co-location and specialisation, arguing that public policy should proactively promote, support, and organise clusters. This approach became very popular, especially during the 1990s and 2000s, with many Porter-like cluster policies introduced worldwide (e.g. Cooke, 2012; Lundequist & Power, 2002). Compared to the IID, Porter's conceptualisation focuses less on the clusters' socio-economic and cultural dimensions, being more interested in the regional economic policy aspects (see also Pecquer, 2002). Another difference between the previous conceptualisations and the Porterian vision of clusters is that IID-like clusters were somewhat spontaneous, unplanned co-locations of firms, at least in their first versions. In contrast, Porter proposes to make them explicit, purposefully promoting and supporting them with public policy. However, Porter's approach is quite vague about clusters' scale that may range from local to national economies.

The fourth, most recent conceptualisation conceives clusters as being mechanisms orienting regional economic development. It also introduces the distinction between the clusters – as geographical concentrations of firms – and their governance (Gadille et al., 2013; Grillitsch & Trippl, 2016; Trippl & Otto, 2009). This perspective encompasses heterogeneous streams of thought on regional innovation policy and organisation studies. Whereas the previous approaches were particularly effective in explaining firms' clustering and 'regional innovation systems' (Asheim et al., 2016; Cooke et al., 1997), this stream of research moves the debate towards the role that clusters play in shaping regional economic development. This notion incorporates the fundamental dimension of time, showing how clusters shape the regional economic development paths (see also Hassink, 2005). The parallel developments from management and organisation studies suggest that clusters can be seen as organised entities endowed with the ability to act collectively upon their environments, at least in some cases (Duprat, 2020; Gadille et al., 2013; Lupova-Henry et al., 2021a). Compared to the previous conceptualisations, the focus is no longer on explaining firms' economic competitiveness but on their evolution and ability to deliberately (re-)shape regional development paths.

Building upon this latter stream of thought, this chapter focuses on 'organised' clusters, that is those having the attributes of formal organisations, such as membership, hierarchy, rules, monitoring, and sanction mechanisms (Ahrne & Brunsson, 2005, 2011). We conceptualise such clusters as being territorially anchored 'meta-organisations' or organisations of independent organisations deliberately engaging in joint decision-making and capable of collective action (Gadille et al., 2013; Lupova-Henry et al., 2021a). This approach suggests a more voluntarist perspective, where clusters are no longer seen as 'an incoherent agglomeration, but a coherent organisation' (Astley & Van de Ven, 1983, p. 258). Furthermore, this view of clusters suggests that these can be seen as 'actors' within their environments (King et al., 2010) and can deliberately 'construct' their actorhood (Lupova-Henry et al., 2021b). We, thus, propose that clusters (can) play an important role in sustainability transitions by taking deliberate action as meta-organisations.

Determinants of cluster agency in sustainability transitions

Research has increasingly recognised the importance of agency in shaping regional development paths (cf. Isaksen et al., 2019) and influencing sustainability transitions (Avelino & Wittmayer, 2016; Geels, 2020). This recognition calls for a better understanding of organised clusters as agents driving these processes, rather than 'geographical areas' being influenced by them. The meta-organisational perspective on clusters offers a suitable lens that can deepen our understanding of the effects of organised clustering on the regional contexts and their (re-)orientation towards sustainability.

Indeed, research adopting the 'meta-organisational' perspective suggests that organised clusters can take deliberate action and be recognised as addressable actors by the external audiences (cf. Berkowitz and Gadille, Chapter 4 in this volume). However, what types of actions clusters may take and to what extent they are perceived as deliberate actors may vary. We suggest that three key factors may determine cluster agency in sustainability transitions: their legitimacy (Garaudel, 2020; Human & Provan, 2000), the levels of organisationality and decisionality (cf. Lupova-Henry et al., 2021b), as well as their ability to leverage collective visions and discourses (cf. O'Dwyer et al., 2015).

First, cluster legitimacy is an essential element defining how clusters may engage in collective action, what strategies they implement, and which resources they leverage, as further discussed by Gebhardt in Chapter 3. Organisational legitimacy can be defined as 'the perceived appropriateness of an organisation to a social system in terms of rules, values, norms, and definitions' (Deephouse et al., 2017, p. 32). It is a nuanced concept as there is a two-way relationship between legitimacy and the access to or ownership of resources, experience, reputation, institutional positions, and connections with other influential actors, such as public authorities (Gulati et al., 2012; Human & Provan, 2000; Raven, Kern, Smith, et al., 2016). Indeed, the ability of organised clusters to act collectively may stem from their being in a position bridging the boundaries of multiple fields (Kostova et al., 2008; Zietsma & Lawrence, 2010). This position may be due to the presence of actors in clusters from various institutional fields, such as universities, industry, and government (cf. Etzkowitz, 2012).

At the same time, the need to navigate complex landscapes with multiple – and sometimes conflicting – stakeholders demands legitimacy. Research has shown that clusters intentionally build their internal and external legitimacy to be perceived as legitimate actors by cluster members (internally) and other economic or societal actors (externally) (Garaudel, 2020; Lupova-Henry et al., 2021b). Legitimacy-building may be even more important for the clusters' role in sustainability transitions since these may need to ensure the acceptance of new sustainable technologies or practices disrupting the existing institutions (cf. Gebhardt, Chapter 4 in this volume).

Second, in the meta-organisational context, organisationality (Dobusch & Schoeneborn, 2015) plays an essential role in shaping cluster agency together with decisionality, as discussed by Berkowitz and Bor's Chapter 2 in this volume. Cluster organisationality is defined as the extent to which the elements of formal organisations are present in a cluster (Dobusch & Schoeneborn, 2015; Lupova-Henry et al., 2021b). These elements involve interconnected decision-making instances regarding membership, hierarchy, rules, monitoring and sanctions, and collective identity (Ahrne & Brunsson, 2005; Lupova-Henry et al., 2021b). The way a cluster implements these elements will influence its ability to act and its recognition as an actor by the external audiences. Decisionality, in turn, refers to the degree to which each of these elements of formal organisations is an object of decision-making. The distinction between different degrees of clusters' organisationality and decisionality can shed light on and invite more nuanced discussions of cluster agency in sustainability transitions. For instance more organisationality and formalisation (e.g. through action plans, constitution and other formal rules) can bring about a higher capacity for agency (Garaudel, 2020) but, at the same time, may result in the 'concentration' of actorhood with a limited group within the cluster (Lupova-Henry et al., 2021b). This will then influence power relations within the cluster and affect its ability to engage in sustainability transitions (Avelino, 2017; Avelino & Wittmayer, 2016).

Finally, clusters' visions and discourses can enable its collective agency, especially in cases where fewer elements of formal organisations are present, as elaborated by Viachka and Duprat in Chapter 5 and Saniossian, Beaucourt, and Lecocq in Chapter 6 of this volume. Although the importance of the 'memory' of clusters has often been under-considered in the literature (cf. Dotti & Colombino, 2018), their agency is temporal. It depends on their mobilisation and interpretation of past events and forward-looking visions to formulate strategies and actions in the present (Garud et al., 2010). Clusters do have collective 'memory' and share lessons learnt with other actors, shaping their viewpoints and influencing their capacity to act (Dotti, 2018a; Moyson & Scholten, 2018). Discourses and visions are also crucial elements enabling new sustainable path development (Hassink et al., 2019; Späth & Rohracher, 2010). Indeed, visions can drive and strategically orient sustainability transitions as they motivate, coordinate, and empower the actions of a variety of stakeholders (Loorbach et al., 2017; Quist et al., 2011). This holds for clusters, where common visions around sustainability can help create governance mechanisms in the absence of hierarchical control, that is in conditions of lower degrees of organisationality and decisionality, as presented in Chapter 5 by Viachka and Duprat and in Chapter 10 by Nadegger and Dobusch.

To sum up, the meta-organisational perspective suggests that clusters may potentially be capable of collective action leading to sustainable transition, but this requires the factors discussed before: legitimacy, organisationality and decisionality, and visions and discourses. The following section will further conceptualise cluster agency for sustainability transitions within an evolutionary framework.

An evolutionary perspective on clusters as drivers of sustainability transitions

The previous discussion outlined how the notion of clusters has evolved and identified the determinants of their agency, namely legitimacy, organisationality and decisionality, and mobilisation of visions and discourses. However, for a deeper understanding of clusters' role in their regional economic ecosystems, we propose integrating the discussion on clusters as collective agents with the evolutionary framework (Geels, 2020; Hassink et al., 2019; Loorbach et al., 2017; Slembeck, 1997). Such an approach aims to conceptualise the role of clusters in (re-)shaping regional development paths.

From the evolutionary perspective, regional economic development is a process where cooperative or competitive actors interact with their environment, and the 'fittest ones' survive. Over time, these evolutionary dynamics shape the ecosystem, thus determining the regional development paths. This principle of the 'survival of the fittest ones' (Dotti & Colombino, 2018) should be unpacked around three fundamental dimensions: heterogeneity, selectivity, and preservation (Geels, 2002; Hall, 1993; Slembeck, 1997; Uyarra, 2010). These dimensions should be seen as general rules about how a regional ecosystem evolves. While an extensive literature elaborates on these three dimensions (Andersson & Karlsson, 2006; Asheim et al., 2011; Cooke et al., 1997; Grillitsch & Trippl, 2016); for our discussion, this evolutionary approach aims to explain the development of regional ecosystems and the role of clusters in this evolution. We suggest that from this perspective, clusters are at the same time the playing field for regional actors and collective agents shaping the ecosystem and orienting regional development paths. Specifically, we suggest that organised clusters can promote the emergence of deviant, innovative behaviours, selecting the sustainable ones and preserving these innovations over time (Flanagan et al., 2011; Uyarra, 2010; Uyarra & Flanagan, 2010). In what follows, we will unpack the three dimensions and shed light on their role in understanding clusters' agency in regional path development.

The first dimension is heterogeneity. Deviant actors interact with the resources available in their environment, developing more or less deliberate strategies to obtain those resources, exploit, and preserve them, balancing cooperation and competition (cf. Schumpeter, 1976). As Schumpeter and following scholars (cf. Nelson & Winter, 1992) proposed, deviant actors are crucial in bringing innovation challenging the existing equilibrium of a (socio-economic) ecosystem. At the same time, innovation also depends on the existing actors that might impede access to resources to preserve the status quo. Along these lines, clusters can be seen as 'playing fields', allowing deviant behaviours to emerge and shielding them from the broader environments. However, clusters can also be seen as collective agents displaying deviant behaviour themselves and changing the rules of their regional ecosystems (cf. Crouch et al., 2009).

Selectivity – the second evolutionary dimension – is the fundamental mechanism enabling innovations to emerge (Hall, 1993, 2013). Selectivity refers to the rules of 'success' shaping actors' access to the resources that determine their survival (see also Dotti, 2018a, 2018b). Thus, deviant actors who survive in a given environment become the 'dominant' ones transferring their 'successful behaviours' to the next generation. In the context of clusters, the dynamics of cooperation and competition within cluster boundaries may shape the selection process defining what actors and behaviours may become dominant, potentially entering and competing in the broader economic ecosystems. On the other hand, as collective actors, clusters deviating from the rules established in their regions may successfully transform them and gain more resources and legitimacy to compete and influence rules and behaviours on a broader scale.

Finally, and related to the previous point, preservation refers to the mechanisms allowing to maintain these successful behaviours over time, particularly by transferring economic assets and successful strategies by innovative actors (Coletti & Dotti, 2021). In the cluster context, this may suggest that the successful (deviant) behaviours within clusters may become the 'norm', and deviant clusters as collective actors may be recognised and legitimised in their broader contexts leading to the preservation of once deviant collective practices.

A dual role for clusters as meta-organisations: between firm- and system-levels

Building on the previous discussion and following evolutionary economic geographers (Isaksen et al., 2019; Zukauskaite et al., 2017), we suggest that clusters may act at two levels: organisation- and system-level. Organisation-level agency refers to creating new organisations or initiating new activities in existing organisations to stimulate innovation. In contrast, system-level agency refers to re-shaping the broader institutional and organisational ecosystem (Isaksen et al., 2019). We suggest that clusters play a dual role in new sustainable path development by linking this perspective on agency with the sustainability transitions research (Geels, 2002, 2020; Loorbach et al., 2017). Specifically, organised clusters may provide protected spaces – or 'niches' – facilitating organisation-level agency, or they can be collective actors driving large-scale change in socio-technical ecosystems.

Indeed, the geographical proximity and the collaboration between a network of stakeholders allow creating a protected space, or 'niche', to 'incubate' new technologies, enabling intra-organisational transformation and its institutionalisation (Barrie et al., 2017; Coenen et al., 2010; Isaksen et al., 2019; Raven, Kern, Smith, et al., 2016). Acting as 'niches', clusters can thus foster heterogeneity, allowing deviant actors to emerge and develop innovations in a space that is more conducive to such innovations than the broader ecosystem, as further elaborated by Cappellano and Calavita's Chapter 7 and Viachka's Chapter 8 in this volume. The internal dynamics of competition and cooperation of these 'protected' ecosystems ensure that only the most successful organisations and innovations survive before competing in the 'mainstream' economic ecosystem. However, to create such niches for sustainable innovations, clusters need to leverage their local contexts and policies, as well as subsidies and political support at the national scale (Raven, Kern, Verhees, et al., 2016). Kutsenko et al. (this volume) demonstrate a possible approach to designing cluster organisational structures taking into account the contextual specifics.

On the other hand, organised clusters can be essential vehicles for system-level collective action (cf. Berkowitz, 2018). Indeed, while autonomous and disconnected actors can carry out system-building, it is often a collective endeavour requiring coordination between multiple organisations (Musiolik et al., 2012). Chaudhury and Stecca Douek (this volume) demonstrate how the meta-organisational framework can be effective in organising such collective action on a global scale. From this perspective, organised clusters can become drivers of institutional change due to the collective power they wield (Lupova-Henry et al., 2021b). Thus, their agency can be directed towards changing existing institutional or organisational structures or practices and preventing such changes in the regional economic ecosystem (Farla et al., 2012). Organised clusters can be seen as collective actors either deviating from the dominant institutional logic or supporting the status quo. In other words, they can act either as the 'drivers' or 'brakes' of sustainability transitions, as further investigated by Bor and O'Shea's Chapter 9 in this volume. Clusters, hence, can act both as niches for sustainable innovations and new sustainable pathways and as system-level actors allowing to empower these latter. The choice of their strategy will depend on how they manage and organise and how they achieve the legitimacy needed to drive the sustainability transitions.

Conclusions

In this conceptual chapter, we explored the agency of clusters as meta-organisations driving sustainability transitions. Given clusters' often-considerable weight in the regional economies, their contribution to sustainable (or unsustainable) regional development can be significant. To date, literature has primarily analysed regional clustering within the framework of sustainability transitions as a way to uncover the pre-existing industrial base and explain industry formation as a path-dependent process (Hansen & Coenen, 2015). However, the meta-organisational view suggests that organised clusters may have agency and the necessary competencies to deliberately change regional ecosystems (Lupova-Henry et al., 2021a).

Adopting the meta-organisational perspective, we explored three determinants of clusters' agency: legitimacy, organisationality and decisionality, as well as visions and discourses. Indeed, clusters' ability to (re-)shape regional development paths and steer them towards sustainability may stem from their acting on the boundaries of multiple fields and interacting with actors pursuing different objectives with heterogenous rules (Dotti & Lupova-Henry, 2020; Hoppe, 2005; Kostova et al., 2008; Zietsma & Lawrence, 2010). In these circumstances, legitimacy, organisationality and decisionality, and mobilisation of visions and discourses are vital factors enabling clusters' agency. For instance degrees of decisionality and organisationality may influence clusters' legitimacy and power distribution within the clusters. These may further affect clusters' ability to drive sustainability transitions and their direction. Finally, the ability to mobilise discourses and visions may be a crucial element determining clusters' role as drivers of sustainability transitions.

We then proposed that clusters play an evolutionary role in shaping regional ecosystems and their evolution over time, that is the regional development paths. Accordingly, clusters move along the fundamental dimensions of heterogeneity, selectivity, and preservation, striving to survive while interacting with their ecosystem shaping its rules. We suggested that clusters have a dual role as 'playgrounds' and 'ecosystem shapers'. Thus, on the one hand, clusters can provide 'niches' – or protective spaces – allowing divergent behaviours and sustainable innovations to survive before competing in the mainstream regional economic ecosystem. On the other hand, at the system level, clusters can act as 'ecosystem builders' to shape the regional economic development paths facilitating the adoption of (sustainable) innovations, thus, ultimately supporting sustainable development.

Our chapter contributes to theory by further developing the meta-organisational perspective on clusters and contributing to a shift in perception of clusters as purely 'geographical areas' to one encompassing cluster agency. This shift aims to correct some potentially risky conceptualisations. Indeed, 'organised' clusters can no longer be seen as purely 'spontaneous' agglomerations of firms and should be perceived as 'organised' entities having the attributes of formal organisations, such as membership and joint decision-making (Ahrne & Brunsson, 2011). This conceptualisation opens the opportunity to conceive them as purposeful entities, that is actors interacting with and shaping their environment to survive. From this perspective, the evolutionary approach provides a positive and normative framework to interpret and orient cluster-related policy. Our conceptual framework can serve as a launchpad for future empirical research exploring the interrelation between the niche and system-level agency in clusters driving the transition towards sustainable development. The following chapters in this volume will elaborate on these notions and provide case studies.

References

Ahrne, G., & Brunsson, N. (2005). Organizations and meta-organizations. *Scandinavian Journal of Management, 21*(4), 429–449. https://doi.org/10.1016/j.scaman.2005.09.005

Ahrne, G., & Brunsson, N. (2011). Organization outside organizations: The significance of partial organization. *Organization, 18*(1), 83–104. https://doi.org/10.1177/1350508410376256

Andersson, M., & Karlsson, C. (2006). Regional innovation systems in small and medium-sized regions. In B. Johansson, C. Karlsson, & R. Stough (Eds.), *The emerging digital economy: Entrepreneurship, clusters and policy* (pp. 55–81). Springer.

Armstrong, H., & Taylor, J. (2000). *Regional economics and policy*. Blackwell.

Asheim, B. T., Boschma, R., & Cooke, P. (2011). Constructing regional advantage: Platform policies based on related variety and differentiated knowledge bases. *Regional Studies, 45*(7), 893–904. https://doi.org/10.1080/00343404.2010.543126

Asheim, B. T., Grillitsch, M., & Trippl, M. (2016). Regional innovation systems: Past-present-future. In R. Shearmur, C. Carrincazeaux, & D. Doloreux (Eds.), *Handbook on the geographies of innovation* (pp. 45–62). Edward Elgar Publishing.

Astley, W. G., & Van de Ven, A. H. (1983). Central perspectives and debates in organization theory. *Administrative Science Quarterly, 28*(2), 245–273. https://doi.org/10.2307/2392620

Avelino, F. (2017). Power in sustainability transitions: Analysing power and (dis)empowerment in transformative change towards sustainability. *Environmental Policy and Governance, 27*(6), 505–520. https://doi.org/10.1002/eet.1777

Avelino, F., & Wittmayer, J. M. (2016). Shifting power relations in sustainability transitions: A multi-actor perspective. *Journal of Environmental Policy & Planning, 18*(5), 628–649. https://doi.org/10.1080/1523908X.2015.1112259

Barrie, J., Zawdie, G., & João, E. (2017). Leveraging triple helix and system intermediaries to enhance effectiveness of protected spaces and strategic niche management for transitioning to circular economy. *International Journal of Technology Management & Sustainable Development, 16*(1), 25–47. https://doi.org/10.1386/tmsd.16.1.25_1

Battilana, J., Leca, B., & Boxenbaum, E. (2009). How actors change institutions: Towards a theory of institutional entrepreneurship. *Academy of Management Annals, 3*(1), 65–107. https://doi.org/10.5465/19416520903053598

Berkowitz, H. (2018). Meta-organizing firms' capabilities for sustainable innovation: A conceptual framework. *Journal of Cleaner Production, 175*, 420–430. https://doi.org/10.1016/j.jclepro.2017.12.028

Brusco, S. (1986). Small firms and industrial districts: The experience of Italy. In D. Keeble & E. Wever (Eds.), *New firms and regional development in Europe*. Croom Helm.

Camagni, R. (2004). Uncertainty, social capital and community governance: The city as milieu. In R. Capello & P. Nijkamp (Eds.), *Urban dynamics and growth*. Elsevier.

Capello, R. (2007). *Regional economics* (R. A. T. in E. and Finance, Ed.). Routledge.

Chaudhury, A. S., & Stecca Douek, C. (this volume). Meta-organisations and clusters in climate regimes. In E. Lupova-Henry & N. F. Dotti (Eds.), *Designing and managing clusters for sustainability*. Routledge.

Coenen, L., Raven, R., & Verbong, G. (2010). Local niche experimentation in energy transitions: A theoretical and empirical exploration of proximity advantages and disadvantages. *Technology in Society, 32*(4), 295–302. https://doi.org/10.1016/j.techsoc.2010.10.006

Coletti, P., & Dotti, N. F. (2021). Knowledge co-production promoting policy change in time of decentralisation: A comparison of two cases from Brussels. *Local Government Studies, 47*(2), 276–295. https://doi.org/10.1080/03003930.2020.1739022

Cooke, P. (2012). From clusters to platform policies in regional development. *European Planning Studies, 20*(8), 1415–1424. https://doi.org/10.1080/09654313.2012.680741

Cooke, P., Gomez Uranga, M., & Etxebarria, G. (1997). Regional innovation systems: Institutional and organisational dimensions. *Research Policy, 26*(4–5), 475–491.

Crevoisier, O., & Camagni, R. (2000). *Les Milieux Urbains: Innovation, Systèmes de Production et Ancrage*. EDES.

Crouch, C., Schröder, M., & Voelzkow, H. (2009). Regional and sectoral varieties of capitalism. *Economy and Society, 38*(4), 654–678. https://doi.org/10.1080/03085140903190383

Deephouse, D. L., Bundy, J., Tost, L. P., & Suchman, M. C. (2017). Organizational legitimacy: Six key questions. In *The SAGE handbook of organizational institutionalism* (pp. 27–52). SAGE Publications Ltd. https://doi.org/10.4135/9781526415066

Dobusch, L., & Schoeneborn, D. (2015). Fluidity, identity, and organizationality: The communicative constitution of anonymous. *Journal of Management Studies, 52*(8), 1005–1035. https://doi.org/10.1111/joms.12139

Doloreux, D., & Porto Gomez, I. (2017). A review of (almost) 20 years of regional innovation systems research. *European Planning Studies, 25*(3), 371–387. https://doi.org/10.1080/09654313.2016.1244516

Dotti, N. F. (2018a). Abundant water, abundant knowledge: Cognitive patterns for policy changes in Brussels' water management system. *European Urban and Regional Studies, 25*(1), 54–71. https://doi.org/10.1177/0969776416677621

Dotti, N. F. (2018b). Knowledge that matters for the "survival of unfittest": The case of the new Brussels' rail junction. *Transport Policy, 63*, 131–140. https://doi.org/10.1016/j.tranpol.2017.12.022

Dotti, N. F., & Colombino, A. (2018). Knowledge for policymaking: An evolutionary perspective to achieve policy resilience. In N. F. Dotti (Ed.), *Knowledge, policymaking and learning for European cities and regions: From research to practice*. Edward Elgar Publishing.

Dotti, N. F., & Lupova-Henry, E. (2020). Creative mediators and their role in the governance of creative clusters. In M. Komorowski & I. Picone (Eds.), *Creative cluster development: Governance, place-making and entrepreneurship* (p. 272). Routledge. www.crcpress.com/Creative-Cluster-Development-Governance-Place-Making-and-Entrepreneurship/Komorowski-Picone/p/book/9780367332747

Duprat, L. (2020). *Favoriser la créativité organisationnelle des organisations créatives au sein d'une méta-organisation territorialisée: Le cas de la Friche la Belle de Mai à Marseille* [Ph.D. Thesis]. Aix Marseille Université. https://tel.archives-ouvertes.fr/tel-02948013

Etzkowitz, H. (2012). Triple helix clusters: Boundary permeability at university-industry-government interfaces as a regional innovation strategy. *Environment and Planning C: Government and Policy, 30*(5), 766–779. https://doi.org/10.1068/c1182

Farla, J., Markard, J., Raven, R., & Coenen, L. (2012). Sustainability transitions in the making: A closer look at actors, strategies and resources. *Technological Forecasting and Social Change, 79*(6), 991–998. https://doi.org/10.1016/j.techfore.2012.02.001

Flanagan, K., Uyarra, E., & Laranja, M. (2011). Reconceptualising the "policy mix" for innovation. *Research Policy, 40*(5), 702–713. https://doi.org/10.1016/j.respol.2011.02.005

Florida, R., Adler, P., & Mellander, C. (2017). The city as innovation machine. *Regional Studies, 51*(1), 86–96. https://doi.org/10.1080/00343404.2016.1255324

Gadille, M., Tremblay, D.-G., & Vion, A. (2013). La méta-organisation territorialisée, moteur d'apprentissages collectifs. *Revue Interventions économiques. Papers in Political Economy, 48*, Article 48. https://journals.openedition.org/interventionseconomiques/2156

Garaudel, P. (2020). Exploring meta-organizations' diversity and agency: A meta-organizational perspective on global union federations. *Scandinavian Journal of Management, 36*(1), 101094. https://doi.org/10.1016/j.scaman.2020.101094

Garud, R., Kumaraswamy, A., & Karnøe, P. (2010). Path dependence or path creation? *Journal of Management Studies, 47*(4), 760–774. https://doi.org/10.1111/j.1467-6486.2009.00914.x

Geels, F. W. (2002). Technological transitions as evolutionary reconfiguration processes: A multi-level perspective and a case-study. *Research Policy, 31*(8), 1257–1274. https://doi.org/10.1016/S0048-7333(02)00062-8

Geels, F. W. (2020). Micro-foundations of the multi-level perspective on socio-technical transitions: Developing a multi-dimensional model of agency through crossovers between social constructivism, evolutionary economics and neo-institutional theory. *Technological Forecasting and Social Change, 152*, 119894. https://doi.org/10.1016/j.techfore.2019.119894

Grillitsch, M., & Trippl, M. (2016). *Innovation policies and new regional growth paths: A place-based system failure framework*. Lund University, CIRCLE – Center for Innovation, Research and Competences in the Learning Economy. https://EconPapers.repec.org/RePEc:hhs:lucirc:2016_026

Gulati, R., Puranam, P., & Tushman, M. (2012). Meta-organization design: Rethinking design in interorganizational and community contexts. *Strategic Management Journal, 33*(6), 571–586. https://doi.org/10.1002/smj.1975

Hall, P. A. (1993). Policy paradigms, social learning, and the state: The case of economic policymaking in Britain. *Comparative Politics, 25*(3), 275–296.

Hall, P. A. (2013). Brother, can you paradigm? *Governance, 26*(2), 189–192. https://doi.org/10.1111/gove.12031

Hansen, T., & Coenen, L. (2015). The geography of sustainability transitions: Review, synthesis and reflections on an emergent research field. *Environmental Innovation and Societal Transitions, 17*, 92–109. https://doi.org/10.1016/j.eist.2014.11.001

Hassink, R. (2005). How to unlock regional economies from path dependency? From learning region to learning cluster. *European Planning Studies, 13*(4), 521–535.

Hassink, R., Isaksen, A., & Trippl, M. (2019). Towards a comprehensive understanding of new regional industrial path development. *Regional Studies, 53*(11), 1636–1645. https://doi.org/10.1080/00343404.2019.1566704

Hoppe, R. (2005). Rethinking the science-policy nexus: From knowledge utilization and science technology studies to types of boundary arrangements. *Poiesis & Praxis, 3*(3), 199–215. https://doi.org/10.1007/s10202-005-0074-0

Human, S. E., & Provan, K. G. (2000). Legitimacy building in the evolution of small-firm multilateral networks: A comparative study of success and demise. *Administrative Science Quarterly, 45*(2), 327–365. https://doi.org/10.2307/2667074

Iammarino, S. (2005). An evolutionary Integrated View of Regional Systems of innovation: Concepts, measures and historical perspectives. *European Planning Studies, 13*(4), 497–519.

Isaksen, A., Jakobsen, S.-E., Njøs, R., & Normann, R. (2019). Regional industrial restructuring resulting from individual and system agency. *Innovation: The European Journal of Social Science Research, 32*(1), 48–65. https://doi.org/10.1080/13511610.2018.1496322

Katz, B., & Wagner, J. (2014, June 9). The rise of innovation districts. *Brookings*. www.brookings.edu/essay/rise-of-innovation-districts/

Kemeny, T., & Storper, M. (2015). Is specialization good for regional economic development? *Regional Studies, 49*(6), 1003–1018. https://doi.org/10.1080/00343404.2014.899691

King, B. G., Felin, T., & Whetten, D. A. (2010). Perspective: Finding the organization in organizational theory: A meta-theory of the organization as a social actor. *Organization Science, 21*(1), 290–305. https://doi.org/10.1287/orsc.1090.0443

Köhler, J., Geels, F. W., Kern, F., Markard, J., Onsongo, E., Wieczorek, A., Alkemade, F., Avelino, F., Bergek, A., Boons, F., Fünfschilling, L., Hess, D., Holtz, G., Hyysalo, S., Jenkins, K., Kivimaa, P., Martiskainen, M., McMeekin, A., Mühlemeier, M. S., . . . Wells, P.

(2019). An agenda for sustainability transitions research: State of the art and future directions. *Environmental Innovation and Societal Transitions, 31*, 1–32. https://doi.org/10.1016/j.eist.2019.01.004

Kostova, T., Roth, K., & Dacin, M. T. (2008). Institutional theory in the study of multinational corporations: A critique and new directions. *Academy of Management Review, 33*(4), 994–1006. https://doi.org/10.5465/amr.2008.34422026

Kutsenko, E., Ismagulova, S., & Ivanova, E. (this volume). Urban super-cluster as a novel approach to clustering in megapolises: The case of Moscow Innovation Cluster. In E. Lupova-Henry & N. F. Dotti (Eds.), *Designing and managing clusters for sustainability*. Routledge.

Loorbach, D., Frantzeskaki, N., & Avelino, F. (2017). Sustainability transitions research: Transforming science and practice for societal change. *Annual Review of Environment and Resources, 42*(1), 599–626. https://doi.org/10.1146/annurev-environ-102014-021340

Lundequist, P., & Power, D. (2002). Putting porter into practice? Practices of regional cluster building: Evidence from Sweden. *European Planning Studies, 10*(6), 685–704.

Lupova-Henry, E., Blili, S., & Dal Zotto, C. (2021a). Clusters as institutional entrepreneurs: Lessons from Russia. *Journal of Innovation and Entrepreneurship, 10*(1), 7. https://doi.org/10.1186/s13731-021-00149-5

Lupova-Henry, E., Blili, S., & Dal Zotto, C. (2021b). Designing organised clusters as social actors: A meta-organisational approach. *Journal of Organization Design, 10*(1), 35–54. https://doi.org/10.1007/s41469-021-00092-5

Lupova-Henry, E., & Dotti, N. F. (2019). Governance of sustainable innovation: Moving beyond the hierarchy-market-network trichotomy? A systematic literature review using the "who-how-what" framework. *Journal of Cleaner Production, 210*, 738–748. https://doi.org/10.1016/j.jclepro.2018.11.068

Markusen, A. (1996). Sticky places in slippery space: A typology of industrial districts. *Economic Geography, 72*(3), 293–313.

Marshall, A. (1890). *Principles of economics*. Macmillan and Co.

Martin, R., & Sunley, P. (2006). Path dependence and regional economic evolution. *Journal of Economic Geography, 6*(4), 395–437. https://doi.org/10.1093/jeg/lbl012

McCann, P. (2013). *Modern urban and regional economics*. Oxford University Press.

Moulaert, F., & Sekia, F. (2003). Territorial innovation models: A critical survey. *Regional Studies, 37*(3), 289–302. https://doi.org/10.1080/0034340032000065442

Moyson, S., & Scholten, P. (2018). Theories on policy learning: Existing approaches and future challenges. In N. F. Dotti (Ed.), *Knowledge, policymaking and learning for European cities and regions: From research to practice* (pp. 27–43). Edward Elgar Publishing.

Musiolik, J., Markard, J., & Hekkert, M. (2012). Networks and network resources in technological innovation systems: Towards a conceptual framework for system building. *Technological Forecasting and Social Change, 79*(6), 1032–1048. https://doi.org/10.1016/j.techfore.2012.01.003

Nelson, R. R., & Winter, S. G. (1992). *An evolutionary theory of economic change*. Harvard University Press.

O'Dwyer, M., O'Malley, L., Murphy, S., & McNally, R. C. (2015). Insights into the creation of a successful MNE innovation cluster. *Competitiveness Review, 25*(3), 288–309. https://doi.org/10.1108/CR-08-2014-0026

Pecquer, B. (2002). *Le développement local*. Alternatives Economiques.

Pflitsch, G. M. (2019). *Micro-dynamics and institutional change in regional transition paths to sustainability*. Philipps-Universität Marburg.

Porter, M. E. (1990). *The competitive advantage of nations*. Free Press.

Porter, M. E. (1998a). Clusters and the new economics of competition. *Harvard Business Review, 76*(6), 77–90.

Porter, M. E. (1998b). *On competition*. Harvard Business School.

Quist, J. N., Thissen, W., & Vergragt, P. J. (2011). The impact and spin-off of participatory backcasting: From vision to niche. *Technological Forecasting and Social Change, 78*(5), 883–897. https://doi.org/10.1016/j.techfore.2011.01.011

Raven, R., Kern, F., Smith, A., Jacobsson, S., & Verhees, B. (2016). The politics of innovation spaces for low-carbon energy: Introduction to the special issue. *Environmental Innovation and Societal Transitions, 18*, 101–110. https://doi.org/10.1016/j.eist.2015.06.008

Raven, R., Kern, F., Verhees, B., & Smith, A. (2016). Niche construction and empowerment through socio-political work: A meta-analysis of six low-carbon technology cases. *Environmental Innovation and Societal Transitions, 18*, 164–180. https://doi.org/10.1016/j.eist.2015.02.002

Schumpeter, J. A. (1976). *Capitalism, socialism and democracy*. Routledge.

Slembeck, T. (1997). The formation of economic policy: A cognitive-evolutionary approach to policy-making. *Constitutional Political Economy, 8*(3), 225–254.

Späth, P., & Rohracher, H. (2010). "Energy regions": The transformative power of regional discourses on socio-technical futures. *Research Policy, 39*(4), 449–458. https://doi.org/10.1016/j.respol.2010.01.017

Storper, M. (1997). Regional economies as relational assets. In *Regional world: Territorial development in a global economy*. Guilford Press.

Strambach, S., & Pflitsch, G. (2020). Transition topology: Capturing institutional dynamics in regional development paths to sustainability. *Research Policy, 49*(7), 104006. https://doi.org/10.1016/j.respol.2020.104006

Tödtling, F., & Trippl, M. (2013). Transformation of regional innovation systems. *Re-Framing Regional Development: Evolution, Innovation, and Transition, 62*, 297.

Trigilia, C. (1992). Italian industrial districts: Neither myth nor interlude. In F. Pyke & W. Sengenberger (Eds.), *Industrial districts and local economic regeneration: Vol. OFF PUBNS ILO*. ILO.

Trippl, M., & Otto, A. (2009). How to turn the fate of old industrial areas: A comparison of cluster-based renewal processes in Styria and the Saarland. *Environment and Planning A: Economy and Space, 41*(5), 1217–1233. https://doi.org/10.1068/a4129

Uyarra, E. (2010). What is evolutionary about "regional systems of innovation"? Implications for regional policy. *Journal of Evolutionary Economics, 20*(1), 115–137. https://doi.org/10.1007/s00191-009-0135-y

Uyarra, E., & Flanagan, K. (2010). From regional systems of innovation to regions as innovation policy spaces. *Environment and Planning C: Government and Policy, 28*(4), 681–695. https://doi.org/10.1068/c0961

Viachka, A. (2013). *Comparing firms' associational strategies across sectors and locations: Cluster initiatives as meta-organizations*. Stockholm School of Economics.

Zietsma, C., & Lawrence, T. B. (2010). Institutional work in the transformation of an organizational field: The interplay of boundary work and practice work. *Administrative Science Quarterly, 55*(2), 189–221. https://doi.org/10.2189/asqu.2010.55.2.189

Zukauskaite, E., Trippl, M., & Plechero, M. (2017). Institutional thickness revisited. *Economic Geography, 93*(4), 325–345. https://doi.org/10.1080/00130095.2017.1331703

2 Meta-organisation as partial organisation

An integrated framework of organisationality and decisionality

Héloïse BERKOWITZ and Sanne BOR

Introduction

To what extent are meta-organisations, that is organisations of organisations, themselves organisations? And on which theoretical bases can we study and compare meta-organisations? In this methodological piece, we develop an analytical framework to account for the structural variations of meta-organisations in terms of membership, hierarchy, rules, monitoring, and sanctions (Ahrne et al., 2016b). In so doing, we enable a systemic comparison of clusters as forms of more or less partially organised meta-organisations.

Clusters constitute one possible empirical form of meta-organisations, those characterised by a spatial or territorial anchorage (Gadille et al., 2013; Lupova-Henry & Dotti, this volume). However, meta-organisations cover many other social phenomena of organised collective action among organisations, from multi-partner alliances to trade associations, cooperatives, or R&D consortia (Berkowitz & Bor, 2018). While each phenomenon has been the object of extensive research in its own right, little work has closely examined how these diverse forms can be compared from a meta-organisation perspective and where clusters stand in a broad spectrum of meta-organisations. Understanding this is essential to recognise the potential of organised clusters to drive sustainability transformations (Berkowitz & Gadille, this volume; Lupova-Henry et al., 2021).

Drawing on recent studies addressing the concept of 'partial organisation' (Berkowitz et al., 2020; Grothe-Hammer, 2019b; Laamanen et al., 2019; Nielsen, 2018), this chapter develops a profiling methodology to study, compare, and visualise the selective combination of organisational components in meta-organisations or structural organisationality (Grothe-Hammer et al., 2022).

We break down each component (membership, hierarchy, rules, monitoring, and sanctions) into operationalisable dimensions that can be studied in meta-organisations, including clusters. We use structural organisationality in combination with the concept of decisionality – that is the degree to which each element is itself organised and the object of decisions. We distinguish this dimension of organisationality from decidability, which refers to actors' ability to reach collective decisions (Berkowitz & Grothe-Hammer, 2021).

DOI: 10.4324/9781003215066-4

We show that the degree of decisionality on membership can vary depending on its formality, the auto-determination of the meta-organisation, the categories of membership, the ability of members to decide on their involvement, and the variety of their contributions. Decisionality on hierarchy depends on whether (and if so, how) authority is vested in the meta-organisation, conceptualised as cooperation and coordination power. Decisionality on rules, monitoring, and sanction can be assessed based on affordances, processuality, and uses. On this basis, we further highlight the potential thinness or thickness of (partial) meta-organisation and the dynamics of meta-organising.

This work moves beyond the few assumptions about organisationality in meta-organisations and the emphasis on membership as their structuring feature (Ahrne & Brunsson, 2008; Arora-Jonsson et al., 2020). We argue that variations in meta-organisations arise because of both the number and type of components they mobilise (organisationality) and also the decisions they make about those components (decisionality). This approach has various implications for organisation studies.

What does partial organisation mean at the meta-organisation level?

Meta-organisations are organisations that are constituted of other organisations. Organisation is here understood as a decided order – that is a system of decisions on organisational components, membership, hierarchy, rules, monitoring, and sanctions (Ahrne & Brunsson, 2011). Using only some of these components is referred to as partial organisation (Ahrne & Brunsson, 2011). Ahrne et al. (2016b) argue that partial organisation can appear under different constellations of organisational components, which should be analysed. Partial organisation also connects with the concept of organisationality – that is the organisational dimensions of organisations (Dobusch & Schoeneborn, 2015; Grothe-Hammer, 2019b). Grothe-Hammer et al. (2022) use structural organisationality to distinguish the selective combination of organisational components from entitative organisationality – that is actorhood and collective identity at the level of the entity. Here, we focus strictly on structural organisationality or partial organisation of meta-organisations.

By analogy, meta-organisations are a decided order that may also selectively embrace membership, hierarchy, rules, monitoring, and sanctions (Ahrne et al., 2016b). As noted by Kerwer, this is to be expected: "[Meta-organisations] making full use of these organisational elements challenge the autonomy of its member organisations. As a consequence, [meta-organisations] only draw on a reduced repertoire of organising" (Kerwer, 2013, p. 43). This also means that meta-organisations differ in their organisationality (Lupova-Henry et al., 2021).

We draw on the partial organisation literature to unpack structural organisationality among meta-organisations and degrees of decisionality. We define decisionality as the extent to which decisions are made about organisational elements. In the cluster context, we study the possible organisational elements that structure this territorialised form of meta-organisation. We also choose to set aside the temporal dimension of meta organising – that is the potential dynamics between partialness and completeness that have been studied at the level of organisations (Dobusch & Schoeneborn, 2015; Schoeneborn & Dobusch, 2019). Temporality remains to be examined at the level of meta-organisations. Developing a framework to study the partial organisation of meta-organisations constitutes the first step in this endeavour.

Development of the framework

To develop our framework, we analyse each organisational component for meta-organisations, namely membership, hierarchy, rules, monitoring, and sanctions, and operationalise their degree of decisionality. To illustrate this, we use two examples of meta-organisations studied in the literature. The first case is the Global Business Initiative (GBI), a global group of businesses collaborating on human rights issues (Berkowitz et al., 2017). The second case we draw on to illustrate our approach is Cluster B, an Australian machine-manufacturing cooperative from the Hunter region in New South Wales (Lupova-Henry et al., 2021). These cases illustrate differences in terms of their partiality since GBI has low organisationality and decisionality, while Cluster B has high organisationality and decisionality. We now proceed to analyse each of the organisational elements separately (see Appendix A for synthesis). For each element, we present theoretical elements we use to analyse their decisionality.

Membership

Membership refers to who belongs and contributes to the meta-organisation (Grothe-Hammer, 2019b; Nielsen, 2018). Meta-organisation theory considers members of the meta-organisation to be those organisations that have been accepted as members. Membership is usually voluntary and rests on the initiative of member organisations, though the meta-organisation itself can have the decision power over accepting members or accepting applicants for membership. Whether the meta-organisation has a formalised membership and whether it holds decision power over membership are considered two different aspects of the organisational element membership.

While most members have decision rights in the organisation (referred to as full members), membership can vary depending on participants' positions or roles and, in particular, on the extent of their decision rights (see the discussion on stratification by Gulati et al., 2012).

The meta-organisation's boundary – that between those who belong and those who do not – can be established by defining types of members and their rights and responsibilities. Meta-organisations' websites often contain lists of members. Membership in meta-organisations may contribute to setting boundaries of competition, and meta-organisations may even organise competition in markets (Arora-Jonsson et al., 2020). However, membership decisions can differ significantly from one meta-organisation to the next. Consider a small meta-organisation with five members acting as a closed club – that is having a strict membership boundary. When an organisation would like to join such meta-organisation, existing members can be expected to be involved in deciding whether to admit the new member. In contrast, for a large meta-organisation, such as the UN Global Compact with more than 10,000 members, the situation is likely to be different. Members may have been involved in drafting criteria under which an organisation can become a member, but members are not always involved in evaluating and accepting new members. That decision might well be taken by an administrative unit rather than members collectively.

While some meta-organisations rule that members must be officially accepted before they can participate in the activity of the meta-organisation, that is not always the case. Cropper and Bor (2018) describe the case of a healthcare partnership where non-members participate and contribute to the meta-organisation and, in a way, still belong to the meta-organisation. Although it is clear that accepted and paying members govern the meta-organisation, other organisations may provide it with essential resources and may influence the work programme without joining the meta-organisation formally. Consequently, membership – in terms of owning or governing the meta-organisation – is often more restricted, but membership in terms of participation or contribution might be less clearly defined, thus blurring its boundaries (Grothe-Hammer, 2019a).

Table 2.1 presents the results of decisionality for membership for both GBI and Cluster B.

Cluster B grew from an initial 14 members to currently approximately 150 members. Cluster B has a list of members, and the meta-organisation determines its membership boundary; the organisation, for example shifted from an emphasis on the quantity of members to one of quality by excluding several members. In addition, the meta-organisation has different types of member categories and provides a different form of value to each (ibid). As illustrated

Table 2.1 Comparison of decisionality degree for membership

	Cluster B	*GBI*
Is there a membership (a list of members)?	1	1
Does the meta-organisation determine who can become a member?	1	1
Do members decide on candidates' entry or other members' exit?	1	0
Are there different, pre-determined categories of membership?	1	0
Are contributions to the meta-organisation and participation in its activity restricted to members only?	1	0
Membership decisionality degree	**5**	**2**

in Table 2.1, Cluster B has an overall membership decisionality score of 5. The GBI is an association that seeks to train its members on human rights issues. It counts 18 major companies across multiple sectors, including Total and Coca-Cola, as members. Members meet at workshops where they learn from the experience of other sectors in dealing with human rights issues at different levels of the firm, for example, in the context of procurement or the safety of exploitation sites. Publicly available information shows that the GBI has a list of members, and its administration decides who can join. There is a single category of members. However, the aforementioned workshops can involve guest contributors and are thus not exclusively for the members of the meta-organisation. In addition, members do not hold a decision power over candidate members' entry or incumbent members' exit from the meta-organisation. The GBI, therefore, has an overall score of 2 for membership decisionality.

Hierarchy

In the context of a meta-organisation, hierarchy describes how authority is vested. 'Extensive delegation of significant decisions' is problematic in meta-organisations, as it threatens their autonomy and thereby the future of member organisations, as Ahrne et al. (2016a) note. Nevertheless, authority to make decisions, however restricted, is vested in the meta-organisation to ensure that it can make at least some decisions.

We conceptually distinguish authority in meta-organisations as cooperation or coordination authority (Bor, 2014; Gulati et al., 2012). A cooperation orientation involves governance questions about the 'joint pursuit of the agreed-on goal(s) in a manner corresponding to a shared understanding about contributions and payoffs' (Gulati et al., 2012, p. 533). A meta-organisation can vest cooperation authority in the collective of full members, a governance board, or a general assembly meeting where representatives of all full members can make collective decisions (Ahrne & Brunsson, 2008). However, when the meta-organisation demands frequent oversight or representation, the members may choose to vest their cooperation authority in a smaller group of representatives of member organisations for a particular period (Rothschild-Whitt, 1979). Coordination is concerned with 'the deliberate and orderly alignment or adjustment of partners' actions to achieve jointly determined goals' (Gulati et al., 2012, p. 537). A meta-organisation can vest coordination authority in one single group or different groups (for various coordination purposes) and split further into sub-groups that form a hierarchy of coordination decisions (Albers et al., 2016). While these different groups may bring representatives of member organisations together, they can also centralise authority to select representatives of members or personnel hired by the meta-organisation, so forming what Provan and Kenis (2008) describe as a network administrative organisation. Table 2.2 illustrates the variations in hierarchical decisionality in Cluster B and GBI. In Cluster B, members decide to delegate authority to the meta-organisation and, specifically, to a secretariat reporting to the cluster's board. Cooperation

Table 2.2 Comparison of the degree of hierarchical decisionality

	Cluster B	*GBI*
Is there a decision from members to vest authority in the meta-organisation?	1	1
Is cooperation authority vested in a collective of members?	1	1
Is cooperation authority further vested in a (or various) smaller internal group(s)?	1	0
Is coordination authority vested in committees/ workgroups (and possible sub-groups)?	0	1
Is coordination authority vested in offices (in an administrative organisation)?	1	1
Hierarchy decisionality degree	**4**	**4**

authority is thus vested in a smaller group, and other members do not partake; the power has thus become centralised. There is no mention of any working groups or committees, but the secretariat does the coordination work. In GBI, the members are expected to work together to determine the meta-organisation's strategic priorities, learning focus areas, and opportunities for engagement with external stakeholders. The collective of members thus makes the cooperation decisions. Members also invest in coordination through participation in bi-annual peer learning meetings. Alongside the involvement of the members, a small steering group undertakes the administrative organisation of GBI and has the authority to make some coordination decisions.

Both examples represent meta-organisations with a relatively high degree of hierarchical decisionality. Indeed, in both cases, authority in the meta-organisation is vested in several devices to pursue collective action, although the forms of collective action vary considerably across the case examples.

Rules

Rules refer to formalised parameters that frame collective actions and members' behaviour (Grothe-Hammer, 2019b; Nielsen, 2018). Rules are determined by generalised expectations of behaviour and duties, input (contributions), output (results), procedure, or process. An organisation may have no defined rules (Dobusch & Schoeneborn, 2015), a very limited number of set rules (Laamanen et al., 2019), or several sets of rules, as is common in formal organisations. The more areas are covered by rules, the more organised (and thus the more predictable) the organisation will be.

Although rules can remain verbal, they are often written down. Written rules have organising strength because they can be checked, recalled, more easily communicated, and therefore have greater decisionality. The agreed rules can thus find their way into meeting memos and various other communications. To ensure rules are easily accessible, however, they are often collected into bodies of rules or collated into rulebooks (which may be incorporated into contracts and other agreements, for example). The more accessible the ruleset is, the greater the chance is that the rules have an organising effect, and therefore the more significant the decisionality of that ruleset is. Research addressing self-regulation and soft law suggests that in the context of meta-organisations, self-regulation has a more substantial effect than regulation from outside (Ostrom, 1990) because the member organisations themselves define the rules and are therefore more likely to follow them (Ahrne & Brunsson, 2011; Brunsson et al., 2012; King & Lenox, 2000). Accordingly, the more rules regulating member behaviour are self-imposed or voluntarily agreed upon, the more impactful they should be.

While in the two cases, at least some decisions are made about rules within the meta-organisation, Cluster B and GBI differ notably in the specification and implementation of those rules (see Table 2.3). Examples of GBI setting a minimum level of rule adherence include the statements,

> Companies commit to the vision and spirit of GBI' and 'We work to shape practice, inspire commitment and build capability to implement respect for human rights, in line with the UN Guiding Principles on Business and Human Rights. We are the only business organisation to focus entirely on human rights.
>
> (GBI website)

However, the specifics of those rules are not detailed and written down. In contrast with GBI, the practice of Cluster B is such that it has clear rules and criteria specified in its constitution or its charter. There do not seem to be different sets of rules for different areas. The voluntary nature of adherence to decisions may be questioned owing to the rather centralised power, monitoring, and sanction regime, which forces the members to follow the rules under the threat of exclusion.

Table 2.3 Comparison of decisionality degree for rules

	Cluster B	*GBI*
Are there decisions made about action and behavioural parameters?	1	1
Are the decided rules written down?	1	0
Are the decided rules collected in 'rule books' or charters?	1	0
Are there different sets of rules for different substantial areas?	0	0
Do members voluntarily comply with decided rules?	0	1
Rules decisionality degree	**3**	**2**

Monitoring

Monitoring implies observing as well as collecting, organising, and sharing information about behaviour, efforts, or results. The organising effect of monitoring depends on several dimensions. One issue of importance is the perceived trustworthiness of the information. Information trustworthiness relates to how the information is gathered, what is known about it, and who collates it. Data gathered systematically, possibly through an automated and transparent process, can be considered more trustworthy than data gathered less systematically and transparently. Another critical element is who collects and analyses the information – that is whether the organisation conducting the monitoring is a trusted actor or not.

Another issue of importance is the channel for information sharing. Information accumulated through monitoring information may be shared via various channels, such as reports, ratings, or rankings. The more actionable, accessible, understandable, clear, and trustworthy information is, the more helpful it is for decision-makers (within or outside the organisation). Rankings and labels can simplify information and thus serve as structuring tools in situations where those who need to make decisions lack the time or the capability to understand the complexity of their choices (Osterloh & Frey, 2015; Sauder & Espeland, 2009).

The steering effect of monitoring is more substantial when monitoring information is available to a wide range of individuals, groups, or organisations, allowing them to make informed decisions (Ahrne et al., 2016a, 2016b; Kerwer, 2013). As member organisations are affected by the results of monitoring decisions, Ahrne, Brunsson, and Seidl expect that there are 'limitations to the amount of monitoring members are willing to accept' (Ahrne et al., 2016b, p. 97). However, external pressures may convince meta-organisation members to monitor their behaviour, efforts, or results and make monitoring information more openly available. Meta-organisations may also aim to influence their wider environment, which can mean that members and non-members are monitored.

As Table 2.4 synthesises, in Cluster B, the board monitors member behaviour and may also act based on the reported behaviour of members, but monitoring is restricted to members. The process is not very clear and seems to be somewhat random. Similarly, reporting does not seem systemic or public outside the meta-organisation. The GBI, in contrast, has made no decision at all about monitoring.

Sanctioning

Sanctioning is defined as a decision to try to influence the behaviour of an individual or group. Ahrne and Brunsson controversially define it as capable of encompassing both punishment and reward (Ahrne et al., 2016b; Ahrne & Brunsson, 2011). Ahrne and Brunsson (2008) note that decisions by meta-organisations to sanction are complicated, and decisions on negative sanctions are likely to be particularly difficult. However, decisions on sanctions may

Table 2.4 Comparison of decisionality degree for monitoring

	Cluster B	*GBI*
Is there a decision by the meta-organisation to monitor behaviour, efforts, or results?	1	0
Are non-members (also) monitored?	0	0
Is the process of gathering observations considered trustworthy by decision-makers?	1	0
Is the reporting of the findings accessible, easily understandable?	0	0
Is the reporting made available outside the meta-organisation?	0	0
Monitoring decisionality degree	**2**	**0**

accumulate over time. This accumulation might increase the organizing effect of sanction over the long run.

The difficulty arises first because members need to agree on sanctions, which would affect them too. Second, if we accept the proposition by Ahrne and Brunsson that sanctions encompass incentives, and meta-organisations often do not have sufficient financial resources to provide significant rewards to members. Sanctions can also take the form of identity-enhancing benefits, such as being allowed to utilise a symbol of certification. Third, meta-organisations depend on their members for their existence, making it more difficult to punish members without punishing the collective, including the meta-organisation.

Ahrne et al. (2016b) do, however, note that sanctions may emerge slowly over a more extended period. Sanctioning decisionality may depend on how systematic (and thus predictable) the sanction is and how much it affects the member organisation's functioning.

First, awards distributed to individual member organisations, or their representatives, can positively affect the concerned organisation. However, the individual nature of these sanctions means they have only a limited organising effect. Second, punishments doled out to individual member organisations have a potentially more substantial organising effect. As Ostrom (1990) pointed out in the context of self-steering systems, the circumstances and history of the issue will often be considered in the decision, and these sanctioning decisions are often graduated, with the stakes or consequences increasing each time. Such negative sanctions mainly affect those who do not follow agreed rules or regulations and are not always systematic. Consequently, some organisations that are important to the meta-organisation may never be punished for disobeying the rules. Third, with more systematic positive sanctions, for instance, being rewarded for meeting a clear set of criteria, the organising power becomes more significant.

There are two difficulties with such sanctioning. First, negative sanctions only have a strong organising effect when the consequence is severe enough for those who break the rules to be concerned. Second, if the sanction is too

Table 2.5 Comparison of decisionality degree for sanction

	Cluster B	*GBI*
Are there decisions made about sanctions (positive or negative)?	1	0
Are non-members (also) sanctioned?	0	0
Is there a defined set of criteria and a process for sanctioning?	1	0
Have negative sanctions actually been enforced?	1	0
Are sanctions used consistently?	0	0
Sanction decisionality degree	**3**	**0**

severe, the organisation may consider terminating its membership in the meta-organisation. The most strongly organising situation is that in which sanctioning decisions are made on a wide range of themes, combining positive and negative sanctions. We expect that the more systematic and frequent sanctioning decisions are, the more routine and rule-based, the easier these will become, whereupon administration bodies will assume a more central role than governance bodies in the decision-making.

As synthesised in Table 2.5, as with the question of monitoring, GBI has made no decision about sanctioning its members. This is in line with the lack of written rules or collective goals that would drive collective action. In contrast, Cluster B sanctions members and may exclude them from the meta-organisation on the basis of the criteria and process set in the charter. Whether these sanctions are used consistently remains unclear from the data presented.

An integrated framework: structural organisationality and decisionality

This chapter provides an integrated framework assessing various criteria of decisionality developed to analyse structural organisationality in meta-organisations. Membership degree of decisionality depends on whether there is a formal membership, on the ability of the meta-organisation to decide about membership (or its auto-determination), on the categories of membership, on the ability of members to decide on their involvement, and the variety of contributions. Similarly, decisionality on hierarchy depends on whether and how authority is vested in the meta-organisation and how cooperation and coordination authority is organised. Decisionality on rules, monitoring, and sanctions can be assessed based on their affordances, processuality, and uses. The more criteria are met, the greater is the degree of each component's decisionality. These criteria are not exhaustive, and more could be added.

By combining degrees of decisionality for each organisational element, we propose an integrative framework to assess and compare forms of meta-organisations. Doing so makes it possible to determine an average decisionality that accounts for decisionality across all components. Table 2.6 illustrates this framework and the average decisionality for Cluster B and GBI. Radar charts can illustrate the variations of structural organisationality. This visualisation helps us outline varying meta-organisational profiles; see Figure 2.1.

Mapping decisionality thus achieves what Ahrne et al. (2016b) called for, an understanding of the constellations of organisational elements. It also answers the call of Ahrne and Brunsson (2005) for a better understanding of the variety of meta-organisation.

We can further conceptualise these constellations depending on structural organisationality and decisionality (see Figure 2.2). We propose to conceptualise structures with lesser organisationality – that is those combining two or fewer organisational elements – as partial meta-organising structures. In comparison, those with greater organisationality – that is many organisational elements (three or more) – can be conceptualised simply as meta-organising structures. We further conceptualise those with greater decisionality as thick and those with lesser decisionality as thin (with similar thresholds as before). By combining organisationality with decisionality, we obtain four categories: 1) thin partial meta-organising with lesser decisionality and lesser organisationality; 2) thin meta-organising with lesser decisionality but greater organisationality; 3) thick

Table 2.6 Decisionality by organisational element and on average

	Cluster B	*GBI*
Membership decisionality	5	2
Hierarchy decisionality	4	4
Rules decisionality	3	2
Monitoring decisionality	2	0
Sanctions decisionality	3	0
Average decisionality	**3.4**	**1.6**

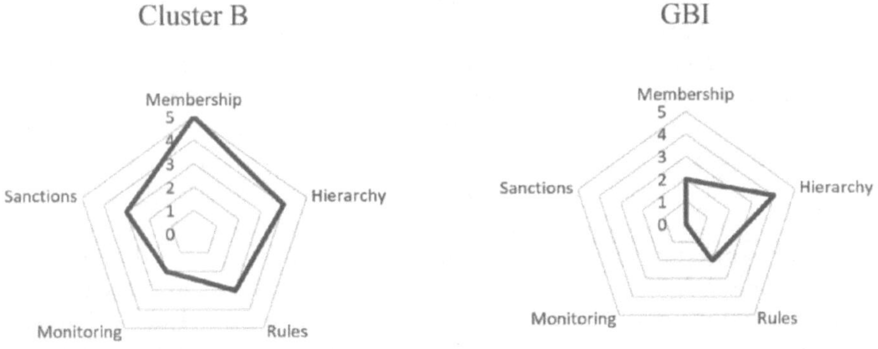

Figure 2.1 Radar charts of meta-organisation structural organisationality and decisionality profiles

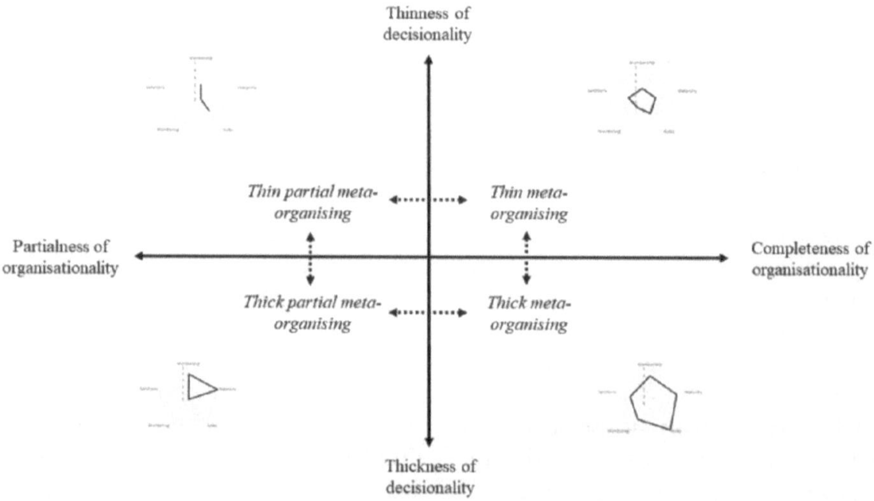

Figure 2.2 Meta-organising: potential transformations in thinness/thickness and partialness/completeness

partial meta-organising with lesser organisationality and greater decisionality; and 4) thick meta-organising, with greater decisionality and greater organisationality. It can be argued that clusters, and other collectives of organisations in general, will align more closely with one of these four profiles.

The thin partial meta-organising profile encompasses weak meta-organisational structures, where only one or two elements are the object of decisions, and less decisionality is observed. Membership plays a specific role in meta-organisation since it is the basis of both its definition and nature. Therefore, we can assume that thin partial meta-organising encompasses associations that at least decide upon membership but impose very few restrictions. An example might be open clubs, a meta-organisation where organisations can join if they wish to, without other members deciding upon this. As a meta-organisation, GBI would fall into this category as it decides only on membership, hierarchy, and rules and has an overall weak average of decisionality (about 1.6, see Table 2.6). Another example of an open club type may be Fab City, an association of municipalities that undertakes little decision-making. Fab City provides a forum to cities with a shared interest in sustainability transition and the use of fab labs (see Capdevila & Zarlenga, 2015).

The thin meta-organising category includes meta-organisational structures where many organisational elements are decided upon but with little decisionality. In other words, a thin meta-organising organisation embraces many organisational elements, from membership to hierarchy. However, few collective decisions are made on those elements, whether because members are reluctant to increase decisionality or because the meta-organisation is too new to have implemented decision-making processes.

The thick partial meta-organising category would encompass a meta-organisation where few organisational elements are decided upon (e.g. membership and hierarchy alone) but where those elements are highly structured – that is, they have a higher degree of decisionality. This could be the case in meta-organisations that serve the collective strategies of their members but do not seek to shape their members' behaviour or actions. Some trade associations could serve as examples of thick partial meta-organising: although these have an organising effect on their members, that effect is strictly limited to specific dimensions.

The final category, thick meta-organising, in contrast, describes meta-organisations that combine many organisational elements with greater decisionality, as is the case with Cluster B. Here, the meta-organisation moves towards a state of completeness of the organisation. This means many decisions are made on every organizational component (Ahrne & Brunsson, 2011; Schoeneborn & Dobusch, 2019) (see Figure 2.2). We can assume that such meta-organisations have strong organising effects on their members and their environments, such as markets and regulators.

While this study has not addressed evolution per se, we can provide a basis for understanding the transformation, stabilisation, and destabilisation processes of meta-organising clusters and collective action among organisations in general. Figure 2.2 shows how meta-organising can vary across two axes: from partial to complete in terms of structural organisationality; and from thinness to thickness in terms of decisionality. Meta-organisations are not fixed in one profile. Indeed, Ahrne and Brunsson (2008) argue that organisations and meta-organisations are constituted by decisions; yet, decisions always remain provisional. They are attempts at an agreement but can always be questioned. Decisions, therefore, produce an irreducible uncertainty – that is organisation is always unstable and can be destabilised further by new decisions (Brunsson & Jutterström, 2018). Figure 2.2 illustrates how destabilisation can occur in meta-organising, where a meta-organisation moves from thick to thin or the other way around. From this perspective, the meta-organising stabilisation and destabilisation processes occur when structural changes affect decisions. In other words, change in a meta-organising profile results from a change to the degree of structural organisationality – that is the presence or absence of decisions on membership, hierarchy, rules, monitoring, sanction, and changes in decisionality – that is the extent to which those elements are the object of decisions.

Discussion, theoretical contributions, and future research

The objective of the current research was to understand to what extent meta-organisations are themselves organised and thus to respond to a repeated call to investigate variations in the organisational structure of such meta-organisations (Ahrne et al., 2016b; Berkowitz & Bor, 2018; Spillman, 2018). Further, we sought to analyse if and how the multiplicity and interrelatedness of decisions systems in meta-organisations affect the meta-organising process. We contribute to the literature on meta-organisations and the study of clusters by providing an integrated framework connecting organisationality and decisionality. Based on the unpacking of structural organisationality and decisionality, we propose four profiles: thin partial meta-organising, thin meta-organising, thick partial meta-organising, and thick meta-organising. This research moves beyond the few predictions provided in the literature about the organisation of meta-organisations. In particular, the current study challenges the implicit assumption that meta-organisations are all similarly organised with little hierarchy, monitoring, or sanction capability. Ahrne et al. (2016b) pointed out that meta-organisations are generally reluctant to be fully organised. That reluctance manifests itself as the selective use of structural organisationality. However, that reluctance may vary across arrangements; for instance certain clusters use standards rather than binding rules, and they usually cannot monitor their members because those members want to retain their autonomy. However, some meta-organisations have more authority and sanctioning power than others. We also show that there can be significant variations in the uses of membership, hierarchy, rules, monitoring, and sanctions as well as their decisionality – that is the extent to which these elements are the object of collective decisions.

We contribute to organisation studies by operationalising the concept of partial organisation (Ahrne & Brunsson, 2011, 2019) or structural organisationality (Grothe-Hammer et al., 2022) at the meta-organisation level. We provide the first integrative analytical framework allowing the study and systemic comparison of meta-organisations. By emphasising the role of decisions in meta-organisations through the concept of decisionality, we extend recent efforts to restore decisions to the centre of organisation studies (Ahrne et al., 2016b; Berkowitz & Grothe-Hammer, 2021; Grothe-Hammer et al., 2022). Our research has implications for the study of collective action in general, as it might finally permit accounting for and understanding the differences between (meta/partial) organisations, networks, and institutions (Ahrne & Brunsson, 2011). Networks and institutions are expected to exhibit lesser decisionality, with varying degrees of organisationality. Exploring these variations would be crucial to understanding processes of institutionalisation of meta-organisations.

Future research might use our framework to develop this theorising further and then build upon, strengthen, challenge, or refine it. It would be useful to study the drivers that may trigger organisationality–decisionality dynamics. The fluidity in meta-organising profiles could be affected by different variables, such as place, time, the composition of membership, tensions between autonomy and hierarchy (Kerwer, 2013), consistency of goals between the meta-organisation and its members (Garaudel, 2020), or tentative organisationality such as collective identity or (responsible) actorhood (Berkowitz & Gadille, this volume). Further, a fruitful avenue of investigation might be to connect organisationality and decisionality to the design of meta-organisations as actors contributing positively or negatively to the transition of our societies to sustainability (Bor & O'Shea, this volume). Last, temporality necessarily affects (partial) organising and meta-organising. Future research could focus on temporal changes in organisationality and decisionality and highlight the resulting evolutionary trajectories of meta-organisations' stabilisation, destabilisation, and institutionalisation.

Appendix

Table 2.7 Key criteria of the partial organisation framework applied to a meta-organisation (MO)

Key criteria of the partial organisation framework applied to a meta-organisation (MO)				
Membership	*Hierarchy*	*Rules*	*Monitoring*	*Sanction*
Is there a membership (a list of members)?	Is there a decision from members to vest authority in the MO?	Are there decisions made about action and/or behavioural parameters?	Is there a decision by the MO to monitor behaviour, efforts, or results?	Are there decisions on sanctions (positive or negative)?
Does the MO decide who can become a member?	Is cooperation authority vested in a collective of members?	Are the decided rules written down?	Are non-members (also) monitored?	Are non-members (also) sanctioned?
Are there different, pre-determined categories of membership?	Is cooperation authority further vested in a or various smaller internal groups?	Are the decided rules collected in rule books or charters?	Is the process of gathering observations considered trustworthy by decision-makers?	Is there a defined set of criteria and a process for sanctioning?
Do members determine other members' access or exit?	Is coordination authority vested in committees/ workgroups (and possible sub-groups)?	Are there different rulesets for different areas?	Is reporting of findings accessible and easily understandable?	Have negative sanctions been applied?
Are contributions to the MO and participation in activities restricted to members only?	Is coordination authority vested in offices (in an administrative organisation)?	Do members voluntarily agree to follow decided rules?	Is the reporting made available outside the MO?	Are sanctions consistently applied?

References

Ahrne, G., & Brunsson, N. (2005). Organizations and meta-organizations. *Scandinavian Journal of Management, 21*(4), 429–449. https://doi.org/10.1016/j.scaman.2005.09.005

Ahrne, G., & Brunsson, N. (2008). *Meta-organizations*. Edward Elgar Publishing.

Ahrne, G., & Brunsson, N. (2011). Organization outside organizations: The significance of partial organization. *Organization, 18*(1), 83–104. https://doi.org/10.1177/1350508410376256

Ahrne, G., & Brunsson, N. (2019). *Organization outside organizations: The abundance of partial organization in social life*. Cambridge University Press.

Ahrne, G., Brunsson, N., & Kerwer, D. (2016a). The paradox of organizing states: A meta-organization perspective on international organizations. *Journal of International Organizations Studies*, 7(1), 5–24.

Ahrne, G., Brunsson, N., & Seidl, D. (2016b). Resurrecting organization by going beyond organizations. *European Management Journal, 34*(2), 93–101. https://doi.org/10.1016/j.emj.2016.02.003

Albers, S., Wohlgezogen, F., & Zajac, E. J. (2016). Strategic alliance structures: An organization design perspective. *Journal of Management, 42*(3), 582–614. https://doi.org/10.1177/0149206313488209

Arora-Jonsson, S., Brunsson, N., & Hasse, R. (2020). Where does competition come from? The role of organization. *Organization Theory, 1*(1), 2631787719889977. https://doi.org/10.1177/2631787719889977

Berkowitz, H., & Bor, S. (2018). Why meta-organizations matter: A response to Lawton et al. and Spillman. *Journal of Management Inquiry, 27*(2), 204–211. https://doi.org/10.1177/1056492617712895

Berkowitz, H., Bucheli, M., & Dumez, H. (2017). Collective CSR strategy and the role of meta-organisations: A case study of the oil and gas industry. *Journal of Business Ethics, 143*(4), 753–769.

Berkowitz, H., Crowder, L. B., & Brooks, C. M. (2020). Organizational perspectives on sustainable ocean governance: A multi-stakeholder, meta-organization model of collective action. *Marine Policy, 118*, 104026. https://doi.org/10.1016/j.marpol.2020.104026

Berkowitz, H., & Gadille, M. (this volume). Meta-organizing clusters as agents of transformative change through "responsible actorhood". In E. Lupova-Henry & N. F. Dotti (Eds.), *Clusters and sustainable regional development: A meta-organisational approach*. Routledge.

Berkowitz, H., & Grothe-Hammer, M. (2021). From a clash of social orders to a loss of decidability in meta-organizations tackling grand challenges: The case of Japan leaving the international whaling commission. *Research in the Sociology of Organizations*. https://halshs.archives-ouvertes.fr/halshs-03271137

Bor, S. (2014). *A theory of meta-organisation: An analysis of steering processes in European commission-funded R&D "network of excellence" consortia* [Doctoral Thesis]. Hanken School of Economics.

Bor, S., & O'Shea, G. (this volume). The roles of meta-organisations in transitions: Evidence from food packaging transition. In E. Lupova-Henry & N. F. Dotti (Eds.), *Clusters and sustainable regional development: A meta-organisational approach*. Routledge.

Brunsson, N., & Jutterström, M. (2018). *Organizing and reorganizing markets*. Oxford University Press.

Brunsson, N., Rasche, A., & Seidl, D. (2012). The dynamics of standardization: Three perspectives on standards in organization studies. *Organization Studies, 33*(5–6), 613–632. https://doi.org/10.1177/0170840612450120

Capdevila, I., & Zarlenga, M. I. (2015). Smart city or smart citizens? The Barcelona case. *Journal of Strategy and Management, 8*(3), 266–282. https://doi.org/10.1108/JSMA-03-2015-0030

Cropper, S., & Bor, S. (2018). (Un)bounding the meta-organization: Co-evolution and compositional dynamics of a health partnership. *Administrative Sciences, 8*(3), 42. https://doi.org/10.3390/admsci8030042

Dobusch, L., & Schoeneborn, D. (2015). Fluidity, identity, and organizationality: The communicative constitution of anonymous. *Journal of Management Studies, 52*(8), 1005–1035. https://doi.org/10.1111/joms.12139

Gadille, M., Tremblay, D.-G., & Vion, A. (2013). La méta-organisation territorialisée, moteur d'apprentissages collectifs. *Revue Interventions économiques. Papers in Political Economy, 48*, Article 48. https://journals.openedition.org/interventionseconomiques/2156

Garaudel, P. (2020). Exploring meta-organizations' diversity and agency: A meta-organizational perspective on global union federations. *Scandinavian Journal of Management, 36*(1), 101094. https://doi.org/10.1016/j.scaman.2020.101094

Grothe-Hammer, M. (2019a). Membership or contributorship? Managing the inclusion of individuals into organizations. In G. Ahrne & N. Brunsson (Eds.), *Organization outside organizations. The abundance of partial organization in social life* (pp. 84–112). Cambridge University Press.

Grothe-Hammer, M. (2019b). Organization without actorhood: Exploring a neglected phenomenon. *European Management Journal, 37*(3), 325–338. https://doi.org/10.1016/j.emj.2018.07.009

Grothe-Hammer, M., Berkowitz, H., & Berthod, O. (2022). Decisional organization theory: Towards an integrated framework of organization. In M. Godwyn (Ed.), *Research handbook on the sociology of organizations* (pp. 30–53). Edward Elgar Publishing Ltd.

Gulati, R., Wohlgezogen, F., & Zhelyazkov, P. (2012). The two facets of collaboration: Cooperation and coordination in strategic alliances. *Academy of Management Annals, 6*(1), 531–583. https://doi.org/10.5465/19416520.2012.691646

Kerwer, D. (2013). International organizations as meta-organizations: The case of the European Union. *Journal of International Organizations Studies, 4*(2), 40–53.

King, A. A., & Lenox, M. J. (2000). Industry self-regulation without sanctions: The chemical industry's responsible care program. *Academy of Management Journal, 43*(4), 698–716. https://doi.org/10.5465/1556362

Laamanen, M., Bor, S., & den Hond, F. (2019). The dilemma of organization in social movement initiatives. In G. Ahrne & N. Brunsson (Eds.), *Organization outside organizations: The abundance of partial organization in social life* (pp. 293–317). Cambridge University Press. https://doi.org/10.1017/9781108604994.014

Lupova-Henry, E., Blili, S., & Dal Zotto, C. (2021). Designing organised clusters as social actors: A meta-organisational approach. *Journal of Organization Design*. https://doi.org/10.1007/s41469-021-00092-5

Lupova-Henry, E., & Dotti, N. F. (this volume). Clusters as collective actors and agents of change for (new) sustainable path development. In E. Lupova-Henry & N. F. Dotti (Eds.), *Clusters and sustainable regional development: A meta-organisational approach*. Routledge

Nielsen, K. R. (2018). Crowdfunding through a partial organization lens: The co-dependent organization. *European Management Journal, 36*(6), 695–707. https://doi.org/10.1016/j.emj.2018.01.006

Osterloh, M., & Frey, B. S. (2015). Ranking games. *Evaluation Review, 39*(1), 102–129. https://doi.org/10.1177/0193841X14524957

Ostrom, E. (1990). *Governing the commons: The evolution of institutions for collective action*. Cambridge University Press.

Provan, K. G., & Kenis, P. (2008). Modes of network governance: Structure, management, and effectiveness. *Journal of Public Administration Research and Theory, 18*(2), 229–252. https://doi.org/10.1093/jopart/mum015

Rothschild-Whitt, J. (1979). The collectivist organization: An alternative to rational-bureaucratic models. *American Sociological Review, 44*(4), 509–527. https://doi.org/10.2307/2094585

Sauder, M., & Espeland, W. N. (2009). The discipline of rankings: Tight coupling and organizational change. *American Sociological Review, 74*(1), 63–82. https://doi.org/10.1177/000312240907400104

Schoeneborn, D., & Dobusch, L. (2019). Alternating between partial and complete organization: The case of anonymous. In G. Ahrne & N. Brunsson (Eds.), *Organization outside organizations: The abundance of partial organization in social life* (pp. 318–333). Cambridge University Press. https://doi.org/10.1017/9781108604994.015

Spillman, L. (2018). Meta-organization matters. *Journal of Management Inquiry, 27*(1), 16–20. https://doi.org/10.1177/1056492616688856

3 What governance for regional innovation clusters? Meta-organisational analysis of the German innovation cluster 'Physics for Food'

Christiane GEBHARDT

Introduction: innovation clusters and regional transformation

In German Innovation Policy, clusters as meta-organisations or 'organisations of organisations' (Ahrne et al., 2016) are considered suitable mechanisms for addressing the complexity of regional transformation. They integrate the many diverse regional players necessary for re-building or creating productive systems and sustainable value chains and for bringing about change in society by activating a critical mass of players with a new joint mission and strategy (Apelt et al., 2017).

In 2017, Germany's Ministry of Education and Research (BMBF) set up the 'WIR! Regional Transformation Programme' to fund innovation clusters (see BMBF Innovation & Strukturwandel, 2022) seen as 'social actors' (Lupova-Henry et al., 2021) with a 'spatial or territorial anchorage' (Gadille et al., 2013) in structurally weak regions. These temporary meta-organisations (MOs) provide the creation of new value chains, technology transfer, and rapid utilisation of scientific knowledge for societal and industrial benefit, as well as the mitigation of problems in regional transformation such as 'brain drain' or unemployment.

This chapter discusses the case of the WIR! 'Physics for Food' cluster in Northeast Germany, focused on agro-food innovations (Physics for Food, 2022a). This innovation cluster challenges environmentally and socially unsustainable practices, supports entrepreneurial spinoffs, and aims to enhance farmers' autonomy. The study employs a meta-organisational analysis to illustrate how strategy-driven organisational design and governance of innovation must be taken into account for regional transformation and sustainable development. The research is based on interviews and action research in cluster strategy meetings (Argyris & Schön, 1989; Dick, 2011). It covers the stages of cluster formation and operation in the funding period 2018–2021.

This chapter analyses regional innovation clusters as a specific meta-organisation (MO). Such clusters are characterised by a high degree of 'organisationality', that is the degree to which a social collective organisation

DOI: 10.4324/9781003215066-5

displays the three following characteristics: (1) interconnected instances of decision-making, (2) actor-hood, and (3) identity (Dobusch & Schoeneborn, 2015). Such clusters employ a rich repertoire of organisational components such as 'membership, hierarchy, rules, monitoring, and sanctions' (Berkowitz & Dumez, 2016) as well as system-building elements, such as strategy and informal communication addressing the 'collective identity' of the member organisations (MO) (Grothe-Hammer & Cour, 2020). Furthermore, innovation clusters can be seen as complete MOs (Berkowitz & Bor, 2018). Indeed, they display such characteristics as a high degree of integration, the particular decision-making structure of a loosely coupled network of diverse stakeholders with complementary functions, and the 'thickness or breadth of decisionality', that is the extent to which decisions are made about organisational elements (Ahrne et al., 2016).

This chapter suggests critically re-examining the role of regional innovation clusters for regional transformation and innovation in the light of organisationality and decisionality. Despite the widespread use of innovation clusters in regional innovation policies (Gebhardt, 2012; Rothgang et al., 2017; Tödtling & Trippl, 2013), it is difficult to evaluate the impact of cluster policies on regional development (Martin & Sunley, 2003, 2011, 2012; Ritala et al., 2013).

Concentrating on the organisational aspects of MOs, the chapter discusses whether regional innovation clusters are an adequate instrument for inducing innovative and entrepreneurial pathways in the region (Audretsch et al., 2016). To do so, the chapter analyses the organisational 'black box' of innovation clusters in relation to the steering problem of MOs (Garaudel, 2020) or the governance of innovation (Cooke et al., 2000) and in the context of the regional system in which they are embedded (Adapa et al., 2020; Rutten & Boekema, 2007). The chapter builds upon the theoretical framework for meta-organisational analysis proposed by Berkowitz and Bor (2018). The question then is, what kind of adaptive governance is necessary to initiate regional growth: that is permit MOs to cope flexibly with conflicts of interest, collectively follow trial-and-error paths of innovation strategies, exit blind alleys of high technologies and innovation pathways. Insights from the innovation cluster 'Physics for Food' will be used to discuss the organisational characteristics of clusters in innovation policy and the adequacy of the related governance employed in the German case.

The following section places innovation clusters within the meta-organisational framework and discusses the literature on governance of innovation and transformation. The action research design of the empirical study and the data collection methods are then outlined. The following sections present the case describing the WIR! Programme and its funding criteria, outlining 'Physics for Food' cluster strategy and organisational design, and revealing the interaction and decision-making structure. The findings are then discussed concerning the adequacy of governance models for MOs and their impact on regional innovation systems. The chapter concludes by presenting the avenues for future research in the governance of innovation clusters.

Theoretical framing

Innovation clusters: MOs in the regional innovation system

Federally funded regional innovation programmes frequently focus on clusters as a mechanism for regional innovation promotion (Hassink, 2005; Rothgang et al., 2017). This instrument points to the increasing importance of meta-organisations in place-based innovation policies (Barca, 2019) and regional transformation (Gebhardt, 2012; Gebhardt & Pohlmann, 2013; Isaksen et al., 2018; Koschatzky & Stahlecker, 2010; Tödtling & Trippl, 2013). Two research agendas in organisational science can be linked to regional innovation and transformation. The first is the meta-organisational perspective on clusters (Beer, 1985; Lupova-Henry et al., 2021); the other is the management of networks and systems (Provan et al., 2007; Schwaninger, 2006; Schwaninger et al., 2006; Sydow, 1992, 2009) and MOs (Berkowitz & Dumez, 2016; Garaudel, 2020).

In an organisational context, regional innovation clusters represent a 'decided social order' comprising five elements – membership, rules, hierarchy, monitoring, and sanctions – resting on collective decisions. The presence of these organisational elements indicates that clusters can be seen as complete MOs (Ahrne et al., 2016; Grothe-Hammer, 2019). The networking structure of clusters allows for plurality, that is participation of many institutional stakeholders (Berkowitz et al., 2020) and citizens (Gebhardt, 2020; Wanner et al., 2018), facilitating change and rapid adaptation to new conditions. From a management viewpoint, innovation clusters are used to avoid the disadvantages of large hierarchical organisations, such as organisational bottlenecks, lack of flexibility, and slowness of decision-making when coping with complexity. Many authors claim that networks, clusters, or systems are suitable instruments for addressing the change dimension inherent in the transformation of regional systems (Castells, 2010; Isaksen et al., 2018; Provan et al., 2007).

Consequently, the rapidly growing literature on transition management and system innovation has provided insight into the evolutionary aspects of transformations, systems orchestration for sustainable development, and regional resilience characterised by the ability to absorb change and recover from disruptions (Donohue et al., 2016; Elmqvist et al., 2003; Ritala et al., 2013). For example Abreu (2011) illustrates the importance of variety for absorptiveness of regions; while Hassink (2005) details the necessity of adaptiveness of regional innovation systems for sustainable development. This range of actors and topics provides many synergies and rich diversity of responses (Elmqvist et al., 2003) – reflected in the debates on regional innovation ecosystems (Farinha et al., 2020; Moser & Rice, 2016).

In this systemic and evolutionary perspective, innovation clusters are seen as experimental testbeds for new developments or 'incubation rooms' allowing to cultivate new 'socio-economic regimes'. Clusters are organisational mediums where new standards, techniques, rules, and laws are created, selected, tested, and rolled out (Geels, 2005; Köhler et al., 2019). In particular, knowledge-based innovation clusters comprising universities, industry, and government – so-called

Triple Helix constellations – can contribute to tapping regional potential (Etzkowitz, 2012; Ruhrmann et al., 2021). They can help regions become 'global economic hot spots where new technologies germinate at an astounding rate and where pools of capital, expertise, and talent foster the development of new industries and new ways of doing business' (Engel, 2015, p. 36).

Given this potential, innovation clusters became, for policymakers, an advanced tool for meeting the complex challenges of regional transformation and evolutionary path development. This perspective bridges concepts such as proximity (Golra et al., 2018) and networking relationships of regional actors (Huggins & Prokop, 2017; Lupova-Henry & Dotti, 2019; Vermeulen & Paier, 2017) with the regional innovation system approach where partners from industry, science, and government create synergies, and systems develop new properties (Cooke, 2013; Ruhrmann et al., 2021). These space-based concepts enrich the current framework to analyse MOs as embedded systems (Berkowitz et al., 2020).

With the popularity of clusters in regional innovation policy, specific requirements in terms of structural organisationality and decisionality of the MO have become a condition for funding. Thus the competence-based, competitive cluster strategy (Gebhardt, 2012) defines cluster boundaries by setting membership criteria and procedures. These ideally provide sufficient transparency for member engagement and autonomous action, space for self-reflection, dialogue, and collective decision-making. Furthermore, cluster members decide on structural elements and organisational rules such as hierarchies and monitoring (Grothe-Hammer & Cour, 2020) suitable for facilitating strategy implementation. Moreover, the communication and interaction of cluster members (Ruhrmann et al., 2021) with regional, national, and global challenges is an essential element for cluster coherence (Lapoutte, 2021) and system building (Gebhardt, 2013; Leydesdorff, 2021).

Adaptive governance of innovation for the dynamics of evolution and transformation

Intervention that disrupts existing institutional arrangements to induce regional and industrial growth remains difficult to legitimise and organise (Cooke et al., 2000). Managing regional transformation and organisational change is complex and prone to conflicts arising from different rationalities of industry, academia, and the state. In addition, the clusters' institutional logics might eventually clash along the regional development path having different regional effects (Boschma et al., 2017; Boschma & Frenken, 2018).

As outlined earlier, the ability of clusters to collectively anticipate and avoid the consequences of declining sectors by inducing regional transformation relies on self-organisation and setting the action-guiding structure for co-evolutionary processes (Boschma et al., 2017; Gong & Hassink, 2019; Isaksen et al., 2018; Martin & Sunley, 2015). Therefore, innovation governance must be adaptive and ideally 'enable actors to be flexible, adaptable to changing circumstances, and experimental' (Clement, 2021). Governance includes 'mechanisms of monitoring and feedback to regularly adjust the way things are done' (Clement, 2021, p. 53). Furthermore, Keping (2018) offers a definition of governance that embraces formal rules, integrative actions, and informal interaction in an evolutionary perspective. Consequently, governance must be understood as a process in which communication and interaction patterns, values, strategy, and commonly established rules become an accepted reality in the system, reinforced by reverberation, interaction, and collective reflection (Schwaninger, 2006; Schwaninger et al., 2006). Governance implies that cluster members and stakeholders of the system are orchestrated, know their role and contribution in the cluster, and balance their interests with the system's environment. Finally, Ranga and Etzkowitz (2013) relate the organisational properties of clusters to the necessity to manage a 'consensus space'.

Research design

This chapter uses a longitudinal study and qualitative research approach and discusses the 'Physics for Food' innovation cluster located in a structurally weak agrarian region in Northeast Germany. The cluster is funded by Germany's Ministry of Education and Research (BMBF) through the WIR! Programme 'Innovation and Structural Transformation'. This programme addresses structurally weak and underdeveloped regions in Eastern Germany. The research took place in 2018–2021 and was based on interviews, documents, and action research in regular strategy meetings, with accompanying action, critical reflection, and learning (Argyris & Schön, 1989; Dick, 2011). Table 3.1 gives an overview of the methods, data sources, and objectives addressing the concept of governance as outlined in the literature.

The backbone of the research was the development and implementation of the cluster strategy. The study sought to obtain insight into the following:

1. The *internal cluster interactions and decision-making processes* to validate the concept of organisationality and decisionality and the degree to which main components were applied.
2. The *thickness of the meta-organisation (MO)* to validate the MO category of the innovation cluster.
3. The congruity of cluster strategy, organisation, and environment for adaptability and cohesion.
4. The adequacy of innovation governance and the policy impact on regional transformation (*i.e. use of innovation clusters in innovation policy*).

Case study: the Physics for Food innovation cluster

Regional situation

In the German Bundesland Mecklenburg-Vorpommern, large-scale structured and industrialised farming prevails. The region has 1.34 million ha of agricultural land, with 4,700 farms employing more than 25,000 persons. Ecological farming accounts for 9.2 per cent of the total area suitable for farming (Mecklenburg-Vorpommern Landesregierung, 2022).

Table 3.1 Methods, data sources, and objectives

Methods	*Data source*	*Research objectives (Governance indicators)*
Unstructured stakeholder interviews	Cluster members from industry and science, all functions (team leaders, team members, spokesmen, advisory body, cluster support functions such as strategy, communication, and monitoring). Interviews with speakers of the core organisations: INP Institute of Cold Plasma Physics (Applied Science); University of Applied Science Neubrandenburg; Ceravis, seed producer in the region and subsidiary of the global company Agravis (industry). Interviews within the agro-food sector.	Previous cluster experiences (acceptance of decisionality and organisational depth). Motivation/rationale for cluster membership (values). Contribution to cluster strategy (Values). Strategy targets of home organisation and conflict of interest (cohesion). Networking, interaction mode (depth, trust). External visibility, strategic fit (cohesion).
Survey	All cluster members	Benefit and value (cohesion). Contribution to cluster mission (values).
White Papers/Reports	Concept, strategy proposal (tenders, terms of reference), and organisational chart, GANNT chart. Cluster reporting. Board of Trustees and General Assembly presentations and minutes. Report to Government agency and Ministry: BMBF and PTJ.	Cluster strategy in relation to regional benefit (adaptability). Trends and drivers in the agro-food sector (disturbances).
Analytical tools employed for discussion	SWOT, PESTLE, critical path, value chain, market intelligence for business models.	Discussion of results and strategy adaptation (cohesion, adaptability, decisionality). Organisational structure (organisationality). Congruity of strategic analysis and cluster strategy (adaptability).
Action research	Formal member meetings. Formal Board meetings. Strategy meetings. Conferences. Thematic workshops.	Proceedings, communication culture, decision-making (adaptability). Intervention patterns (adaptability). Organisational elements.

Currently, the structurally weak region is characterised by large agricultural fields, rigid and globally defined value chains 'from farm to fork', and unsustainable practices in terms of land use and use of fertilisers and pesticides (Mecklenburg-Vorpommern Landesregierung, 2022). The headquarters of the AgroSciences industry are located outside the region, but local farmers depend on them for chemically treated seeds, fertilisers, and pesticides for regional crops cultivated in monocultures. Retailing in Germany is similarly centralised and dictates the prices for agricultural goods. Farmers complain that the lack of autonomy in these rigid value chains and changing biodiversity legislation in Germany make their business unattractive and economically unreliable (Physics for Food, 2019b). At the same time, the sector offers a relevant potential for sustainability gains and needs to adapt to new biodiversity targets and sustainability taxonomies (Lyal et al., 2008). The Physics for Food innovation cluster responds directly to these sectoral and regional challenges. Table 3.2 summarises the cluster developmental stages.

Set-up phase

To obtain funding in the framework of the WIR! Programme, innovation clusters needed to relate to the Ministry's specific objectives to meet its funding criteria. These objectives included creating new innovative activities in underdeveloped regions, long-term potential for job creation and economic growth, and improving quality of life. Moreover, existing regional competencies must be considered a foundation for new developmental paths. Thus, proposed solutions needed to focus on areas where the region already had economic, scientific–technological, or social activities. Another requirement was the participation

Table 3.2 Cluster development, topics, and governance indicators

Period	*Cluster development stage*	*Topics*	*Governance indicators*
2018	Set up and short mission paper	Cluster competition Programme design and funding criteria	Solution-driven mission
2018 – Autumn 2018	Conceptual phase (Two cluster strategy workshops/all members)	Development of cluster strategy, project strategies, and organisational design	Competence-based strategy as a joint task Organisational design Joint learning, establishing rules, and code of conduct
2019 to Autumn 2019	Scientific front-runner projects	Proof of principle	Science and evidence-driven innovation
2019–2022	Strategy implementation phase	Operation, evaluation, and strategy alignment	Decision-making regional impact

of and collaboration between many regional actors, such as firms (SMEs and young firms), universities, and research institutes. In addition, for groups with no experience in innovation, the citizens concerned needed to be involved in the regional development process. Education and training could be included if relevant to regional innovativeness (BMBF Innovation & Strukturwandel, 2022). Thus, the clusters needed to specify the innovation concept, present a coherent strategy, and define suitable cluster members and the organisational structure. Funding was provided for the concept phase to define a joint strategy and – after assessment by an expert jury – for strategy implementation. Of 44 proposals, 23 were eventually funded (BMBF Innovation & Strukturwandel, 2022).

After 2 years, clusters assessed the progress and outlined the plan to implement the strategy further. In a best-case scenario, the funding period covered 6 years from initial draft to implementation, with funding of a maximum of 15 million Euros given directly to the participating members based on funding quotas and financial planning defined in the cluster strategy. The funding period of 6 years was granted based on a self-evaluation exercise covering proof of principles (science part), the portfolio of activities, a forecasted strategy check, and the progress of strategy implementation (actions part). The cluster community carried out self-evaluation with the help of an advisory body installed by the cluster.

Conceptual phase (strategy definition)

In the Physics for Food case, the research institute INP took the lead in organising the proposal phase. This institute enjoyed an excellent track record of winning BMBF cluster programmes (BMBF Innovation & Strukturwandel, 2022) and other research tenders and managing interdisciplinary clusters. INP, together with Ceravis, a seed supplier, and the Neubrandenburg University of Applied Sciences developed a short mission paper for collaboration. The BMBF welcomed this mission paper inviting the cluster to design a strategy concept. The cluster's mission was to build an innovative value chain with reduced use of chemicals in a Triple Helix setting involving scientists, the business sector (the German Farmers' Association), and policymakers.

The cluster pursued the following aims (Physics for Food, 2019a): reduction of the use of chemical pesticides, protection of crop yields endangered by climate change, technology transfer, protection of seeds and resilience of crops, optimisation of agricultural resources for food processing and reduction of harmful substances in food production, creation of and securing employment through technology, and treatment of agricultural water. Figure 3.1 shows the participating sectors and actors.

Strategy development in the conceptual phase involved up to 49 members and followed a systematic process. In the first strategy workshop, the current situation and the group members' competencies related to the mission were assessed. In the second workshop, the participants considered the possible trends and drivers in the agricultural and food industry and the potential impact of

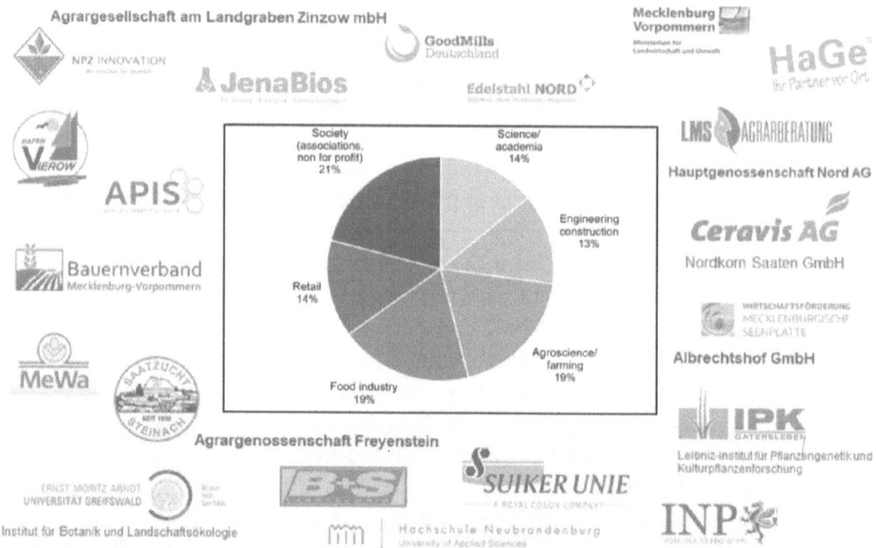

Figure 3.1 Cluster members

Source: Physics for Food, 2019a

replacing the chemical treatment of seeds and plants with alternative methods. Based on SWOT analysis, cluster members agreed on the critical challenges and developed a range of project ideas to answer these challenges. This exercise was followed by the definition of feasible key projects that had the potential to disrupt or modernise the existing value chain, lead to start-up creation, or contribute to the development of new products and processes for non-chemical seed treatment. The cluster members then designed four science-industry projects and three to facilitate technology transfer through legal services, strategy process management, and communication. The cluster decided upon an organisational structure to clarify responsibilities and tasks and define the degree of integration and mode of co-working of the participating members in different locations (source: Physics for Food, 2019a, and interviews).

The mission statement and strategy of the Physics for Food cluster that resulted from the workshops focused on the development and testing of innovative technologies to reduce the use of chemical fertilisers and plant protection products, and to improve the durability of seeds in an environmentally safe manner, without yield decrease (Physics for Food, 2022a). Figure 3.2 summarises these mission statements.

Proof of principle for the technology outside the laboratory was an important project milestone and was, therefore, the initial focus of the cluster. Accordingly, a basic front-runner research project started before the other strategic projects. Equally, certification, patenting, and quality standards played a significant role

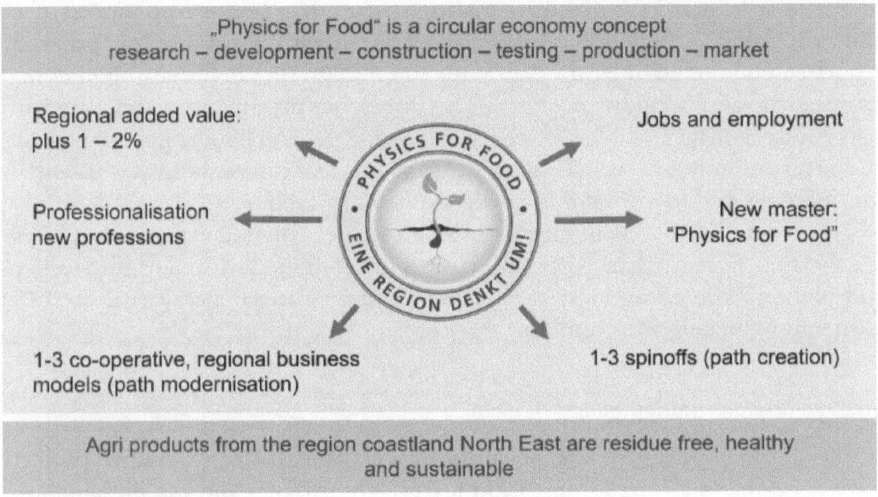

Figure 3.2 Mission statements (dark shading) and strategic objectives (light shading) of the cluster

Source: Physics for Food, 2019a

in the sustainability of the new industrial path. They were accommodated in a supporting project that dealt with technology transfer issues and approval of new engineering procedures.

Concurrently, and in collaboration with local universities, the cluster set out to support the emergence of start-up firms by creating new business models with students and providing innovation input for local SMEs and the agro-industry. The innovation cluster wanted to facilitate new firm formation through incubators and food-related 'hackathons' to develop citizen-, student-, and farmer-driven business models. Thus, participatory governance models for the farming and food industries were integrated elements of the strategic initiative. These models offered new job prospects and incentivised students and young farmers to stay in the region. The cluster strategy focused on Bundesland Mecklenburg-Vorpommern regional priority areas such as health, food production, and biotechnology and relied on the locally cultivated and exported crops. Membership in the cluster was formalised by Letters of Intent, and key roles were defined for members, such as leading the strategy projects or cluster support functions such as communication, monitoring, and strategy development. The team leaders or responsible persons were approved by their home organisations. Spokespeople for the innovation cluster represented it in public, and the media and came from three core member organisations. They also were responsible for troubleshooting and organising decision-making processes with external, volunteer advisory boards comprising representatives of the German Farmers' Association, the regional Chamber of Commerce, a global enterprise in the food industry, local SMEs, the regional consumer organisation, and an expert in regional innovation studies. In a bottom-up process, the cluster approved a 'light-touch' monitoring system with short monthly progress reports, a code of conduct for patenting and publishing the results, open communication, and periodic meetings. The three core organisations appointed an operations manager to oversee the proceedings and strategy implementation and escalate problems, if necessary. Bottom-up decision-making was essential for openness and trust-building in the cluster (see Table 3.1).

The Physics for Food cluster was awarded limited funding at the end of 2019 for the two front-runner proposals: basic science projects in plant physiology and physics. The entire cluster concept was also financed at the end of 2019 with approximately €7.1 million.

Strategy implementation phase

In the implementation phase, scientific results from the front-runner project were accepted as a sound foundation for further research and the initialisation of technology transfer and commercialisation. However, divergent interests and varying pace of the thematic development paths represented a challenge for the cluster. Specifically, the front-runner project implied building local production facilities, but these were delayed by validation of results in the field. In cluster meetings, members assessed competitive technologies outside the cluster, conducting detailed benchmarking of the European and global markets rather than considering the regional context. Moreover, although laboratory trials of alternative seed treatment technologies gave promising first results concerning seed germination, plant vigour, root growth, and plant resilience (Mitra et al., 2014), the industry was reluctant to invest in the new technologies.

At the same time, local enterprises that experienced the negative financial impact of the COVID-19 crisis urged scientists to adopt a faster pace, something not congruent with usual scientific methods. Furthermore, traditional pathogen and crop-driven patenting requirements contradicted the integrative plant resilience and protection approach. The complexity inherent in combining different crops, technologies, and soil and weather-dependent field research became obvious. At every stage, decontamination and removal of seed surface diseases, propagation, viability, germination, sprouting, rooting, and establishment of plants had to be tested, with different path developments arising as a consequence. While decontamination of seed and plant environments generated some industry interest, seed vigour and plant resilience projects, which offered a disruptive path of innovation, began to attract other research groups in Asia and Russia but alarmed local cluster-member SMEs. Activities in social innovation such as cooperative financial models were neglected, and citizen participation, such as student-based start-up workshops, was postponed due to COVID-19 restrictions and the prevailing business-to-business orientation of the strategy. The cluster members held several workshops to discuss these conflicts. In 2021, the BMBF asked for a strategy check for the funding period 2022–2025; cluster members jointly worked for the strategic objective of commercialisation within the given time frame and looked for new industrial partners to support that goal. In autumn 2021, the cluster prepared a self-evaluation and extended strategy concept for continuation and strategy realisation (funding phase 2022–2025), the total funding for which was an additional €6 million (Physics for Food, 2022b).

Discussion

The meta-organisational perspective thus has brought insight into the main characteristics of cluster governance. In particular, the findings of this research indicate that the strategy process turned out to be the most decisive governance element. Indeed, to obtain funding within the WIR! Programme, clusters were required by BMBF to develop and formalise their strategy, joint projects, and organisational design to cope with the complexity inherent in such initiatives. The INP, an experienced recipient of public funding in cluster programmes, organised a highly participative, bottom-up process with the members to discuss and decide on the channels for information sharing, rules for behaviour and collaboration, and even escalation modes in case of conflict. The following structuring elements allowed the adaptive cluster governance: formalised rules and monitoring; formal organisational design; well-defined strategy; continuing informal dialogue with a reflection on roles, values, and strategy contribution; decision-making; and conflict mitigation.

Organisationality and decisionality

The principal components of organisationality (Ahrne et al., 2016) were present and explicitly defined. Despite a decentralised financial model (funding was allocated to the cluster members and not centralised), the autonomy of member organisations was restricted by monitoring. However, the cluster management did not have the power to impose sanctions. Every member could leave the cluster and abandon the strategy without financial penalties; however, in the interviews, members told the researchers that they would stay. Ultimately, they recognised the benefits of participating in the cluster because they understood its purpose and shared the mission and many values. Sense-making was thus a solid organisational element (Weick, 1995).

Transparency was very high in the conceptual phase due to the physical meetings. In the plenaries, failures and delays were openly and respectfully discussed. This approach allowed for monitoring by social control of cluster members as they had a shared understanding of the interdependency of their actions and projects. Frequent physical meetings established a robust informal culture of collaboration based on formal rules. The objectification of goals by a strategy process created a safe space for discussing possible scenarios, outcomes, and drawbacks.

Equally, membership was reflected in the cluster strategy and joint mission, and the mode of membership was accepted by organisations and individuals involved. In addition, the initial selection of cluster members was made by matching competencies and strategic objectives roughly outlined in the first idea sketch and later in a detailed concept for strategy implementation. This fact helped assign roles to individuals in member organisations according to their expertise and implementation capacity.

Despite the bottom-up decision-making process, the cluster succeeded in establishing a transparent hierarchy. Specifically, the cluster adopted a flat hierarchy widely accepted culturally in all member organisations, including academia and industry. A cluster management organisation was created predominantly as a service provider rather than a centralised authority. If problems occurred, these could be escalated according to predefined and jointly made rules and addressed collectively. Moreover, rules were extended to include a code of conduct and communication (information sharing, publication planning, spokespersons, and external and internal communication rules). The cluster agreed to remain open to ideas on how to deal with external competition. This information was made visible in strategy checks, and external rival innovations – new solutions that challenged the cluster's purpose – were discussed openly. New entrants were considered if they fit the requirements of the strategy. New requirements arising from results and progress of the strategy implementation were a frequent topic, and there was room for this discussion in the meetings.

Although there was a relatively high level of formal organisationality, informal face-to-face communication and the redundancy of interaction channels also contributed to the robustness of the cluster. Moreover, the latter used a strongly participative mode of decision-making and involved members in the design phase: this increased the workload but might also have had positive effects on motivation and collaboration. Due to the inherent complexity of clusters and the external challenges the cluster faced, decision-making was frequent, and the 'togetherness' of cluster members was manifestly transparent and a topic of discussion. Finally, the extent of decisionality in the innovation cluster was high. In particular, the purpose and form of organisational elements were discussed intensively within the cluster organisation in the first phase of cluster design. The innovation cluster can thus be classified as a complete MO due to the high degrees of both organisationality and decisionality (Berkowitz & Bor, this volume).

To sum up, this research identified the following components contributing to the high degrees of organisationality and decisionality of the Physics for Food innovation cluster:

- Room for reflection and joint decision-making and learning.
- Accumulated tacit knowledge.
- Intense and transparent interaction.
- Communication on and management of conflicts of interests.
- Clear definition and consistent implementation of cluster strategy.

Innovation clusters for intervention in regional systems?

The perceived congruity of cluster strategy and its environment and the high level of cohesion and viability of the cluster implies a high level of resilience. However, trends and innovations in the global agri-food markets might overshadow the idea of contributing to an existing regional innovation system in an underdeveloped region: cluster members are increasingly challenged to become agents of change that disrupts local practices.

The strong cohesion between members, together with the trust-building through shared practices and jointly managed conflicts, can contribute to the survivability of the cluster after the funding period ends. Indeed, even though individuals in the clusters work in relatively independent projects and are bound by the institutional rules of their home organisations, the cluster might become more than just a new transitory experience – even if public funding stops. However, this research shows that the development paths from the cluster to the region and further to the global value chains are unclear both for cluster members and the funding ministry. Attracting industrial investment and innovation adoption beyond the cluster boundaries remain problematic: clusters risk becoming isolated beacons in the region. As a result, the use of innovation clusters as appropriate organisational tools for regional transformation needs to be researched further from a multi-governance perspective.

Furthermore, while the funding conditions set by the Ministry have been crucial for innovation governance in the cluster, these might limit its autonomy in decision-making and present a barrier for the strategic alignment between cluster members. Equally, strategy realisation, the limitations of the funding period, and commercialisation might eventually clash with the culture of openness and flexibility of clusters and threaten the cohesive nature of the MO.

This study has its limitations. As with most studies of clusters, data have been gathered over a too short period and contain temporal gaps. This limitation affects the ability to state with confidence whether changes in regional entrepreneurial dynamics or investments arise from this specific innovation cluster or long-term responses of the regional assemblage of clusters, institutional funding activities, or world market effects. As a result, the organisational analysis of the cluster in the context of regional studies reveals opportunities for further research on the transformation of regional innovations systems and government intervention for ecosystem building.

Conclusion: towards better governance of innovation

A systemic perspective on management and steering was employed to analyse innovation clusters as regionally embedded MOs. It was suggested that these could be viable or transitory due to their degree of organisationality and decisionality. The empirical study made it clear that the studied innovation cluster within the German WIR! Programme has a high organisationality and decisionality. Moreover, it represents an MO with a distinct experimental design of its organisation structure, management, and adaptive governance. The strategic backbone of the cluster that accounts for its environment and the knowledge-based Triple Helix design for diversity are powerful design elements. These allow for the selection of members, group cohesion, and the cluster's adaptivity to changes in external conditions. The study has demonstrated that innovation clusters are MOs that function in high-level social and technical complexity situations. Innovation policy funds such clusters as mechanisms of regional transformation on the condition that they adopt a participative, decentralised governance model. In addition to numerous funding criteria, the design of the WIR! Programme introduced new elements of citizen participation to open innovation to laypeople. The programme thus aimed to enable mutual learning and address the problem of societal acceptance of science-driven high-technology solutions.

However, the impact of the innovation cluster on the transformation and resilience of the structurally weak region must be questioned. Indeed, it seems doubtful whether public investments help the region become a 'global economic hot spot' (Engel, 2015) and whether cluster activities will eventually foster a vibrant regional innovation system with significant private investment in the new development path. Despite the congruity of cluster strategy, organisation, and cluster environment, these MOs are still not the powerhouses driving transitions in structurally weak regions. It remains to be seen whether these political instruments can fulfil their intended purpose for such regions.

Equally, rapid successful upscaling of cluster initiatives and their further development into virtual cooperation platforms or holdings can have controversial effects on the diversity necessary for resilience. A measured approach might therefore be more acceptable for regional transformation. Alternatively, the transfer of cluster activities to regions with a high density of talents and investment opportunities or withdrawal from blind innovation alleys needs to be tolerated by innovation policy – even though this might negatively affect regional employment and accelerate brain drain. Generally, the question needs to be raised about whether structurally weak regions are the correct testbed for strategy-driven innovation clusters.

However, the major weakness for adaptive governance might be the high level of the bureaucracy of the Ministry and the rigid financial and legal controls of the funding agency. Indeed, traditional financial control and assessment forms prevail in the Ministry and the innovation agency. This research suggests that the Ministry needs to adopt more flexible approaches enabling experimentation and joint learning that evolve alongside the cluster programme. This joint learning journey has still to be initiated, and there is currently no room for self-reflection in concert with the BMBF in its role as the public initiator and sponsor of these MOs. The present case illuminates the need for a new governance model that includes all formal and informal elements of governance in a functional and systemic perspective.

References

Abreu, M. (2011). Absorptive capacity in a regional context. In P. Cooke, B. Asheim, R. Boschma, R. M. D. Schwartz, & F. Tödtling (Eds.), *Handbook of regional innovation and growth*. Edward Elgar.

Adapa, S., Sheridan, A., & Yarram, S. R. (2020). *Entrepreneurship in regional communities: Exploring the relevance of embeddedness, networking, empowerment and communitarian values* (1st ed. 2021 edition). Palgrave Macmillan.

Ahrne, G., Brunsson, N., & Seidl, D. (2016). Resurrecting organization by going beyond organizations. *European Management Journal, 34*(2), 93–101. https://doi.org/10.1016/j.emj.2016.02.003

Apelt, M., Besio, C., Corsi, G., Groddeck, V., Grothe-Hammer, M., & Tacke, V. (2017). Resurrecting organisation without renouncing society: A response to Ahrne, Brunsson and Seidl. *European Management Journal, 35*(1), 8–14.

Argyris, C., & Schön, D. A. (1989). Participatory action research and action science compared: A commentary. *American Behavioral Scientist, 32*(5), 612–623. https://doi.org/10.1177/0002764289032005008

Audretsch, D., Lehmann, E., Meoli, M., & Vismara, S. (2016). *University evolution, entrepreneurial activity and regional competitiveness*. Springer International Publishing.

Barca, F. (2019). Place-based policy and politics. *Renewal: A Journal of Labour Politics, 27*(1), 84–95.

Beer, S. (1985). *Diagnosing the system for organizations* (1st ed.). Wiley.

Berkowitz, H., & Bor, S. (2018). Why meta-organizations matter: A response to Lawton et al. and Spillman. *Journal of Management Inquiry, 27*(2), 204–211. https://doi.org/10.1177/1056492617712895

Berkowitz, H., & Bor, S. (this volume). Meta-organisation as partial organisation: An integrated framework of organisationality and decisionality. In E. Lupova-Henry & N. F. Dotti (Eds.), *Clusters and sustainable regional development: A meta-organisational approach*.

Berkowitz, H., Crowder, L. B., & Brooks, C. M. (2020). Organizational perspectives on sustainable ocean governance: A multi-stakeholder, meta-organization model of collective action. *Marine Policy, 118*, 104026. https://doi.org/10.1016/j.marpol.2020.104026

Berkowitz, H., & Dumez, H. (2016). The concept of meta-organization: Issues for management studies. *European Management Review, 13*(2), 149–156. https://doi.org/10.1111/emre.12076

BMBF Innovation & Strukturwandel. (2022). *WIR! The programme*. Federal Ministry of Education and Research – BMBF Innovation & Strukturwandel. www.innovation-strukturwandel.de/strukturwandel/en/innovation-and-structural-change/wir-the-programme/wir-the-programme_node.html

Boschma, R., Coenen, L., Frenken, K., & Truffer, B. (2017). Towards a theory of regional diversification: Combining insights from evolutionary economic geography and transition studies. *Regional Studies, 51*(1), 31–45.

Boschma, R., & Frenken, K. (2018). Evolutionary economic geography. In G. Clark, M. Gertler, M. P. Feldman, & D. Wójcik (Eds.), *The new Oxford handbook of economic geography* (pp. 213–229). Oxford University Press.

Castells, M. (2010). *The rise of the network society: The information age: Economy, society, and culture v* (2nd ed., Vol. 1). Wiley-Blackwell.

Clement, S. (2021). *Governing the Anthropocene: Novel ecosystems, transformation and environmental policy*. Palgrave Macmillan (Springer International Publishing).

Cooke, P. (Ed.). (2013). *Re-framing regional development: Evolution, innovation, and transition*. Routledge.

Cooke, P., Boekholt, P., & Tödtling, F. (2000). *The governance of innovation in Europe: Regional perspectives on global competitiveness*. Pinter.

Dick, B. (2011). Action research literature 2008–2010: Themes and trends. *Action Research, 9*(2), 122–143.

Dobusch, L., & Schoeneborn, D. (2015). Fluidity, identity, and organizationality: The communicative constitution of anonymous. *Journal of Management Studies, 52*(8), 1005–1035. https://doi.org/10.1111/joms.12139

Donohue, I., Hillebrand, H., Montoya, J. M., Petchey, O. L., Pimm, S. L., Fowler, M. S., Healy, K., Jackson, A. L., Lurgi, M., McClean, D., O'Connor, N. E., OGorman, E. J., & Yang, Q. (2016). Navigating the complexity of ecological stability. *Ecology Letters, 19*(9), 1172–1185.

Elmqvist, T., Folke, C., Nyström, M., Peterson, G., Bengtsson, J., Walker, B., & Norberg, J. (2003). Response diversity, ecosystem change, and resilience. *Frontiers in Ecology and the Environment, 1*(9), 488–494.

Engel, J. S. (2015). Global clusters of innovation: Lessons from Silicon Valley. *California Management Review, 57*(2), 36–65. https://doi.org/10.1525/cmr.2015.57.2.36

Etzkowitz, H. (2012). Triple helix clusters: Boundary permeability at University-Industry-Government interfaces as a regional innovation strategy. *Environment and Planning C: Government and Policy, 30*(5), 766–779. https://doi.org/10.1068/c1182

Farinha, L., Santos, D., Ferreira, J. J., & Ranga, M. (2020). Regional helix ecosystems and sustainable growth: The interaction of innovation, entrepreneurship and technology transfer. In L. Farinha, D. Santos, J. J. Ferreira, & M. Ranga (Eds.), *Studies on entrepreneurship, structural change and industrial dynamics*. Springer International Publishing.

Gadille, M., Tremblay, D.-G., & Vion, A. (2013). La méta-organisation territorialisée, moteur d'apprentissages collectifs. *Revue Interventions économiques. Papers in Political Economy, 48*, Article 48. https://journals.openedition.org/interventionseconomiques/2156

Garaudel, P. (2020). Exploring meta-organizations' diversity and agency: A meta-organizational perspective on global union federations. *Scandinavian Journal of Management, 36*(1), 101094. https://doi.org/10.1016/j.scaman.2020.101094

Gebhardt, C. (2012). The entrepreneurial state: The German entrepreneurial regions' programme as an attenuator for the financial crisis. *European Planning Studies, 20*(9), 1469–1482.

Gebhardt, C. (2013). The making of plasma medicine: Strategy driven clusters and the emerging roles of cluster management and government supervision. *Journal of Technology Transfer, 38*(4), 401–414.

Gebhardt, C. (2020). The impact of participatory governance on regional development pathways: Citizen-driven smart, green and inclusive urbanism in the Brainport Metropolitan Region. *Triple Helix, 6*, 69–110.

Gebhardt, C., & Pohlmann, M. C. (2013). Managing the organisation 2.0: Entrepreneurial spirit and general management competences as early indicators for cluster success and sustainable regional development: Findings from the German Entrepreneurial Regions Programme. *Journal of High Technology Management Research, 24*(2), 153–160.

Geels, F. W. (2005). *Technological transitions and system innovations: A co-evolutionary and socio-technical analysis*. Edward Elgar.

Golra, O., Rosiello, A., & Harrison, R. (2018). Proximity and its impact on the formation of technical networks of product and process innovation. *4th Geography of Innovation Conference*.

Gong, H., & Hassink, R. (2019). Co-evolution in contemporary economic geography: Towards a theoretical framework. *Regional Studies, 53*(9), 1344–1355.

Grothe-Hammer, M. (2019). Membership or contributorship? Managing the inclusion of individuals into organizations. In G. Ahrne & N. Brunsson (Eds.), *Organization outside organizations: The abundance of partial organization in social life* (pp. 84–112). Cambridge University Press. https://doi.org/10.1017/9781108604994.004

Grothe-Hammer, M., & Cour, A. (2020). Membership and contributorship in organisations: An update of modern systems theory. *Systems Research and Behavioural Science*, *37*(3), 482–495.

Hassink, R. (2005). How to unlock regional economies from path dependency? From learning region to learning cluster. *European Planning Studies*, *13*(4), 521–535.

Huggins, R., & Prokop, D. (2017). Network structure and regional innovation: A study of university-industry ties. *Urban Studies*, *54*(4), 931–952.

Isaksen, A., Martin, R., & Trippl, M. (Eds.). (2018). *New avenues for regional innovation systems: Theoretical advances, empirical cases and policy lessons*. Springer International Publishing.

Keping, Y. (2018). Governance and good governance: A new framework for political analysis. *Fudan Journal of the Humanities and Social Sciences*, *11*(1), 1–8.

Köhler, J., Geels, F. W., Kern, F., Markard, J., Onsongo, E., Wieczorek, A., Alkemade, F., Avelino, F., Bergek, A., Boons, F., Fünfschilling, L., Hess, D., Holtz, G., Hyysalo, S., Jenkins, K., Kivimaa, P., Martiskainen, M., McMeekin, A., Mühlemeier, M. S., . . . Wells, P. (2019). An agenda for sustainability transitions research: State of the art and future directions. *Environmental Innovation and Societal Transitions*, *31*, 1–32. https://doi.org/10.1016/j.eist.2019.01.004

Koschatzky, K., & Stahlecker, T. (2010). A new challenge for regional policy-making in Europe? Chances and risks of the merger between cohesion and innovation policy. *European Planning Studies*, *18*(1), 7–25.

Lapoutte, A. (2021). Resilience of a meta-organisation: The case of a food commune. *Annals of Public and Cooperative Economics*, *92*(1), 79–100.

Leydesdorff, L. (2021). *The evolutionary dynamics of discursive knowledge: Communication: Theoretical perspectives on an empirical philosophy of science*. Springer International Publishing.

Lupova-Henry, E., Blili, S., & Dal Zotto, C. (2021). Designing organised clusters as social actors: A meta-organisational approach. *Journal of Organization Design*, *10*(1), 35–54. https://doi.org/10.1007/s41469-021-00092-5

Lupova-Henry, E., & Dotti, N. F. (2019). Governance of sustainable innovation: Moving beyond the hierarchy-market-network trichotomy? A systematic literature review using the "who-how-what" framework. *Journal of Cleaner Production*, *210*, 738–748. https://doi.org/10.1016/j.jclepro.2018.11.068

Lyal, C., Kirk, P., Smith, D., & Smith, R. (2008). The value of taxonomy to biodiversity and agriculture. *Biodiversity*, *9*(1–2), 8–13. https://doi.org/10.1080/14888386.2008.9712873

Martin, R., & Sunley, P. (2003). Deconstructing clusters: Chaotic concept or policy panacea? *Journal of Economic Geography*, *3*(1), 5–35.

Martin, R., & Sunley, P. (2011). Conceptualizing cluster evolution: Beyond the life cycle model? *Regional Studies*, *45*(10), 1299–1318. https://doi.org/10.1080/00343404.2011.622263

Martin, R., & Sunley, P. (2012). Forms of emergence and the evolution of economic landscapes. *Journal of Economic Behaviour and Organisation*, *82*(2–3), 338–351.

Martin, R., & Sunley, P. (2015). On the notion of regional economic resilience: Conceptualisation and explanation. *Journal of Economic Geography*, *15*(1), 1–42.

Mecklenburg-Vorpommern Landesregierung, M. für K. (2022). Landwirtschaft, ländliche Räume und Umwelt. *Landwirtschaft*. Mecklenburg-Vorpommern Landesregierung, Ministerium Für Klimaschutz, Landwirtschaft, Ländliche Räume Und Umwelt. www.regierung-mv.de/Landesregierung/lm/Landwirtschaft/Landwirtschaft/

Mitra, A., Mitra, A., Li, Y.-F., Li, Y.-F., Klämpfl, T. G., Klämpfl, T. G., Shimizu, T., Shimizu, T., Jeon, J., Jeon, J., Morfill, G. E., Morfill, G. E., Zimmermann, J. L., & Zimmermann, J. L. (2014). Inactivation of surface-borne microorganisms and increased germination of seed specimen by cold atmospheric plasma. *Food and Bioprocess Technology*, 7(3), 645–653.

Moser, H., & Rice, C. (2016). *Transformative innovation for international development: Operationalising innovation ecosystems and smart cities for sustainable development and poverty reduction.* Center for Strategic and International Studies.

Physics for Food. (2019a). *Cluster Proposal: White paper.* (internal document).

Physics for Food. (2019b). *Cluster Survey: White paper.* (internal document).

Physics for Food. (2022a). *Physics for food.* https://physicsforfood.org/english-summary/

Physics for Food. (2022b, March 7). Forschungsprojekt geht in die zweite Runde. *Physics for Food.* https://physicsforfood.org/news/forschungsprojekt-geht-in-die-zweite-runde/

Provan, K. G., Fish, A., & Sydow, J. (2007). Interorganisational networks at the network nevel: A review of the empirical literature on whole networks. *Journal of Management, 33*(3), 479–516.

Ranga, M., & Etzkowitz, H. (2013). Triple Helix systems: An analytical framework for innovation policy and practice in the knowledge society. *Industry and Higher Education, 27*(4), 237–262.

Ritala, P., Agouridas, V., Assimakopoulos, D., & Gies, O. (2013). Value creation and capture mechanisms in innovation ecosystems: A comparative case study. *International Journal of Technology Management, 63*(3/4), 244–267.

Rothgang, M., Cantner, U., Dehio, J., Engel, D., Fertig, M., Graf, H., Hinzmann, S., Linshalm, E., Ploder, M., Scholz, A. M., & Töpfer, S. (2017). Cluster policy: Insights from the German leading edge cluster competition. *Journal of Open Innovation, 3*(1), 1–20.

Ruhrmann, H., Fritsch, M., & Leydesdorff, L. (2022). Synergy and policy-making in German innovation systems: Smart Specialisation Strategies at national, regional, local levels? *Regional Studies, 56*(9), 1468–1479. https://doi.org/10.1080/00343404.2021.1872780

Rutten, R., & Boekema, F. (2007). Regional social capital: Embeddedness, innovation networks and regional economic development. *Technological Forecasting and Social Change, 74*(9), 1834–1846.

Schwaninger, M. (2006). Theories of viability: A comparison. *Systems Research and Behavioral Science, 23*(3), 337–347. https://doi.org/10.1002/sres.731

Schwaninger, M., Janovjak, M., & Ambroz, K. (2006). Second-order intervention: Enhancing organizational competence and performance. *Systems Research and Behavioral Science, 23*(4), 529–545. https://doi.org/10.1002/sres.780

Sydow, J. (1992). *Strategische Netzwerke.* Evolution und Organisation SpringerGabler.

Sydow, J. (2009). Zur Zukunft der Netzwerkorganisation. *Zeitschrift Führung + Organisation, 78*(5), 225.

Tödtling, F., & Trippl, M. (2013). Transformation of regional innovation systems. *Re-Framing Regional Development: Evolution, Innovation, and Transition, 62*, 297.

Vermeulen, B., & Paier, M. (Eds.). (2017). *Innovation networks for regional development: Concepts, case studies, and agent-based models.* Springer International Publishing.

Wanner, M., Hilger, A., Westerkowski, J., Rose, M., Stelzer, F., & Schäpke, N. (2018). Towards a cyclical concept of real-world laboratories. *DisP: The Planning Review, 54*(2), 94–114. https://doi.org/10.1080/02513625.2018.1487651

Weick, K. E. (1995). *Sensemaking in organisations (Foundations for organisational science).* Sage Publications Inc.

4 Meta-organising clusters as agents of transformative change through 'responsible actorhood'

Héloïse BERKOWITZ and Martine GADILLE

Introduction

Tackling grand challenges and ensuring sustainability transitions of our societies require deep, multi-level, and systemic transformations of our production and consumption modes (Geels, 2002). Recent literature on transition studies calls for a new framing of innovation policies centred on transformative change through local experimentations and deliberative governance processes (Schot & Steinmueller, 2018). The roles clusters can play in these multi-level system transformations for sustainability are generally implicitly downplayed, as they are considered outmoded policy instruments (Schot & Steinmueller, 2018). However, there is no one best way to transition towards sustainability. On the contrary, transition studies argue that multiple actors, directionalities, and pathways can have transformative change power at the system level (ibid). In addition, the geography of transitions literature calls for a place-based approach to sustainability transition (Binz et al., 2020), which, we argue, requires investigating clusters. So, how can clusters stimulate system-level transformative change?

Clusters, a focus of science, technology, and innovation (STI) policy in the 1980s, incarnate the strategic choice of public policy to concentrate on specific activities in a given territory (Castells & Hall, 1994). Initially, sustainability was not clusters' core focus (Martin & Mayer, 2008). However, this situation is changing with the development of eco-industrial clusters (Cooke, 2011) and third sector or solidarity economy clusters and similar arrangements (Lemaître & Helmsing, 2012; Petrella et al., 2021; Saniossian et al., this volume; Viachka & Duprat, this volume). In this evolution of both clusters and STI policy, we still understand relatively little about the ways to organise and shape these important territorial players so they can contribute to sustainability transitions.

This chapter assumes that clusters can be (re)designed to act as agents of transformative change for sustainability. In other words, these can be seen as places of local experimentations and as governance devices facilitating inclusive deliberation processes. We argue that one condition for this is that clusters achieve what we call 'responsible actorhood'. By responsible actorhood, we mean that clusters and, more generally, collaborative arrangements among organisations, or meta-organisations, 1) become organisational actors – that

DOI: 10.4324/9781003215066-6

is they become externally perceived as actors (King et al., 2010) and 2) make active steps towards sustainability transformation. This chapter adopts the meta-organisational perspective on clusters and explores how they can enact 'responsible actorhood' and produce transformative change. In particular, it suggests that achieving 'responsible actorhood' involves solving the issues of answerability, path dependency to growth and labour mobility. This is possible through 1) developing mechanisms ensuring 'meta-organisational accountability' towards stakeholders, 2) nurturing 'transformative mediated reflexivity' about technological ruptures and environmental performance, and 3) enabling 'negotiated professional restructuring' to establish new knowledge processes at work. We thus contribute to more critical discussions on meta-organisations and responsibility (Carmagnac et al., 2022).

The roles of clusters in STI and sustainability transitions

Clusters constituted one of the main policy tools in the 1980s to foster R&D, innovation, and entrepreneurship (Schot & Steinmueller, 2018). They were mostly designed to enhance competitiveness (ibid) and raised several governance issues (Cooke, 2001). While they have sometimes successfully triggered significant business disruptions, clusters have been accompanied by growing inequalities, especially at the international level. According to Schot and Steinmueller (2018), these effects result from the very nationally anchored models of innovation clusters traditionally incarnate. Conversely, system transition, they argue, must involve a new model of innovation based on local niches and experimentations, deliberative governance, and transformative change (ibid).

Three synergistic levels matter in system transitions towards sustainability: socio-technical landscape, which encompasses the macro-political economy, social values, and culture; a meso-level of socio-technical systems, called 'regimes' with their institutions, rules, and practices; and a micro-level of niches where experimentations can take place (Geels, 2002). In the latter level, innovation can emerge and eventually displace incumbent, unsustainable regimes and produce transformations at other levels (Schot & Geels, 2008). From this perspective, we can assume that regions or territories, through clusters, can become spaces for local experimentation leading to broader change at the national level (Cooke, 2015).

While clusters have not always been designed for sustainability (Martin & Mayer, 2008), 'eco-industrial clusters' are increasingly being set up. In this specific kind of cluster, sustainable innovations can take various forms, from Product-Oriented, Flagship-Oriented, to Territory-Oriented, or Institution-Oriented (Kebir et al., 2017). They may thus contribute to developing social or environmental innovations for the transition. This kind of cluster presents two specific characteristics of social interactions: 1) their members include professional groupings or associations gathering companies or research and education players as well as NGOs, public authorities, citizens, or consumers; and 2) they are governed by new multi-scalar laws and regulations (ibid).

Clusters as meta-organisations

Clusters can be conceptualised as a specific type of meta-organisation with a territorial anchorage (Berkowitz & Bor, this volume; Lupova-Henry & Dotti, this volume). Owing to their increasingly hybrid membership, some clusters can further be conceived as multi-stakeholder meta-organisations (Berkowitz, 2018). These relate to and involve, more or less closely, third-sector organisations, the social or solidarity economy (SSE) (Lemaître & Helmsing, 2012; Petrella et al., 2021; Saniossian et al., this volume). Member-organisations composing such clusters present a diversity of institutional statuses and imply clusters' role in coordinating new activities, sectors, and functionalities in the territory. For Rullani (2011), a theorist of industrial networks transformations, this consists of creating or reinforcing spaces with new physical, legal, and moral constraints, for example third places (Berkowitz, 2018; Viachka & Duprat, this volume).

Clusters' quest for legitimacy in transition studies and STI literature and the assessment of clusters' relatively weak contribution to sustainability transitions so far call for new steering practices. Re-designing old clusters or designing new ones as transformative agents requires rationalisations both at their governance level (the meta-organisation) and at the level of member-organisations and employees' work (sectors involved). Clusters can be organised as actors rather than simply resulting from environmental or institutional pressures that shape a geographical zone (Lupova-Henry et al., 2021). This involves drawing on organisational components, like membership, hierarchy, rules, monitoring and sanctions (i.e. structural organisationality), and actorhood or collective identity (i.e. entitative organisationality) (Grothe-Hammer et al., 2022). Meta-organisations may present more or less structural organisationality (Berkowitz & Bor, this volume). Following the same argument, meta-organisations can achieve entitative organisationality or fail to do so.

However, organising and recognising players in a cluster as a formal meta-organisation are not sufficient per se to ensure transformative change. The development of labour adapted to the implementation of transition processes is necessary. Taking into account employees in clusters is essential as systemic sustainability transition involves profound transformations of vocational education and training, upskilling, or reskilling of the workforce (Hazelkorn & Edwards, 2019). How to address these issues in the design of clusters is the object of the next section.

Meta-organising clusters for transition

We propose that clusters can be designed as transformative meta-organisations if they gain responsible actorhood for the transition. Hereafter, we develop the notion of responsible actorhood as a combination of three properties – that is multi-directional, meta-organisational accountability for decisions; transformative mediated reflexivity about socio-environmental effects; and negotiated professional restructuring. See Table 4.1 for synthesis.

Table 4.1 Achieving responsible actorhood

Concept	*Definition*	*Main outcome*
Responsible actorhood	A system of autonomous decision-making externally recognised as an actor, which decisions highlight care for future generations and a commitment to enacting a sustainable future	Enabling clusters and meta-organisations in general to have transformative outcomes
Multi-directional, meta-organisational accountability	Complex ties of accountability between the meta-organisation and its members and between the meta-organisation, members, and external publics	Addressing the answerability issue
Transformative mediated reflexivity	A continuous process mediated by the meta-organisation and consisting in identifying, reflecting upon, and integrating external changes as well as impacts on all publics (including non-human publics)	Mitigating the path dependency towards growth
Negotiated professional restructuring	A deliberative process enabling cluster's stakeholders to renew and adapt their professional and labour activities to technological or social ruptures, especially as a result of meta-organisational accountability and transformative mediated reflexivity	Transforming risks of labour resistance into labour adaptation to the new professions and sectors of the transition

Responsible actorhood

A paradoxical tension in meta-organisations exists between dependence on member-organisations to exist and a form of autonomy that is necessary to gain organisational actorhood: 'meta-organisations are autonomous actors with autonomous actors as members' (Ahrne et al., 2019, p. 392). We follow the classical view of actorhood as an external recognition – that is the organisational attribute that an organisation gains when it becomes externally perceived as an addressable actor (Dobusch & Schoeneborn, 2015; Grothe-Hammer et al., 2022; King et al., 2010). Therefore, actorhood differs from agency in the sense that organisations can have agency, that is take actions and have an organising effect, without necessarily achieving actorhood (Berkowitz et al., 2020). Like Lupova-Henry et al. (2021), we assume that actorhood can be constructed. We conceive it as a form of organisationality at the level of the entity or entitative organisationality (Grothe-Hammer et al., 2022).

Actorhood thus implies the existence of an autonomous system of decision at the level of the meta-organisation and the external attribution of responsibility for these decisions (Dobusch & Schoeneborn, 2015; Grothe-Hammer, 2019).

'Responsible actorhood' refers to 'a collective commitment of care for the future' (Owen et al., 2013, p. 36) – that is taking action that ensures the realisation of socially desirable outcomes (Berkowitz, 2018). It follows that responsible actorhood does not mean solely taking responsibility for decisions but, instead, taking decisions that enact a sustainable future.

Achieving responsible actorhood at the meta-organisational level while maintaining members' autonomy empowers territories to develop sustainable and responsible innovations through experimentations. Meta-organisational responsible actorhood of clusters is, thus, embedded in regions, territories, and place-making (Berkowitz et al., 2020). The emergence of territorial or place identity in transition studies (Binz et al., 2020) is coupled with the growing importance of self-organising (Berkowitz et al., 2020). In that context, there can be tension between territories as vehicles for innovation policy, and territories as places with their own resources, identity, and regional development trajectories (François et al., 2013). Meta-organising clusters as agents of transformative change, through responsible actorhood, can make them valuable intermediaries (Kivimaa et al., 2019) that develop place-based collective reflection and transition strategy.

Hereafter we argue that responsible actorhood results from three meta-organisational properties that aim to solve three issues. The first issue is the lack of answerability for decisions, which is solved by developing multi-directional, meta-organisational accountability mechanisms. The second issue is path dependency towards growth, which, we argue, can be mitigated through transformative mediated reflexivity. Finally, the issue of labour forces' adaptation to change can be tackled through negotiated professional restructuring.

Multi-directional, meta-organisational accountability

One main issue of meta-organisations in general, and clusters in particular, when it comes to transitioning towards sustainability, is the lack of answerability for socio-environmental impacts. Contrary to businesses, particularly publicly listed ones, meta-organisations generally have no obligation to report on their sustainability progresses. Owing to their opacity and discursive strategies, meta-organisations can escape responsibility attribution or strategically shift responsibility to specific actors (Carmagnac et al., 2022). We understand relatively little about their positive or negative contributions to sustainability (Berkowitz & Bor, 2018; Carmagnac et al., 2022). Against this backdrop, gaining responsible actorhood means that meta-organisations must become accountable for their decisions as autonomous actors and their socio-environmental impacts.

Accountability has a double meaning. By being (held) accountable, an organisation is taking responsibility for its decisions and actions and being held responsible by external agents (Cornwall et al., 2000). Owing to this double dynamics and the dependence-autonomy tension, it follows that accountability dynamics in meta-organisations are quite specific and complex (Ahrne et al., 2019). Member organisations do not merge into meta-organisations but retain their actorhood, identity, and decision-making processes (Ahrne & Brunsson, 2008). Meta-organisations, therefore, constitute organisations where social orders and decision-making processes are layered (Grothe-Hammer et al., 2022). This has implications for accountability, making it challenging to understand who is accountable to whom and how and to set accountability mechanisms as member organisations can deny responsibility (Berkowitz & Bor, 2018). This is particularly the case in the absence of actorhood.

The nature of meta-organisations can explain their specific accountability (Bor, 2019). Meta-organisations are voluntary associations of members that are themselves organisations (Ahrne & Brunsson, 2008). Owing to their high dependence on their members to whom they provide services (Berkowitz & Bor, 2018), meta-organisations may naturally imply some form of accountability systems. However, accountability is also necessarily multi-directional in meta-organisations (ibid.). Member-organisations are made accountable to the meta-organisation, and the meta-organisation is made accountable to its members (Bor, 2019). Both member-organisations and the meta-organisation are also made accountable to various external agents: for instance non-members providing resources, such as states or the EU (Bor, 2014, 2019).

However, in meta-organisations tackling grand challenges or contributing to sustainability transitions, accountability also involves a broader range of stakeholders like society as a whole and even nature (Laine, 2010; Starik, 1995). Dewey (2016) argued for the integration of all publics: human as well as entities such as soils, atmosphere, rivers, forests, and their biological diversity. It is crucial that organisations and meta-organisations are held accountable to these nonhuman publics as well. Only then can they take full responsibility for the problems arising from the direct and indirect consequences of social action in complex societies. From that perspective, responsible actorhood means jointly developing and agreeing upon specific rules of transparency, mechanisms, and tools of accountability towards these various stakeholders or publics (Mirvis & Worley, 2013). Multi-stakeholder meta-organisations that internalise various publics may develop specific accountability criteria, including information transparency, the inclusion of affected stakeholders, procedural fairness, and efficacy (Hennchen & Schrempf-Stirling, 2020).

The case of Suwa industrial region in Japan illustrates the challenges of meta-organisational accountability of an industrial cluster initially specialised in the machinery and metal industry (Sato & Okamoto, 2017). This specialisation led to the reuse of advanced technologies in eco-friendly products, renewable energy, and services for life quality (care for older people). The meta-organisation, SUWAMO, was created by stakeholders such as chambers of commerce and industry, employer associations, and municipalities (which also deal with care services for older adults at home). The objective was to form a cross-regional and cross-departmental agency whose stakeholders were extended to representatives of central government services, support agencies, and universities (including outside the region). SUWAMO's multi-directional form of accountability results from a transformation of local networks through the actions of the region, the State, and local firms.

When they achieve meta-organisational responsible actorhood, member-organisations can no longer hide behind the collective for jointly made decisions. They become jointly answerable through the meta-organisation, thanks to multi-directional accountability mechanisms. This idea of a complex configuration of multi-directional, meta-organisational accountability echoes the multi-level perspective on innovation that some researches in the field of sustainable regions and transitions suggest (Gibbs, 2018). Meta-organisational accountability for cluster transitions requires a place-based approach in a multi-level perspective. The interplay of actors, places, identities, resources, and political alliances committed to sustainability transitions gives it meaning and direction, therefore, building the essential ties of accountability.

Transformative mediated reflexivity

Drawing on Dryzek and Pickering's (2018) analysis of institutions, we can argue that clusters follow a pathological path dependency towards economic growth due to their use as competitiveness policy instruments. According to Dryzek and Pickering (2018), ecological reflexivity can help adapt to grand challenges. Reflexivity is needed to 1) identify and acknowledge changes in socio-ecological systems, 2) reflect on these changes and how institutions may adapt to them, and 3) reconfigure norms, discourses, and instruments in consequence.

Therefore, we can argue that mediated reflexivity (Gadille, 2008; Gadille et al., 2013a; Xhauflair, 2013) – that is the active and continual accounting for and discussion of one's performativity – is crucial for clusters' transition. More specifically, this mediated reflexivity needs to address technological ruptures and the cluster's environmental performance. Literature has shown that the governance of clusters involves mediation to move beyond contradictions existing among stakeholders (Dotti & Lupova-Henry, 2020).

Taking inspiration from the aforementioned works, we suggest that 'transformative mediated reflexivity' ensures that clusters' actions do not remain limited to energy or resource efficiency but trigger deep, transformative change. This reflexivity is mediated because it happens at the level of the meta-organisation. In the context of 'polycentric city-regions' (Soja, 2015), it may require going beyond the sectoral boundaries of the cluster. The objective is to favour sustainable innovations by encouraging experimentations (Rogge et al., 2020) and by developing new combinations of activity involving 'related and unrelated variety' at cross-sectoral and inter-cluster levels (Boschma et al., 2017; Frenken et al., 2007; Gadille & Gallego-Bono, 2021). A cluster can redefine its boundaries to survive and change its relatedness both with stakeholders and public policies.

Reflexivity mediated by the meta-organisation can also result from an external intervention on behalf of the collective. For instance Gadille et al. (2013b) show that the intervention of social scientists revealed the critical role of medium-tech subcontractors in the aeronautics and space cluster. They thus highlighted the importance of creative competencies. Commissioned by the meta-organisation secretariat, these researchers examined the evolution of jobs and skills as well as the relationship between purchasers and the small- and medium-sized suppliers in the cluster. The latter felt that their added value, and even their intellectual property, were discredited by the main purchasers. Local suppliers were indeed placed in head-on competition with suppliers in low-cost countries, who did not yet propose any innovation in the sub-systems supplied for an aircraft. This reflexivity was crucial in understanding the necessary changes in the cluster to foster more sustainable development.

Lupova-Henry et al. (2021) also show that the secretariat, usually studied as an executor of the board of directors and the advisory committee's decisions, can play a tacit role in producing new knowledge feeding the reflexivity of the member organisations. In this case, the secretariat called upon a third external actor (an academic consultant) to diagnose the practices and strategies of the cluster members and examine the possibility to diversify other sectors of activity. In so doing, the secretariat made it possible to shift the cluster's boundaries and extend its activities beyond the mining sector. Therefore, it has taken on the task of helping members understand that they can move into other areas such as medical equipment, food, and a range of other activities. In this case, reflexivity helps raise awareness that membership in an industry association does not necessarily restrict an organisation to that industry.

Therefore, reflexivity is not only stimulated by the shared knowledge production within the meta-organisation and third parties. It can also result from the capacity of this knowledge to reveal the functioning of a social order in which the actors act 'naturally' without being aware of it. By revealing its functioning, the meta-organisation can thus extend or move the social order's boundaries.

Reflexivity and accountability are connected. Transformative mediated reflexivity can question the meta-organisational autonomy as a condition to be externally recognised and accountable actor. From this perspective, the transformative mediated reflexivity of a cluster deals with multi-directional translation activities between stakeholders, public policymakers, and public problems. Thus, these publics can also be taken into account and integrated into meta-organisational processes of reflexivity.

Social and solidarity organisations as stakeholders of a cluster face the same limits as for-profit organisations do in their capacity to steer transformative change and improve their environmental performance. Sahakian (2016) argues that the concept of the social and solidarity economy fully embraces the 'social equity' dimension of ecological performance transformation. However, according to Dewey's definition, this concept is people-centric but not public-centric. We can call it people-centric rather than simply anthropocentric because it aims to place service to communities above profit. It also embraces the notion of reciprocity through social entrepreneurship, crowdfunding, fair trade, community currencies, and some forms of peer-to-peer sharing. This conception is essential for the transformative mediated reflexivity of meta-organisations, but it is not sufficient. We suggest that the capacity to take all publics into account through the meta-organisation depends on the meta-organization's ability to intermediate interactions between for-profit and not for-profit organisations involved in collective experiments and initiatives as well as non-human publics.

Ultimately, reflexivity at the cluster or meta-organisation level is transformative when it contributes to the construction of a 'grammar' of territory and territoriality defined by the aim 'to affect, influence or control people, phenomena and relationships by delimiting and asserting control over a geographic area' (Sack, 1986, p. 19; as cited by Paasi et al., 2018). Mediated reflexivity becomes transformative when it changes social order for more sustainability. Designing clusters for sustainability necessarily acknowledges the spatial and geophysical dimensions of clusters and system transitions. Reflexivity thus means taking into account the identity of the cluster's place or territory, its specific resources, and context (Binz et al., 2020; François et al., 2013). However, being reflexive also raises issues of labour adaptation to these necessary changes.

Negotiated professional restructuring

Another issue is the adaptation of professions in the cluster, or more generally the meta-organisation's members, to the transition. Professions and organisations of the regime may resist transformations towards sustainability (Geels, 2014). Therefore, we suggest that 'negotiated professional restructuring' is crucial to organise clusters as transformative agents. Negotiated professional restructuring consists of a deliberative process enabling cluster stakeholders to renew and adapt their professional and labour activities to technological or social ruptures, especially resulting from meta-organisational accountability and transformative mediated reflexivity. Further drawing on Dewey (2016), if meta-organisational responsible actorhood means accounting for all impacts on all publics, including the biosphere, then it follows that meta-organisations must be able to transform their activities, knowledge processes, and empowerment mechanisms to take on that responsibility.

Professionality refers to individuals' purposes and capacities to acquire and actualise new knowledge and skills. Production processes adopted at the company level leave little margin of autonomy for sustainable professionality (Marasco, 2018). Thus, transitioning clusters requires a transformation of professionalities on the basis of a process of place-making or 'territorialisation' – that is anchoring them in territories. Employees and member organisations must develop new skills to address the challenge of sustainable innovation and transition. However, they also need to use international networks contributing to knowledge exchanges and, at the same time, re-organise production locally. A meta-organisation becomes an agent of transformative change when it succeeds in taking on an intermediary role in such transformations. Moreover, it needs to balance the constant back-and-forth between the expectations and competencies of its stakeholders with the collective commitment to take responsibility for the future towards the publics.

De Rosa and Trabalzi's (2017) study of the failure of an agricultural meta-organisation can be illustrative of this. They highlight the lack of back-and-forth interactions enabling professional restructuring. The 'Campagna Amica' Foundation was created in Rome to sustain the rurban territorial system. It sought to build a meeting place for farmers and citizens in the three main areas of direct sales, tourism, and eco-sustainability. Its members are mainly farming cooperatives. It has been promoted by Coldiretti, the main farmers' trade union in Italy, and extended through all the Italian regions with local networks of marketplaces where citizens can access local products. De Rosa and Trabalzi (2017) show that the meta-organisation failed to adapt to and draw on the needs of a local actor – the School Meal program. This program aims at supplying organic and local, quality food to public schools in Rome and has been promoted by the municipality, teachers, families, and dieticians since the mid-2000. However, the local productive system failed to provide for it. The program had to procure food from further away. One main explanation for this failure was the exclusion of stakeholders from the coordination of the meta-organisation. The transformation of its members' knowledge towards civil society's expectations – that is organic farming for local schools – might have had a better chance of success if embedded in a professional restructuring at the local system level. However, the link between the meta-organisation and the national farm union deterred the development of new relationships with other local actors. It thus prevented them from building multi-directional accountability, transformative reflexivity, and professional restructuring.

The changing professionality operates at two levels: that of cluster members and that of employees hired by the meta-organisation to pool resources. As members of clusters, universities necessarily play a key role in this. However, this restructuring can be piloted by the meta-organisation itself to better coordinate these various transformations in training, upskilling, and reskilling. While this restructuring operates at a very local level, it also needs to involve national and transnational frameworks and agents. This is especially relevant for policies that impact vocational education strategies (such as the EU's Smart Specialisation Strategy (RIS3) or the European Green Deal) (see for instance Hazelkorn & Edwards, 2019). Ultimately, clusters can only play a transformative role in sustainability transitions due to this multi-scalar meta-organisational re-composition of objectives, accountability, and socialisation processes.

Discussion and conclusion

How to organise clusters as local agents of transformative change – that is players that actively contribute to systemic sustainability transitions anchored in territories? Recent literature on Transition Studies, and more specifically on Science and Technology Innovation policy, argues that a new frame of STI policy is needed, one that focuses on transformative change, experimentations, and deliberative governance (Köhler et al., 2019; Schot & Steinmueller, 2018). Within this framework, clusters tend to be somewhat overlooked as an outdated policy instrument of the 1980s. However, their geographical omnipresence in Europe and the rest of the world makes them important tools that need to be integrated into transition strategies and strengthened or re-designed for this very purpose. In this chapter, we investigated under which conditions clusters can stimulate system-level transformative change for sustainability transition.

Bridging industrial ecology literature and Science and Technology Innovation policy, we took a meta-organisational perspective on the design of clusters for sustainability. Furthering Lupova-Henry et al. (2021), we proposed that gaining 'responsible actorhood' is a necessary organisational condition for clusters to act as local agents of transformative change. Only under this condition can meta-organised clusters solve several obstacles to transformative change – that is lack of answerability, path dependency to growth, and lack of labour adaptation to sustainability. Responsible actorhood means that the meta-organisation presents a system of autonomous decision making and is externally recognised as an actor ('entitative organisationality', as in Grothe-Hammer et al., 2022). It further means that this autonomous, addressable actor is committed to a sustainable future (Berkowitz, 2018). We develop 'responsible actorhood' around three main properties needed to meta-organise clusters for transition purposes – that is to (re)design the industrial system at the meta-organisational level for sustainability. We synthesise these properties in Figure 4.1.

We first argue that responsible actorhood of a meta-organisation involves developing mechanisms to ensure multi-directional, meta-organisational accountability to ensure answerability. This means that meta-organisations are (held)

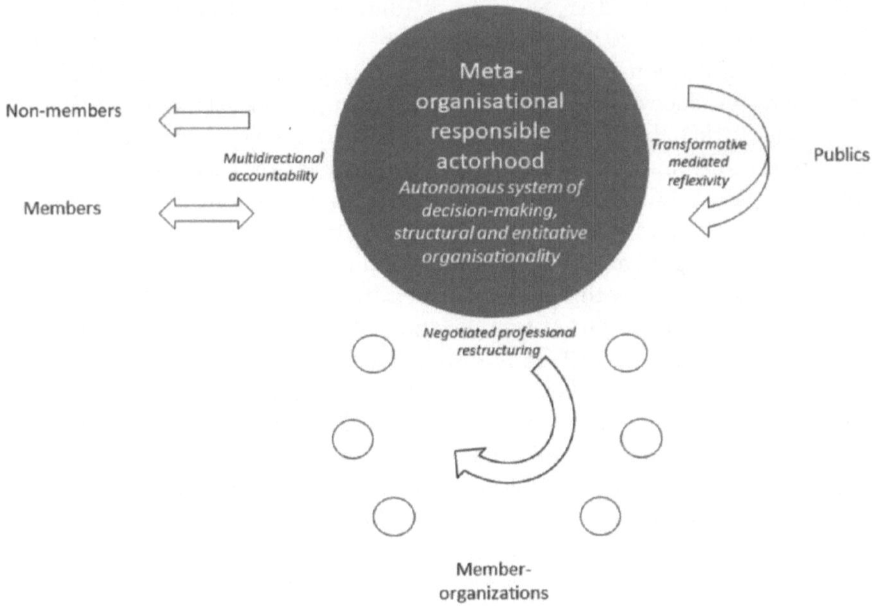

Figure 4.1 A model of meta-organisational responsible actorhood

accountable for their actions and that this accountability concerns several publics from civil society to non-human publics like the biosphere. This further translates into nurturing 'transformative mediated reflexivity' at the meta-organisational level about technological ruptures and environmental performance. Transformative mediated reflexivity means solving the issue of path dependency to growth by taking a public-centric approach to impacts – that is accounting for impacts on both people and the biosphere. Last, multi-directional meta-organisational accountability and transformative mediated reflexivity require enabling 'negotiated professional restructuring' to establish new knowledge processes at work and thus tackle the risk of a low labour mobility for sustainability.

This work contributes to several streams of literature. First, it contributes to STI, transition studies, and cluster literature (Baldassarre et al., 2019; Schot & Steinmueller, 2018) by bridging these approaches and unpacking the organisational conditions under which clusters can become transformative agents for the transition. We emphasise the importance of place-making in the transition of clusters towards sustainability and discuss how they can become intermediaries for such a transition (Binz et al., 2020; Kivimaa et al., 2019). We further contribute to this extensive literature by highlighting the value of clusters as meta-organisations that can foster local experimentation and deliberative governance for the transition of territories.

We also contribute to the growing meta-organisation literature (Ahrne & Brunsson, 2008; Berkowitz & Bor, 2018; Spillman, 2018) by analysing the territorial anchorage of meta-organisations such as clusters (Gadille et al., 2013b; Lupova-Henry et al., 2021). Most works in the meta-organisation literature have focused on cases disconnected from the territory or space, mostly operating at the national (Berkowitz & Souchaud, 2019; Spillman, 2018) or international level (Ahrne et al., 2019; Carmagnac et al., 2022). We, in particular, add to the recent critical discussion about meta-organisations' roles in sustainability, their potential dark side, and discuss how counter-productive strategies can be prevented (Carmagnac et al., 2022).

We suggest that the re-design of established industrial players for sustainability transitions might be understood using a meta-organisational approach and, more generally, an evolutionary, regional multidisciplinary approach of local systems dynamics. This means highlighting the immaterial aspects of 'territorial capital' (cognitive, social, relational, and identity capital) inherited from slow historical processes that are not necessarily oriented towards economic goals (Camagni et al., 2009). As such, we go beyond the Neo-Marshallian view focused on interpreting small firms' systems rather than innovation processes.

Our findings are transferable to other settings, especially to emerging countries. In the context of re-territorialised globalisation, our findings need to be attuned to the differentiated policy and urban trajectories forged by geo-historical relations of power (colonialism, imperialism, global capitalism) in order to foster inclusive alternatives and directionalities of sustainability transition (Kanai & Schindler, 2018; Pansera & Owen, 2018). Our work also has policy and practical implications for the design and steering of eco-industrial clusters, in particular, in settings other than clusters based in developed countries.

References

Ahrne, G., & Brunsson, N. (2008). *Meta-organizations*. Edward Elgar Publishing. www.e-elgar.com/shop/gbp/meta-organizations-9781847209504.html

Ahrne, G., Brunsson, N., & Kerwer, D. (2019). The partial organization of international relations: International organizations as meta-organizations. In G. Ahrne & N. Brunsson (Eds.), *Organization outside organizations: The abundance of partial organization in social life* (pp. 390–418). Cambridge University Press.

Baldassarre, B., Schepers, M., Bocken, N., Cuppen, E., Korevaar, G., & Calabretta, G. (2019). Industrial Symbiosis: Towards a design process for eco-industrial clusters by integrating Circular Economy and Industrial Ecology perspectives. *Journal of Cleaner Production, 216*, 446–460. https://doi.org/10.1016/j.jclepro.2019.01.091

Berkowitz, H. (2018). Meta-organizing firms' capabilities for sustainable innovation: A conceptual framework. *Journal of Cleaner Production, 175*, 420–430. https://doi.org/10.1016/j.jclepro.2017.12.028

Berkowitz, H., & Bor, S. (2018). Why meta-organizations matter: A response to Lawton et al. and Spillman. *Journal of Management Inquiry, 27*(2), 204–211. https://doi.org/10.1177/1056492617712895

Berkowitz, H., & Bor, S. (this volume). Meta-organisation as partial organisation: An integrated framework of organisationality and decisionality. In E. Lupova-Henry & N. F. Dotti (Eds.), *Clusters and sustainable regional development: A meta-organisational approach*. Routledge.

Berkowitz, H., Crowder, L. B., & Brooks, C. M. (2020). Organizational perspectives on sustainable ocean governance: A multi-stakeholder, meta-organization model of collective action. *Marine Policy, 118*, 104026. https://doi.org/10.1016/j.marpol.2020.104026

Berkowitz, H., & Souchaud, A. (2019). (Self-)Regulation of sharing economy platforms through partial meta-organizing. *Journal of Business Ethics, 159*(4), 961–976. https://doi.org/10.1007/s10551-019-04206-8

Binz, C., Coenen, L., Murphy, J. T., & Truffer, B. (2020). Geographies of transition: From topical concerns to theoretical engagement: A comment on the transitions research agenda. *Environmental Innovation and Societal Transitions, 34*, 1–3. https://doi.org/10.1016/j.eist.2019.11.002

Bor, S. (2014). *A theory of meta-organisation: An analysis of steering processes in European commission-funded R&D "network of excellence" consortia* [Doctoral Thesis]. Hanken School of Economics.

Bor, S. (2019). Understanding accountability in the context of meta-organizations. *Proceedings of the 33rd Annual Conference of the British Academy of Management, 104*.

Boschma, R., Coenen, L., Frenken, K., & Truffer, B. (2017). Towards a theory of regional diversification: Combining insights from evolutionary economic geography and transition studies. *Regional Studies, 51*(1), 31–45.

Camagni, R., Capello, R., & Nijkamp, P. (2009). Territorial capital and regional development. In *Handbook of regional growth and development theories* (pp. 118–132). Edward Elgar Cheltenham.

Carmagnac, L., Touboulic, A., & Carbone, V. (2022). A wolf in sheep's clothing: The ambiguous role of multistakeholder meta-organisations in sustainable supply chains. *M@n@gement, 25*(4), forthcoming.

Castells, M., & Hall, P. (1994). *Technopoles of the world: The making of the 21st century*. Routledge.

Cooke, P. (2001). Regional innovation systems, clusters, and the knowledge economy. *Industrial and Corporate Change, 10*(4), 945–974.

Cooke, P. (2011). Transition regions: Regional: National eco-innovation systems and strategies. *Progress in Planning, 76*(3), 105–146.

Cooke, P. (2015). Green governance and green clusters: Regional & national policies for the climate change challenge of Central & Eastern Europe. *Journal of Open Innovation: Technology, Market, and Complexity, 1*(1), 1. https://doi.org/10.1186/s40852-015-0002-z

Cornwall, A., Lucas, H., & Pasteur, K. (2000). Introduction: Accountability through participation: Developing workable partnership models in the health sector. *IDS Bulletin, 31*(1), 1–13. https://doi.org/10.1111/j.1759-5436.2000.mp31001001.x

De Rosa, M., & Trabalzi, F. (2017). Innovative rurban networks in Rome. In L. Kebir, O. Crevoisier, P. Costa, & V. Peyrache-Gadeau (Eds.), *Sustainable innovation and regional development* (pp. 153–169). Edward Elgar Publishing. www.elgaronline.com/view/edcoll/9781784712204/9781784712204.00016.xml

Dewey, J. (2016). *The public and its problems: An essay in political inquiry*. Swallow Press.

Dobusch, L., & Schoeneborn, D. (2015). Fluidity, identity, and organizationality: The communicative constitution of anonymous. *Journal of Management Studies, 52*(8), 1005–1035. https://doi.org/10.1111/joms.12139

Dotti, N. F., & Lupova-Henry, E. (2020). Creative mediators and their role in the governance of creative clusters. In M. Komorowski & I. Picone (Eds.), *Creative cluster development: Governance, place-making and entrepreneurship* (p. 272). Routledge. www.crcpress.com/Creative-Cluster-Development-Governance-Place-Making-and-Entrepreneurship/Komorowski-Picone/p/book/9780367332747

Dryzek, J. S., & Pickering, J. (2018). *The politics of the Anthropocene*. Oxford University Press.

François, H., Hirczak, M., & Senil, N. (2013). De la ressource à la trajectoire: Quelles stratégies de développement territorial? *Géographie, Économie, Société, 15*(3), 267–284.

Frenken, K., Van Oort, F., & Verburg, T. (2007). Related variety, unrelated variety and regional economic growth. *Regional Studies, 41*(5), 685–697.

Gadille, M. (2008). Le tiers comme agent de réflexivité et accélérateur d'apprentissages collectifs: Le cas du dispositif des pôles de compétitivité. *Humanisme et Entreprise, 289*(4), 61–79.

Gadille, M., & Gallego-Bono, J. R. (2021). Rebuilding a Cluster While Protecting Knowledge within Low-Medium-Tech Supplier SMEs: A Spanish and French Comparison. *Sustainability, 13*, 11313. https://doi.org/10.3390/su132011313

Gadille, M., Tremblay, D.-G., & Vion, A. (2013a). La méta-organisation territorialisée, moteur d'apprentissages collectifs. *Revue Interventions économiques. Papers in Political Economy, 48*, Article 48. https://journals.openedition.org/interventionseconomiques/2156

Gadille, M., Méhaut, P., & Courault, B. (2013b). Compétences et régulation des marchés du travail dans les pôles de compétitivité: le cas du pôle Pégase. *Revue d'Economie Regionale Urbaine, 2*, 339–361.

Geels, F. W. (2002). Technological transitions as evolutionary reconfiguration processes: A multi-level perspective and a case-study. *Research Policy, 31*(8), 1257–1274. https://doi.org/10.1016/S0048-7333(02)00062-8

Geels, F. W. (2014). Reconceptualising the co-evolution of firms-in-industries and their environments: Developing an inter-disciplinary Triple Embeddedness Framework. *Research Policy, 43*(2), 261–277.

Gibbs, D. (2018). Sustainable regions. In A. Paasi, J. Harrison, & M. Jones (Eds.), *Handbook on the geographies of regions and territories* (pp. 182–194). Edward Elgar Publishing Ltd. www.elgaronline.com/view/edcoll/9781785365799/9781785365799.00024.xml

Grothe-Hammer, M. (2019). Organization without actorhood: Exploring a neglected phenomenon. *European Management Journal, 37*(3), 325–338. https://doi.org/10.1016/j.emj.2018.07.009

Grothe-Hammer, M., Berkowitz, H., & Berthod, O. (2022). Decisional organization theory: Towards an integrated framework of organization. In M. Godwyn (Ed.), *Research handbook on the sociology of organizations* (pp. 30–53). Edward Elgar Publishing Ltd.

Hazelkorn, E., & Edwards, J. (2019). *Skills and smart specialisation: The role of vocational education and training in smart specialisation strategies*. Publications Office of the European Union. https://s3platform.jrc.ec.europa.eu/documents/20182/81824/Skills+and+Smart+Specialisation+The+role+of+Vocational+Education+and+Training+in+Smart+Specialisation+Strategies/3bf420ed-c7f6-4507-aabe-a9a2a60901d6

Hennchen, E., & Schrempf-Stirling, J. (2020). Fit for addressing grand challenges? A process model for effective accountability relationships within multi-stakeholder initiatives in developing countries. *Business Ethics: A European Review, beer.12325*. https://doi.org/10.1111/beer.12325

Kanai, J. M., & Schindler, S. (2018). Regional urbanization: Emerging approaches and debates. In *Handbook on the geographies of regions and territories*. Edward Elgar Publishing Ltd.

Kebir, L., Peyrache-Gadeau, V., Crevoisier, O., & Costa, P. (2017). Introduction: Sustainability, innovative milieus and territorial development. In L. Kebir, O. Crevoisier, P. Costa, & V. Peyrache-Gadeau (Eds.), *Sustainable innovation and regional development* (pp. 1–24). Edward Elgar Publishing. www.elgaronline.com/view/edcoll/9781784712204/9781784712204.00007.xml

King, B. G., Felin, T., & Whetten, D. A. (2010). Perspective: Finding the organization in organizational theory: A meta-theory of the organization as a social actor. *Organization Science*, *21*(1), 290–305. https://doi.org/10.1287/orsc.1090.0443

Kivimaa, P., Hyysalo, S., Boon, W., Klerkx, L., Martiskainen, M., & Schot, J. (2019). Passing the baton: How intermediaries advance sustainability transitions in different phases. *Environmental Innovation and Societal Transitions*, *31*, 110–125. https://doi.org/10.1016/j.eist.2019.01.001

Köhler, J., Geels, F. W., Kern, F., Markard, J., Onsongo, E., Wieczorek, A., Alkemade, F., Avelino, F., Bergek, A., Boons, F., Fünfschilling, L., Hess, D., Holtz, G., Hyysalo, S., Jenkins, K., Kivimaa, P., Martiskainen, M., McMeekin, A., Mühlemeier, M. S., . . . Wells, P. (2019). An agenda for sustainability transitions research: State of the art and future directions. *Environmental Innovation and Societal Transitions*, *31*, 1–32. https://doi.org/10.1016/j.eist.2019.01.004

Laine, M. (2010). The nature of nature as a stakeholder. *Journal of Business Ethics*, *96*(S1), 73–78. https://doi.org/10.1007/s10551-011-0936-4

Lemaître, A., & Helmsing, A. H. J. (Bert). (2012). Solidarity economy in Brazil: Movement, discourse and practice analysis through a Polanyian understanding of the economy. *Journal of International Development*, *24*(6), 745–762. https://doi.org/10.1002/jid.2865

Lupova-Henry, E., Blili, S., & Dal Zotto, C. (2021). Designing organised clusters as social actors: A meta-organisational approach. *Journal of Organization Design*, *10*(1), 35–54. https://doi.org/10.1007/s41469-021-00092-5

Lupova-Henry, E., & Dotti, N. F. (this volume). Clusters as collective actors and agents of change for (new) sustainable path development. In E. Lupova-Henry & N. F. Dotti (Eds.), *Clusters and sustainable regional development: A meta-organisational approach*. Routledge.

Marasco, F. (2018). Il ruolo dell'associazione datoriale tra mercato del lavoro e tutela della professionalità. *Labour & Law Issues*, *4*(2), 72–87.

Martin, S., & Mayer, H. (2008). Sustainability, clusters, and competitiveness: Introduction to focus section. *Economic Development Quarterly*, *22*(4), 272–276. https://doi.org/10.1177/0891242408325702

Mirvis, P. H., & Worley, C. G. (2013). Organizing for sustainability: Why networks and partnerships? *Organizing for Sustainable Effectiveness*, *3*, 1–34.

Owen, R., Bessant, J., & Heintz. (2013). *Responsible innovation: Managing the responsible emergence of science and innovation in society* (M., Ed.). John Wiley & Sons, Ltd. https://doi.org/10.1002/9781118551424.ch5

Paasi, A., Harrison, J., & Jones, M. (2018). New consolidated regional geographies. In *Handbook on the geographies of regions and territories*. Edward Elgar Publishing.

Pansera, M., & Owen, R. (2018). Framing inclusive innovation within the discourse of development: Insights from case studies in India. *Research Policy*, *47*(1), 23–34. https://doi.org/10.1016/j.respol.2017.09.007

Petrella, F., Simsa, R., Pape, U., Pahl, J. B., Brandsen, T., Richez-Battesti, N., & Zimmer, A. (2021). Dealing with paradoxes, manufacturing governance: Organizational change in European third-sector organizations. *Nonprofit and Voluntary Sector Quarterly*, *08997640211005849*. https://doi.org/10.1177/08997640211005849

Rogge, K. S., Pfluger, B., & Geels, F. W. (2020). Transformative policy mixes in socio-technical scenarios: The case of the low-carbon transition of the German electricity system (2010–2050. *Technological Forecasting and Social Change*, *151*, 119259. https://doi.org/10.1016/j.techfore.2018.04.002

Rullani, E. (2011). L'economia della conoscenza nel capitalismo delle reti. *Sinergie Italian Journal of Management*, *76*, 67–90.

Sack, R. D. (1986). *Human territoriality: Its theory and history* (Vol. 7). CUP Archive.

Sahakian, M. (2016). The social and solidarity economy: Why is it relevant to industrial ecology? In *Taking stock of industrial ecology* (pp. 205–227). Springer.

Saniossian, J., Beaucourt, C., & Lecocq, X. (this volume). Managing social and sustainability issues in a territory through multi-stakeholder meta-organizations. In Lupova-Henry & N. F. Dotti (Eds.), *Clusters and sustainable regional development: A meta-organisational approach*. Routledge.

Sato, M., & Okamoto, Y. (2017). From regional production system to regional innovation system: Evolutional changes of Suwa industrial region in Japan. In L. Kebir, O. Crevoisier, P. Costa, & V. Peyrache-Gadeau (Eds.), *Sustainable innovation and regional development* (pp. 225–246). Edward Elgar Publishing. https://ideas.repec.org/h/elg/eechap/16153_11.html

Schot, J., & Geels, F. W. (2008). Strategic niche management and sustainable innovation journeys: Theory, findings, research agenda, and policy. *Technology Analysis & Strategic Management*, *20*(5), 537–554.

Schot, J., & Steinmueller, W. E. (2018). Three frames for innovation policy: R&D, systems of innovation and transformative change. *Research Policy*, *47*(9), 1554–1567. https://doi.org/10.1016/j.respol.2018.08.011

Soja, E. (2015). Accentuate the regional. *International Journal of Urban and Regional Research*, *39*(2), 372–381.

Spillman, L. (2018). Meta-organization matters. *Journal of Management Inquiry*, *27*(1), 16–20. https://doi.org/10.1177/1056492616688856

Starik, M. (1995). Should trees have managerial standing? Toward stakeholder status for non-human nature. *Journal of Business Ethics*, *14*(3), 207–217. https://doi.org/10.1007/BF00881435

Viachka, A., & Duprat, L. (this volume). We are all in this together: The significance of meta-organisations for cluster policy. In E. Lupova-Henry & N. F. Dotti (Eds.), *Designing and managing clusters for sustainability*. Routledge.

Xhauflair, V. (2013). Apprentissage collectif et réflexivité systémique: Le rôle des acteurs tiers dans la structuration des méta-organisations. *Revue Interventions économiques. Papers in Political Economy*, *48*, 1–18.

Part 2

Internal dynamics of clusters as meta-organisations

5 From a wasteland to a creative community

The significance of meta-organising for cluster policy

Assia VIACHKA and Lola DUPRAT

Introduction

Policy initiatives that use the cluster concept to promote economic development have become common in recent decades. These policies target not only specific types of organisations, primarily firms but also other actors such as academic and public institutions, which are often mobilised and organised into business collectives within the policy framework. Clusters are understood as 'geographic concentrations of interconnected companies, specialised suppliers, service providers, firms in related industries, and associated institutions' (Porter, 2000, p. 15) and are believed to be important for economic growth. In this respect, the central role of cluster policies is to foster the development of collaborative and collectively competitive regional ecosystems of related actors. Therefore, the outcome of such policies depends on the establishment of collective action within geographical clusters. However, despite the importance of collective organisation in clusters, relatively few empirical studies have addressed this topic.

Our intention with this chapter is to explore the role of a meta-organisation, which is a formal organisation composed of other formal organisations (Ahrne & Brunsson, 2005, 2008), in the process of organising clusters. Moreover, we examine the role of meta-organising in establishing cooperative and socially sustainable communities of organisations that can 'sustain and reproduce themselves at an acceptable level of functioning' (Dempsey et al., 2011, p. 293). It has been suggested that meta-organising is a useful strategy for establishing collective action between competing entities (Azzam & Berkowitz, 2018). Competition is common in clusters (Porter, 2000). However, the meta-organisation framework has not yet incorporated a geographic dimension, and the role of a meta-organisation in a geographical cluster remains unclear. This research aims to develop our knowledge of meta-organising among co-located organisations, which could facilitate the implementation of cluster-based policy.

This chapter presents the exploratory single-case study of 'La Friche la Belle de Mai' (henceforth, La Friche), a meta-organisation made up of arts and culture sector organisations. La Friche is located in Marseille (France) in a cultural wasteland. A wasteland is an abandoned urban space of industrial buildings and

DOI: 10.4324/9781003215066-8

sites that have been taken over – sometimes illegally or for very low rent – by cultural actors and artists in need of a place to create (Thorion, 2005). These actors gradually restructure cultural wastelands and, in some cases, as in La Friche, even develop their own governance structure for the long-term management of projects. The governance structure of La Friche has been identified as a 'territorialised meta-organisation' (TMO) 'with dimensions of classical meta-organisation and with the addition of territorialisation' (Duprat, 2020, p. 113). TMOs are meta-organisations that are strongly anchored in their territory – that is their geographical and socio-economical surroundings. This case examines the role of the meta-organisation in the urban transformation of La Friche and the importance of the territorial dimension in its survival and the social sustainability of the community. Social sustainability refers to the social goals of sustainable development, an often overlooked but important dimension (cf. Vallance et al., 2011). One of the elements of social sustainability is the presence of a sustainable community – that is one that meets the needs of present and future residents and is a place where people 'want to live and work, now and in the future' (Dempsey et al., 2011, p. 290). Industrial clusters are rooted in specific geographic places. Therefore, social sustainability is highly relevant to the long-term ability of a region to sustain industrial ecosystems and communities around them.

This chapter is structured as follows. First, we briefly address the link between geographical clusters, organising, and social sustainability and analyse the role of meta-organising in geographical clusters. This is followed by a description of La Friche and a discussion of its role in the development of the district. We show that the meta-organisation provided the conditions for the emergence of a cooperative community of creative organisations and facilitated the urban restructuring of the area. We then discuss the implications for organising clusters and ensuring the social sustainability of organised communities.

Organised clusters and social sustainability

The literature associated with economic clustering is vast and complex and provides many accounts of similar and related economic activity co-location in a defined geographical area. 'Cluster theory' (Maskell & Kebir, 2006) includes terms such as agglomerations, localised industries, industrial districts, spatial concentrations, growth poles, and innovative milieu, each providing an interpretation of the inter-organisational dynamics that take place at a particular place and time. These terms are, however, not synonyms. They represent distinct theoretical approaches and are not in agreement on all aspects. One of these approaches has been proposed by the business economist Michael Porter (1998, 2000). Porter's framework suggests that clusters should be identified and supported to foster economic development and national competitiveness.

Many attempts have been made to put the cluster framework into practice in a wide range of industrial and economic settings (see, e.g. Borrás & Tsagdis, 2008). These have sought to improve agglomerations through organising collective action, upgrading company sophistication and business environment quality (Ketels, 2013). A central tenet of the cluster approach is that changing collective behaviour can promote the emergence of a self-sustaining system of innovation and commercial renewal (Raines, 2002). This typically involves collaboration between the organisations that have been selected for and organised into a collective entity, often called 'a cluster'. However, such an 'organised' cluster does not necessarily include all the economic actors in an agglomeration. Indeed, the composition of the cluster is defined by such factors as public policy, the purpose of collaboration, and the willingness of actors to participate in the initiative.

Lindqvist et al. (2013) explain that 'organised clusters' are often used as political tools to enhance innovation, growth, and competitiveness, the most successful regional cluster policies building on an established organising capacity (Kiese & Hundt, 2014). Organising capacity is considered to be the ability of a region to enlist and engage all actors that are important to cluster growth, using elements such as shared vision/strategy, political/societal support, and public–private partnerships (van den Berg et al., 2001). The importance of collective action in clusters has been recognised (cf. De Langen & Visser, 2005). However, the literature has paid little attention to how co-located organisations collectively arrange their relationships and the implications of different types of organising at the macro-level and the firm level. Cluster theory has predominately focused on informal and unintentional organising. A regional network, for example, is a social order evolving out of dynamic and complex interactions (e.g. exchange of goods, knowledge and information sharing). There is no common consciousness to create a goal-directed entity (Garaudel, 2020). Organised clusters, however, represent a 'decided social order' (Ahrne et al., 2016). They are established following a decision to arrange relations between organisations.

Furthermore, the role organised clusters play in the social sustainability of industrial communities has recently begun to attract attention. Saniossian et al. (this volume), for example explore the role of territorial clusters for economic cooperation – a new breed of organised clusters in France – in fostering the social and solidarity economy. Saniossian et al. suggest that the meta-organisational framework can be a valuable tool for analysing the role of clusters in social sustainability. Our intention, in this chapter, is to contribute to this line of investigation by exploring how a decision to organise collectively can affect the relationship between actors and their community, which is an important element of social sustainability. Dempsey et al. (2011) explain that, at the urban scale, social sustainability involves the development of communities in which people want to live today and in the future. Such sustainable communities are perceived as being safe and secure, inclusive, and equitable, the residents tending to remain in the community for a long time, to identify with it, interact with each other, and participate in collective aspects of social life. These dimensions of social sustainability are important to achieving local level environmental goals, as a positive sense of attachment leads to increasing resident motivation to see a place endure and grow in the long run.

This chapter discusses collective organising formalised through the establishment of a formal meta-organisation. Meta-organising creates the conditions for establishing a decided social order and is considered important for economic clustering (cf. Lupova-Henry et al., 2021). We focus on exploring how a meta-organisation can shape the interactions between co-located actors and the implications this can have for organising geographical clusters. Furthermore, we show how meta-organising can create a positive attachment between organisations and their community by fostering a common meta-organisational identity and thus helping develop a sense of place and shared culture as elements of social sustainability (Colantonio et al., 2009).

Meta-organising clusters

Meta-organisations (e.g. associations, federations, business groups) have a number of fundamental characteristics (Ahrne & Brunsson, 2005, 2008, 2011; Berkowitz & Dumez, 2016; Garaudel, 2020): (1) they are formal organisations, (2) their members are organisations, 3) membership is voluntary and can be discontinued at any time, and 4) members preserve their organisational and strategic autonomy. Thus, joining a meta-organisation involves a voluntary application by a prospective member and may depend on collective acceptance.

Meta-organisations are defined by boundaries, hierarchy, constitution, and autonomy – attributes that can be useful in the context of organised clusters. Meta-organising allows shaping a cluster into a structure that has boundaries but is flexible enough to accommodate different actors. A meta-organisation can also adjust its membership criteria to exclude some organisations in the geographical cluster or bring in organisations that are otherwise not connected to the collective. Meta-organising also implies the presence of a hierarchy and the formation of a new 'centre of authority' (Ahrne & Brunsson, 2008). Rules can therefore be issued, and actions can be ordered to guide the behaviour of members and solve conflicts. By formalising the conditions of interaction, meta-organising reduces unpredictability in the local business environment. Formalising also makes relationships in the cluster visible (Ahrne et al., 2016), allowing outsiders to easily identify and connect with the collective. Instead of creating a strong central authority, meta-organising creates an arena where socio-economic differences are manifested and negotiated. However, members would not join an organised cluster unless they accept the rights and obligations membership brings. Therefore, they all agree on the principles that guide their partnership (a constitution). Furthermore, a meta-organisation is a source of collective identity that unifies the members.

The long-term effect of meta-organising is somewhat unclear. As its long-term importance increases (Ahrne & Brunsson, 2005), a meta-organisation is likely to be perceived as an independent actor that works with other organisations to advance the interests of the entire cluster in ways not achievable by single organisations. A meta-organisation is, however, not only a device of collective action. It is also an independent organisation that acts in its own right and strives to secure its survival and prosperity (Garaudel, 2020). Therefore, a meta-organisation may try to steer the cluster in a specific direction and influence its members to strive for a specific goal (e.g. Hodges, 2019).

Research into meta-organisations has addressed many aspects of the meta-organising of collective action. However, the literature has yet to consider the specific case of organising co-located organisations. Geography typically appears in the literature as a specificity of purpose (Garaudel, 2020), indicating the level at which a meta-organisation operates (e.g. a national or a regional organisation). It has not been used as an analytical lens to address the effects of distance between members. Geographical clusters are made up of co-located organisations that operate in the same or related sectors. Therefore, there is a continuous tension between competition and collaboration in these clusters, representing a challenge for cooperation. Co-location facilitates interactions and provides opportunities to share knowledge, pool resources, and stay ahead of the competition. However, the overriding imperative remains of being more competitive than everyone else, including other local organisations (Newlands, 2003).

The case presented in this chapter sheds light on how collective action between co-located organisations can be formalised by establishing a meta-organisation. The study's first objective was to understand how the collective was organised and how the meta-organisation conditioned the social interactions at La Friche. Ketels et al. (2012) did not refer directly to the meta-organisation framework in their study of organised clusters (or 'cluster organisations'). They, however, found empirical evidence of a formal membership structure promoting a higher level of collaboration between firms. We were therefore intrigued to find out whether there was a tension between competition and cooperation at La Friche, and whether the activities of the meta-organisation promoted collaboration between members. The research also investigated the meta-organisation's role in transforming the cultural wasteland from an abandoned industrial site to a thriving urban community, thus contributing to the social sustainability of the area. La Friche, as a 'territorialised' meta-organisation (TMO) (Duprat, 2020), is a collective that is organised as a territory and is defined by the area within which all members and almost all collective activities are found. Therefore, we were interested in understanding whether the territorial dimension was significant in the survival of the meta-organisation and the social sustainability of the community at La Friche.

La Friche was founded in 1992 by a collective of local actors and through the support of the City of Marseille's culture delegate. However, the story of the collective began some years earlier when artists determined that the industrial SEITA wasteland in the district of Belle de Mai was a suitable site for hosting their creative pursuits. The tobacco factory previously located here closed in 1990, leaving 120,000 m^2 of abandoned buildings. These could be occupied for a small cost or even for free. The artists had scoured the district for several years before finding a location and creating an association, 'Système Friche Théâtre' (SFT), to organise the collective. Other actors, artistic groups, and cultural operators later joined the collective, establishing La Friche as a cultural wasteland and a place for artistic production.

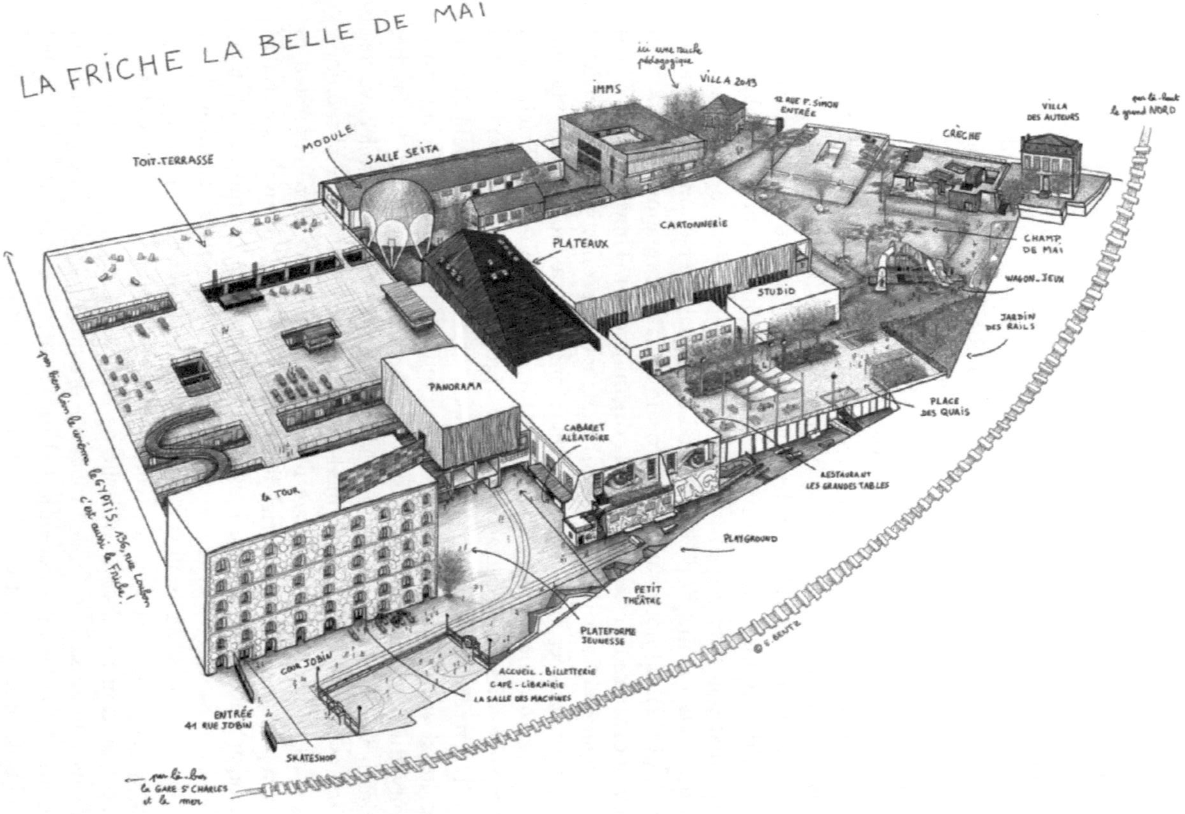

Figure 5.1 La Friche la Belle de Mai

Image credit: Emmanuelle Bentz. *Source:* Friche La Belle de Mai, 2022

The collective, over the years, moved around and gradually renovated the immense site, aided by the financial support of the city. A number of blueprints were used to help structure the wasteland and turn it into the city's cultural hotspot. La Friche is today a 45,000 m^2 site that hosts more than 70 creative organisations. It is still managed by an association and has maintained its strong links to local communities and public institutions, almost 30 years after the collective was first established.

Methodology

La Friche, which was selected for its theoretical contribution (Eisenhardt, 1989), presented an opportunity to study a meta-organisation composed of co-located organisations operating in the same sector. Structural changes took place between 2011 and 2013, leading to a change of governance and the establishment of a 'Société Coopérative d'Intérêt Collectif' (SCIC, in English 'cooperative company of collective interest'), which replaced the SFT association. In French law, a SCIC is a firm using a cooperative form of organising. The SCIC is a formal organisation of permanent employees who oversee the infrastructure and represent and organise the collective. La Friche is also a formal organisation of independent organisations and, therefore, strongly corresponds to a meta-organisation. Membership is voluntary. However, new members must be accepted by the board of directors and can leave La Friche at any time, providing there are no unfulfilled contractual obligations. Being part of the collective requires being located at La Friche. However, the organisational identity of each member continues to be recognised within and outside the collective. Members participate in the governance and operations of the association, the vote of each member having equal weight within their electoral college.

This research sought to create a rich and detailed account of the meta-organisation. Therefore, an abductive approach was adopted, data and theory being permitted to converge (Avenier & Thomas, 2015). Qualitative data collection through documentary analysis, passive observation, and structured open-ended interviews was carried out in three stages: 1) a series of interviews with a large number of key stakeholders (including members, SCIC employees, and even external partners) accompanied by a consultation of documents, 2) a study of a creative project led by a member organisation of the TMO, and 3) additional interviews to provide further insights, interviewees selected based on the initial analysis. The data was collected from June 2017 to July 2019. The transcribed data was encoded twice using the multi-thematic abductive method to look for themes by identifying meaning in context. The final analysis contained 45 hours of interviews and all the data points that could confirm, reject, or explain the context of the case.

Results

The cultural wasteland, over time, attracted members from many artistic fields, ranging from contemporary art to professional training, digital art, music, and dance. La Friche is a place where ideas are shared, despite member organisations being in direct or indirect competition. Members openly discuss their creative plans, preferring to develop similar artistic ideas together rather than competition and believe that the road to bigger and better projects starts with collaboration. The following analysis presented highlights a number of key aspects of the meta-organisation's modus operandi, such as engineered co-location, meta-organised interaction and collaboration, meta-organisational culture, and identity.

First, *engineered co-location* is one of the key aspects of La Friche's functioning. The meta-organisation played a central role in the initial growth of the collective, the founders encouraging key arts and culture actors to establish at the wasteland. This had a snowball effect, with others joining the collective. At the same time, the formal organisation received public funding to reconstruct the wasteland and worked with public authorities to ensure that the site was suitable for artistic production. Spacious premises, the easy transport of artwork, and the availability of materials were factors mentioned by interviewed artists in their decision to locate at La Friche.

Not every application to locate at La Friche was, however, accepted. Before accepting an organisation, the Board of Directors evaluated 1) the potential contribution to the artistic portfolio of the cultural wasteland and 2) social compatibility with the rest of the group. The strict formal procedure ensured that accepted members would be able to access La Friche's social network and that the collective grew in a controlled way. Therefore, the meta-organisation, at least to some degree, influenced the overall creative direction of the collective.

Second, SCIC's facilitation of *interaction and collaboration* between members brought stability and allowed members to explore collaborations without having to re-negotiate expectations. SCIC uses standards to regulate behaviour but not to a significant extent. Standard rental (lease) agreements and project financing contracts ensure that common practices are followed. Standards also exist for communication with the general public (graphic charter, templates) via La Friche's official website. SCIC also governs large-scale projects and facilitates the establishment of relationships within the cultural wasteland. The meta-organisation encourages individual artists to start projects and brings actors together in projects to ensure that no members are excluded from the interaction. Therefore, SCIC tries to provide all members with opportunities to exchange knowledge and establish connections within the wasteland.

La Friche also works to ensure that inspiration is sourced from beyond the cultural wasteland and frequently invites external partners to participate in artistic projects. The meta-organisation also gradually opened more and more of its territory to the public and even built a new skatepark to attract visitors. Adopting the La Belle de Mai name of the surrounding neighbourhood also sent a signal to the public that non-members were welcome to visit the space and be part of the cultural buzz. Most of the site is currently open to the public from morning until late at night. Metal gates and door codes, however, cordon off private working areas.

The meta-organisation has, from the start, worked to forge close links with local public authorities, the urban transformation of La Friche not being possible without the City of Marseille's delegate for culture, who facilitated the initial funding of the initiative. The city and the regional council are both represented at the SCIC general assembly, with La Friche today regularly collaborating with local authorities and hosting many of the city's cultural events.

Moreover, *meta-organisational culture* has been an important element for La Friche. The meta-organisation gives members significant freedom to conduct their day-to-day work and manage collaborations. Members are free to choose whom to partner with, and the collaborations they carry out are not overseen. The only performance monitoring at La Friche is an annual financial review, which reports the results to the main investors. The meta-organisation also does not use sanctions or explicit rewards but instead devised a different mechanism for framing the collective: a formalised vision of what they were to become together. The vision was described in a formal document. The document established a code of conduct and defined what members should strive for as culture operators and artists. It also contained the founders' view on the arts and culture and their core values and common beliefs about the artistic process (such as openness to different audiences, creative freedom and experimentation, and actions against elitism). These are explicitly communicated and weighed during new member evaluation.

The document became the blueprint for establishing what could only be described as a meta-organisational culture of shared ways of thinking and behaving, which in turn encouraged mutual commitment. These ideals further promote cooperation and, through the opportunity to interact daily, contributed to the internalisation of the culture by all organisations located at La Friche. Therefore, the members instinctively trust that everyone will behave in the best interest of the collective, irrespective of whether they enjoy each other's company or not. Culture as an invisible guideline lessens the need for hierarchical control. For example instead of designing copyright procedures, the meta-organisation relied on the appropriation of ideas being seen to be a contravention of the values of the community. This, therefore, represents a significant reputation risk and a member quickly no longer being accepted at La Friche.

Finally, *identity* is another key element of the meta-organisation. Today, La Friche has workspaces along with living quarters, performance venues, a community garden, a skatepark, a bookstore, a restaurant, and even a playground, all giving it a feeling of neighbourhood. The meta-organisation's identity is strongly linked to the district, the services provided at La Friche (e.g., training and culture dissemination) and the many cross-disciplinary events and exhibitions held there every year. Organisations located at La Friche become 'frichistes', some even adding the meta-organisation to their official name (e.g. 'Zinc La Friche'). Not all would call themselves frichistes. Those interviewed who did so had been at La Friche for many years. The interviewees also repeatedly expressed an emotional attachment, pride, and a sense of belonging to the cultural wasteland. When asked whether they would consider leaving, an artist who complained about the meta-organisation's management answered that La Friche was their home, and they would never leave.

Discussion: what could La Friche teach us about organising clusters?

This case provides valuable insights into the role of a meta-organisation in a geographical cluster. The La Friche community displays a number of features that are desired outcomes of an organised cluster. Member organisations, instead of behaving as competitors, seek collaboration and trust that all members will respect the values of the community. La Friche, therefore, stands as proof that a cooperative and creative milieu can be built if co-located actors have a shared vision of what they want to achieve together. The meta-organisation has been instrumental in setting a strategic direction for the cultural wasteland. Furthermore, carefully crafted meta-organisational boundaries ensured that the collective is composed of socially and creatively compatible members from many artistic fields. Geographic proximity is important to creativity. Organisations must, however, also share some (but not too many) cognitive and social similarities if they are to benefit from co-location (Boschma, 2005). Locating in a geographical area does not presuppose any formal acceptance. The outcome of economic clustering, therefore, is difficult to predict. However, La Friche's selection procedure ensured that the membership base was homogeneous and that members' skills and artistic projects were diverse enough to trigger creativity. The wasteland may, without the meta-organisation, have been inhabited by more diverse organisations, making collaboration less likely.

Locating in a geographical cluster does not guarantee any interaction with other local actors. It has, in fact, been suggested that organisations might sometimes even be 'too close' for collaboration to occur, especially if the local context is characterised by intense rivalry (Letaifa & Rabeau, 2013). The La Friche meta-organisation worked actively to arrange and encourage projects among members and between members and external partners. The creation of a centre of authority also meant that standards could be used to bring stability and promote cooperation between organisations. Furthermore, the meta-organisation used its constitution to organise interaction between members, rather than relying on a hierarchy. Thus, members' choices and actions in the collective were guided by formalised fundamental values of the meta-organisation. Institutionalising a code of conduct to dictate ways of living and interacting in the wasteland was used to ensure that members' behaviour was in line with the collective interests. Geographic proximity also played an important role in translating the constitution into a strong internal culture at La Friche, co-location helping actors internalise values through observation and interaction. Therefore, this culture supported the development of an environment that promotes cooperation by reducing behaviour uncertainty and increasing similarity between members. As if in the air, the founders' vision became embedded in the wasteland. La Friche became a place for arts and expression and was recognised for its openness, solidarity, experimentation, and creative freedom. The emergence of an internal culture helped it solidify the collective and support the formation of a stable community. Furthermore, the fact that some organisations call themselves 'frichistes' points to the presence of a strong common identity and self-identification.

The presence of a strong common identity, and a high level of internal coordination and similarity between members (Ahrne & Brunsson, 2008), helped the meta-organisation influence and change the environment. Indeed, La Friche influenced the urban development of the wasteland to ensure that the needs of the residents were met; having begun from an abandoned industrial area, La Friche became a place of economic opportunities where everyone can experience art and socialise. Even the children of La Belle de Mai are welcome to spend time in the wasteland, skate, and enjoy the art. Through constructing a neighbourhood-like environment, the meta-organisation, therefore, blurred the borders between the cultural wasteland and the district, giving a sense of 'placeness' to La Friche (Seamon & Sowers, 2008). Having developed a positive attachment to the cultural wasteland, visitors and residents are likely to want to see it sustained in the long run.

Therefore, the territorial dimension is of great importance to the survival of the meta-organisation. As a TMO, La Friche is not an abstract space constructed around the relations and collective experiences of the members. It also is a territorial space that segregates and protects the creative organisations from the rest of the city. By limiting space accessibility to outsiders, the TMO does not let them freely participate in the community's life. It controls the extent to which non-members interact at La Friche. The meta-organisation also provides access to material and non-material resources (including collaboration projects) that organisations would not necessarily find outside the wasteland. This and a democratic decision-making process that gives all members equal rights to influence the future direction of the collective greatly contributed to the social sustainability of the community. Perceiving La Friche as their home and being firmly anchored in the wasteland, members are likely to act in the interest of the community, preserve it, and ensure the longevity of the meta-organisation.

Several case observations come to mind as implications for cluster policy. The initial co-location of a few artists was driven by the convenience of the location, the group deciding collectively to settle down in the Belle de Mai district and quickly formalising their interaction. The presence of a formal meta-organisation ensured that subsequent community growth was not chaotic but followed an agreed-upon strategic direction. The intensity and variety of interactions at La Friche was also controlled via physical gates and membership limitations. Therefore, the underlying dynamics of group formation and interaction at La Friche differ from that which typically occurs when organisations cluster geographically. The geographical concentration of creative organisations at La Friche was, in other words, not the result of self-selection, the formal organisation guiding development towards the establishment of a cooperative artistic community. However, the territorial dimension was essential in the creation of an organising capacity for the wasteland. Organisations were not permitted to locate at La Friche without being a member of the meta-organisation and had to relocate if they no longer wished to be part of the collective. Therefore, La Friche is a creative territory, and one needs to enter it to interact with the TMO members. Scientific parks and business incubators are two types of settings that are of interest in cluster policy. They have a similar territorial dimension, sometimes also hosting a specific category of organisations. Therefore, the lessons learned at La Friche about organising a cooperative and socially sustainable community could be very valuable to these settings.

We believe that an organised cluster is, in most cases, an abstract organisational structure and not a gatekeeper of physical space. Members and non-members of organised clusters coexist and can be co-located. However, even when a meta-organisation does not own space and cannot stipulate where member organisations are to locate, it can have an organising capacity. The collective actor has access to elements that can be used to facilitate cooperation within the clusters (e.g. standards, monitoring) and is motivated to ensure the longevity of the collective. The TMO, acting in the interest of its own survival, designed an environment that supports the social sustainability of La Friche. Elements such as interaction, sense of place, common culture, and identity increase the likelihood that organisations will participate in an organised cluster and contribute to the sustainable growth of their industrial agglomeration and urban community. McCauley and Stephens (2012) studied organised clusters in the sustainable energy domain and suggested that policy should pay more attention to the social and cultural dimension, as community development is important in establishing successful green energy clusters. In this chapter, we suggest that meta-organising could be a valuable strategy for addressing these concerns and creating organised and socially sustainable cluster communities.

Limitations

La Friche is composed of organisations that are homogeneous in terms of size, sector, and organisational characteristics. The results, therefore, are not directly applicable to more heterogeneous settings. Furthermore, this chapter does not discuss the importance of locational (e.g. culture, institutions) and sectoral (e.g. technological/market dynamics, innovation pace) characteristics in the development of the case. The arts and culture sectors are, for example, not as dependent on technological innovation and patenting as other sectors, which may have reduced the need for TMO control. Meta-organising is also suggested here as a strategy for organising collective action between competitors. However, the emergence of meta-organising in highly competitive settings (e.g. in mature industrial clusters) might be difficult. Collective organising began early at La Friche, and the meta-organisation worked from the start to support collaboration. The setting, therefore, never became highly competitive. However, the difficulties that can arise from high competition are very relevant and should be addressed. The chapter, finally, does not discuss the difficulties of meta-organising. For example meta-organising involves the inclusion of some actors and the exclusion of others by design. This could generate conflicts and even become an obstacle for policy implementation.

Conclusions

This chapter presents the case of La Friche la Belle de Mai, a meta-organisation composed of geographically co-located organisations (TMO). The formal organisation initially was made up of a nomadic group of artists, the organisation helping them obtain the public support necessary to establish a cultural wasteland. La Friche, as its importance increased, became an independent actor that participates in the city's cultural life, organising and hosting numerous cultural events. By striving to engineer an environment that facilitates cooperation, the meta-organisation contributed to forming a socially sustainable community that focused its collective efforts on transforming an industrial wasteland into a lively creative district. The chapter discusses the results in the context of cluster policy, highlighting how meta-organising can support the establishment of collective action in geographic clusters. Future research should investigate the factors that affect the willingness of actors to join meta-organised clusters. Meta-organisations, unlike geographical clusters, have organisational boundaries and cannot exist if potential members do not accept them.

Acknowledgement

The authors would like to thank Emmanuelle Bentz for allowing to use her drawing of La Friche La Belle de Mai in this chapter.

References

Ahrne, G., & Brunsson, N. (2005). Organizations and meta-organizations. *Scandinavian Journal of Management, 21*(4), 429–449. https://doi.org/10.1016/j.scaman.2005.09.005

Ahrne, G., & Brunsson, N. (2008). *Meta-organizations*. Edward Elgar Publishing. www.e-elgar.com/shop/gbp/meta-organizations-9781847209504.html

Ahrne, G., & Brunsson, N. (2011). Organization outside organizations: The significance of partial organization. *Organization, 18*(1), 83–104. https://doi.org/10.1177/1350508410376256

Ahrne, G., Brunsson, N., & Kerwer, D. (2016). The paradox of organizing states: A meta-organization perspective on international organizations. *Journal of International Organizations Studies*, 7(1), 5–24.

Avenier, M.-J., & Thomas, C. (2015). Finding one's way around various methodological guidelines for doing rigorous case studies: A comparison of four epistemological frameworks. *Systèmes d'information et Management, 20*(1), 61–98.

Azzam, J. E., & Berkowitz, H. (2018). Patterns of coopetition in meta-organizations. In *Routledge companion to coopetition strategies* (pp. 280–291). Routledge.

Berkowitz, H., & Dumez, H. (2016). The concept of meta-organization: Issues for management studies. *European Management Review, 13*(2), 149–156. https://doi.org/10.1111/emre.12076

Borrás, S., & Tsagdis, D. (2008). *Cluster policies in Europe*. Edward Elgar Publishing.

Boschma, R. (2005). Proximity and innovation: A critical assessment. *Regional Studies*, *39*(1), 61–74.

Colantonio, A., Dixon, T., Ganser, R., Carpenter, J., & Ngombe, A. (2009). *Measuring socially sustainable urban regeneration in Europe*. Oxford Institute for Sustainable Development (OISD).

De Langen, P. W., & Visser, E.-J. (2005). Collective action regimes in seaport clusters: The case of the Lower Mississippi port cluster. *Journal of Transport Geography*, *13*(2), 173–186.

Dempsey, N., Bramley, G., Power, S., & Brown, C. (2011). The social dimension of sustainable development: Defining urban social sustainability. *Sustainable Development*, *19*(5), 289–300.

Duprat, L. (2020). *Favoriser la créativité organisationnelle des organisations créatives au sein d'une méta-organisation territorialisée: Le cas de la Friche la Belle de Mai à Marseille* [Ph.D. Thesis]. Aix Marseille Université. https://tel.archives-ouvertes.fr/tel-02948013

Eisenhardt, K. M. (1989). Building theories from case study research. *Academy of Management Review*, *14*(4), 532–550.

Friche La Belle de Mai. (2022). *Les Lieux*. Friche la Belle de Mai. www.lafriche.org/la-friche/lieux/

Garaudel, P. (2020). Exploring meta-organizations' diversity and agency: A meta-organizational perspective on global union federations. *Scandinavian Journal of Management*, *36*(1), 101094. https://doi.org/10.1016/j.scaman.2020.101094

Hodges, E. (2019). *A mixed methods study exploring organisational factors influencing the development of services for people with dementia in English hospices* [Ph.D.]. Keele University. https://eprints.keele.ac.uk/7137/

Ketels, C. (2013). Recent research on competitiveness and clusters: What are the implications for regional policy? *Cambridge Journal of Regions, Economy and Society*, *6*(2), 269–284. https://doi.org/10.1093/cjres/rst008

Ketels, C., Lindqvist, G., & Sölvell, Ö. (2012). Strengthening clusters and competitiveness in Europe: The role of cluster organisations. *The Cluster Observatory*, *56*, 56.

Kiese, M., & Hundt, C. (2014). Cluster policies, organising capacity and regional resilience: Evidence from German case studies. *Raumforschung Und Raumordnung*, *72*(2), 117–131.

Letaifa, S. B., & Rabeau, Y. (2013). Too close to collaborate? How geographic proximity could impede entrepreneurship and innovation. *Journal of Business Research*, *66*(10), 2071–2078.

Lindqvist, G., Ketels, C., & Sölvell, Ö. (2013). *The cluster initiative greenbook 2.0*. Ivory Tower Publishers.

Lupova-Henry, E., Blili, S., & Dal Zotto, C. (2021). Designing organised clusters as social actors: A meta-organisational approach. *Journal of Organization Design 10*, 35–54.

Maskell, P., & Kebir, L. (2006). The theory of the cluster: What it takes and what it implies. *Clusters and Regional Development. Routledge*, 30–49.

McCauley, S. M., & Stephens, J. C. (2012). Green energy clusters and socio-technical transitions: Analysis of a sustainable energy cluster for regional economic development in Central Massachusetts, USA. *Sustainability Science*, 7(2), 213–225. https://doi.org/10.1007/s11625-012-0164-6

Newlands, D. (2003). Competition and cooperation in industrial clusters: The implications for public policy. *European Planning Studies*, *11*(5), 521–532.

Porter, M. E. (1998, November 1). Clusters and the new economics of competition. *Harvard Business Review*. https://hbr.org/1998/11/clusters-and-the-new-economics-of-competition

Porter, M. E. (2000). Location, competition, and economic development: Local clusters in a global economy. *Economic Development Quarterly*, *14*(1), 15–34. https://doi.org/10.1177/089124240001400105

Raines, P. (2002, May). The challenge of evaluating cluster behaviour in economic development policy. *International RSA Conference: Evaluation and EU Regional Policy: New Questions and Challenges*.

Saniossian, J., Beaucourt, C., & Lecocq, X. (this volume). Managing social and sustainability issues in a territory through multi-stakeholder meta-organizations. In Lupova-Henry & N. F. Dotti (Eds.), *Clusters and sustainable regional development: A meta-organisational approach*. Routledge.

Seamon, D., & Sowers, J. (2008). Place and placelessness (1976): Edward Relph. In *Key texts in human geography* (pp. 43–52). SAGE Publications Ltd. https://doi.org/10.4135/9781446213742

Thorion, G. (2005). Espaces en friche, des lieux dédiés à l'expérimentation et à la création culturelle. *Communication et organisation. Revue scientifique francophone en Communication organisationnelle, 26*, 114–126.

Vallance, S., Perkins, H. C., & Dixon, J. E. (2011). What is social sustainability? A clarification of concepts. *Geoforum, 42*(3), 342–348.

van den Berg, L., Braun, E., & van Winden, W. (2001). Growth clusters in European cities: An integral approach. *Urban Studies, 38*(1), 185–205. https://doi.org/10.1080/00420980124001

6 Managing sustainability issues of a territory through multi-stakeholder meta-organisations

Jennifer SANIOSSIAN, Christel BEAUCOURT and Xavier LECOCQ

Introduction

Sustainability issues are increasingly visible worldwide, demonstrating the necessity to act collectively to address these challenges. Weather and health crises like hurricanes and COVID-19 confirm the necessity to develop innovative practices at the individual and organisational levels. These issues are highlighted in the United Nations' Sustainable Development Goals (SDGs) that concern areas such as education, air, water, biodiversity, sustainability economy, gender equality, and local economy. It increasingly appears that taking care of the planet and society by developing sustainable practices at local and global levels can only be possible through cooperation and partnerships.

Various forms of collective action – such as implicit networks, local clusters, meta-organisations, or vertical partnerships – can facilitate cooperation between actors to answer sustainability issues (Lupova-Henry & Dotti, 2019). Recently, the importance of collective action for addressing sustainability challenges has been studied in industrial clusters and meta-organisations (Battaglia et al., 2010; Berkowitz et al., 2017; Davies, 2013; Fayyaz et al., 2017; Tvedt, 2019). Indeed, clusters can be seen as important actors in developing local sustainability initiatives and drivers of sustainability transitions on a larger scale (Lupova-Henry & Dotti, this volume). In this respect, cluster studies demonstrate the importance of relationships between members allowing them to share skills and knowledge, develop policies, and carry out collaborative activities (Borrás & Tsagdis, 2008). However, this stream of research has mainly been focused on industrial clusters (Brenner & Mühlig, 2013; Davies, 2013; Fayyaz et al., 2017), while sustainability and social issues may cut across multiple activities and sectors. For instance the mobility issue on a given territory goes beyond what is traditionally labelled as the mobility sector (e.g. cars, buses, bikes) to include tourism and leisure activities and concerns private companies, groups of citizens, and public actors.

We suggest the meta-organisational theory (Ahrne & Brunsson, 2005, 2008) and, more specifically, the multi-stakeholder meta-organisation approach (Berkowitz & Dumez, 2015; Saniossian, 2020) can be a relevant theoretical lens for observing how various stakeholders can collectively address sustainability and social issues on a territory. In particular, our research aims to elucidate how

DOI: 10.4324/9781003215066-9

multiple trans-sectoral members in organised clusters work together under a meta-organisational framework to address sustainability issues on a given territory.

In this chapter, we observe the development of cooperation between different types of organisations to manage sustainability issues at the territorial level. These include local authorities, governments, non-governmental organisations, companies, social and solidarity economy companies, and research centres. To account for the territorial aspect, we bridge the meta-organisational approach with cluster studies and examine the case of a territorial cluster through the lens of a multi-stakeholder meta-organisation theory.

The territorial clusters for economic cooperation – 'Poles Territoriaux de Cooperation Economique' (PTCE) in French – have been introduced by the French Law for Social and Solidarity Economy ('Loi Relative à l'Economie Sociale et Solidaire') in 2014 to promote social and solidarity economy. We can consider these clusters as organised clusters (Lupova-Henry et al., 2021b). In that sense, they concern the grouping of different organisations in a specific territory, which 'deliberately "construct" themselves both as organisations and social actors' (Lupova-Henry et al., 2021b). More specifically, these PTCEs constitute a case of a geographically embedded multi-stakeholder meta-organisation (MSMO) (Saniossian, 2020) which 'aims at sustainable local development' (Article 9, Loi Relative à l'Economie Sociale et Solidaire, 2014). Based on an in-depth single case study (Yin, 2009) of 'La Maison d'Economie Solidaire' (MES), or the House of Solidarity Economy – a PTCE legally established in 2002 – we investigate how various member organisations collectively address sustainability issues on a given territory.

Our results suggest that geographically embedded MSMOs allow the development of territorial sustainability and social activities through two dimensions: by being concerned with the same sustainability issues and by facilitating social and shared innovation activities between various stakeholder organisations. These actions could result from three processes present in an MSMO: the negotiation of common goals between actors around territorial issues, the activity-oriented integration of members, and the use of internal and external communication to engage member organisations in the MSMO.

Our chapter is organised as follows: we first discuss the literature related to the multi-stakeholder meta-organisation phenomenon and show its relevance for addressing sustainability issues at the territorial level. Then, we present the methods implemented and the case before discussing the results of the empirical analysis. Finally, we present our findings and discuss the role of MSMOs in the management of sustainability issues at the territorial level.

Multi-stakeholder meta-organisations (MSMOs) and the management of sustainability issues

Sustainability issues at the territorial level

Sustainability issues can be understood through three dimensions: economic, ecological, and social (Vifell & Thedvall, 2012). These refer, for instance, to the necessity of employment, mobility, food, access to primary resources for the people, and the necessity to preserve wildlife and the natural environment. Moreover, Voegtlin and Scherer (2017) specify that the sustainable development goals must integrate the social needs of the populations and those of the planet to facilitate the development of sustainability practices and activities.

Sustainability issues also exist in a particular form at the territorial level, as they are linked to the local needs. For example in some areas, the mobility issue may concern slow mobility (using soft transport such as cycling, public transport and walking), while in others, it concerns solidarity mobility for older people. Hence, identifying sustainability issues at the territorial level allows organisations to consider the territory and produce geographical analyses (Coenen et al., 2012). Raulet-Croset (2014) suggests that organisations need to consider the territory as a management variable because it connects 'a set of heterogeneous resources, both human and geographic'. Hence, the territory is 'a lever' to facilitate the engagement of multiple stakeholders in joint actions (Raulet-Croset, 2008; Zardet & Noguera, 2013). In this sense, cooperation among organisations appears important for managing these multidimensional issues and promoting sustainability transitions (Loorbach et al., 2017).

Role of organisations and clusters in solving sustainability issues

Research suggests that cooperation among organisations facilitates the production of social innovation and the development of the territory (Ceschin & Gaziulusoy, 2016). Social innovations aim to address social and solidarity issues concerning youth, persons with disabilities, employment, and elderly persons. Thus, cooperation is seen as a way for spatially co-located actors to develop social innovations and facilitate sustainability transitions (Loorbach et al., 2017).

Some authors studied the management of specific types of cooperation among organisations to solve sustainability issues, especially the clusters for sustainability. Porter defines a cluster as 'a geographically proximate group of interconnected companies and associated institutions in a particular field, linked by commonalities and complementarities' (Porter, 2000, p. 16). Some authors point out that, in some cases, clustering can facilitate the formalisation of corporate social responsibility (CSR) policies, tools and practices (Battaglia et al., 2010; Fayyaz et al., 2017), and their integration into the business strategy of cluster members (von Weltzien Høivik & Shankar, 2011). It can also foster the development of collaborative knowledge and innovation platforms (Tvedt, 2019). Research also highlights that the management of these clusters supposes close relationships between members and strong communication of the cluster strategy (Battaglia et al., 2010).

However, research has suggested that the contribution of clusters to solving sustainability challenges could be improved if they involve a wider variety of members (Davies, 2013). Indeed, it would be interesting to observe the development of trans-sectoral clusters involving various stakeholders. While there is growing recognition of the role organised clusters can play in driving the sustainability transitions, empirical research into the intra-cluster processes and mechanisms needed to enable this role is still scarce. Following Lupova-Henry and Dotti (this volume) and Berkowitz and Gadille (this volume), this chapter questions how multiple trans-sectoral members in organised clusters work together under a meta-organisational framework to address sustainability issues on a given territory.

Multi-stakeholder meta-organisations: a cooperation form for sustainability

Recently, cluster literature has been taking the meta-organisational lens to better understand the mechanisms of organising in clusters. Meta-organisations are defined as organisations 'having organisations as members' (Ahrne & Brunsson, 2008, p. 3). These members are autonomous organisations of various types that are free to join or leave the meta-organisation, retain their independence, and are equal in the decision-making processes (Ahrne & Brunsson, 2008). A formal organisation of organisations has the following characteristics: membership, hierarchy (decision-making process, vote, respect of decisions), rules and norms, monitoring (compliance with rules and evaluation of members' performance), and sanctions (Ahrne & Brunsson, 2011). While MSMOs have some characteristics that are similar to traditional meta-organisations – for example they encompass other independent organisations – they have the particularity to rely on various types of members such as companies, governments, civil society, local authorities, or NGOs (Berkowitz et al., 2020; Berkowitz & Dumez, 2015; Saniossian, 2020). The rationale for the creation of meta-organisations ranges from the desire to change the 'conditions of interaction between members' (Ahrne & Brunsson, 2008, p. 66) to the willingness to eliminate a part of the environment (see also Berkowitz & Bor, 2018), to answer complex issues (Valente & Oliver, 2018), or to 'act collectively to shape their environments' (Lupova-Henry et al., 2021a, p. 1). We suggest that an organised cluster is a type of MSMO because it involves the creation of a formal organisation to coordinate a variety of members and engage them in collective action.

Furthermore, the meta-organisational framework has been applied to discuss the role of collective action in addressing sustainability issues (Berkowitz, 2016, 2018; Berkowitz et al., 2020; Carmagnac & Carbone, 2019; Cropper & Bor, 2018). Indeed, Berkowitz (2016) suggests that MSMOs can help answer sustainability issues by providing services facilitating the performative discourse of sustainable development. She highlights that these services and processes involve the organisation of meetings for discussion, co-construction of skills and capabilities, and the implicit diffusion of sustainable norms and practices. Carmagnac and Carbone (2019) explain that the role of meta-organisation is to create and promote the principles and mechanisms of sustainable development. Viachka and Duprat (this volume) demonstrate the role of meta-organising in building sustainable communities as a component of sustainable local development. Thus, while empirical research on the role of meta-organisations in sustainable local development remains scarce, extant sources suggest that MSMOs could help address sustainability issues at the territorial level.

The PTCE as a geographically and socially embedded MSMO

The territorial clusters for economic cooperation (PTCE in the French Law) can be seen as geographical agglomerations of actors in the social and solidarity economy (SSE) sector. These may include companies, local government bodies, research centres, higher education and research institutions, training bodies, and other actors. They collaborate to implement a joint strategy supporting innovative economic and social activities and sustainable local development through the creation of jobs, improvement of social services, or support for local consumption (Law of Social and Solidarity Economy, France, 2014). Figure 6.1 provides a graphic representation of a PTCE.

These PTCEs display the characteristics common to MSMOs (Saniossian, 2020). Specifically, they have a legal form of meta-organisation and include several types of organisations as members; the members have a trans-sectoral affiliation, retain their autonomy and identity, and are free to join or leave and have equal rights; and the meta-organisation 'secretariat' plays a crucial role in stakeholder management (Ahrne & Brunsson, 2008; Berkowitz et al., 2020; Berkowitz & Dumez, 2015).

Moreover, previous studies on PTCEs highlight that these forms of organisation can address sustainability issues at the territorial level. These capabilities come from cooperation, mutualisation, sharing practices, and joint activities

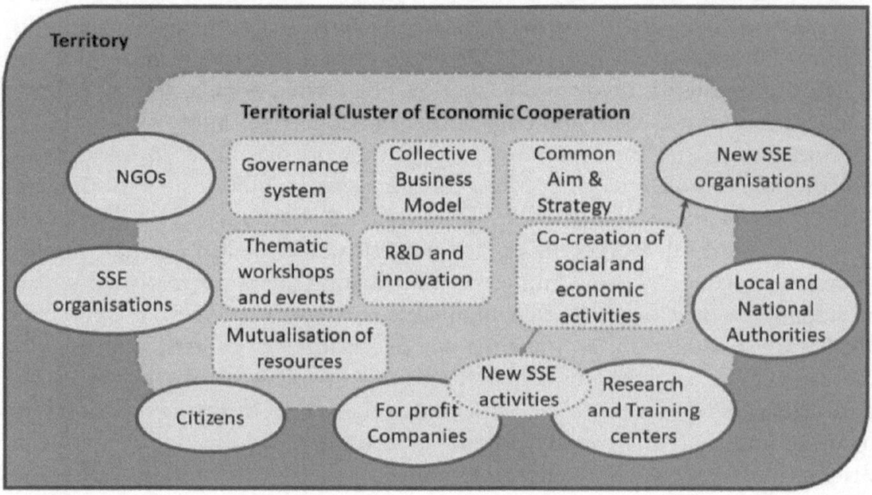

Figure 6.1 A territorial cluster of economic cooperation (PTCE)

of various members of the collective organisation (Bourbousson & Richez-Battesti, 2017; Saniossian, 2020). Indeed, PTCEs also aim to foster social innovation activities, improve the geographical embeddedness of their members, and promote social and economic activities to solve local sustainability issues. Thus, we can consider PTCEs as a specific form of a geographically embedded MSMO aiming to solve sustainability issues at the territorial level (Saniossian, 2020).

In-depth case study of a geographically embedded MSMO

Case study of the 'Maison d'Economie Solidaire'

To study how MSMOs can solve sustainability issues at the territorial level, we chose a specific case of PTCE, using an in-depth case study methodology (Yin, 2009). 'La Maison d'Economie Solidaire' (MES) – or House of Solidarity Economy – is an MSMO created and established as a legal entity in 2002 and funded since 2014 as PTCE under the Social and Solidarity Economy Law. This MSMO comprises 40 organisations: local authorities and institutions, social and solidarity economy companies, traditional companies, NGOs, citizens, and research centres. MES was initially established as a cooperative company for collective interest (SCIC) – 'Société Coopérative d'Intérêt Collectif' in French – which allows for all organisations and citizens to become members and investors of the collective organisation on equal ground. It means that all the members have an equal part in the decision-making process for the PTCE and are free to join or leave it.

This SCIC is anchored territorially. Indeed, MES is located in the 'Pays de Bray' area, a rural area situated 1 hour away from Paris by car or train, in the North of France. The 'Pays de Bray' is a bounded administrative territory, but MES' activities also extend to other neighbouring areas. As MES is a geographically embedded MSMO, its members are organisations and citizens present in this specific territory. Moreover, MES created shared and mutualised offices and other spaces in the centre of the 'Pays de Bray' area for activities and experimentations led by member organisations.

MES' general aim is to 'develop the regional economy through social and professional integration'. The SCIC, with all the member organisations involved, aims to solve several sustainability issues like waste management and circular economy, personal services, social inclusion and training, and craft entrepreneurship. Since 2002, they have carried out a number of new economic activities for the territory, such as creating a place for new craft entrepreneurs; developing a new service for employment and education in personal services with older adults; a place to recycle, select, and sell second-hand objects; and the development of tourism with shared tiny houses. All these new services and products are either developed collaboratively by member organisations or by new organisations created within the SCIC. All these activities aim to facilitate employment for the inhabitants of the area.

Moreover, since 2002, MES has been involving new member organisations and citizens within the SCIC as well as updating its strategic projects and activities. Our study aims to investigate the processes by which MES retains and renews dissimilar organisations operating on the territory and involves them in the co-creation of sustainability activities at the territorial level. More specifically, this research focuses on MES' new strategic project – 'Solidarium' – that aims to integrate individual knowledge and expertise of citizens and volunteers to support MES' objectives.

Methodology

We conducted an in-depth single case study (Yin, 2009) of MES to investigate how multiple trans-sectoral members in organised clusters work together under a meta-organisational framework to address sustainability issues on a given territory. This research has been facilitated by the partnership between MES and one of the authors. It allowed her to observe, analyse, and support MES in designing its governance system, research and development, innovation of activities, and cooperation between organisations and communication.

More specifically, the authors conducted an exploratory study with a collective interview of MES CEOs and two guided visits of MES in 2017. Moreover, one of the authors was present in several meetings and events since 2017 to observe, analyse, and understand MES processes resulting in around 200 hours of participant observations. This was complemented by 12 informal interviews with MES' staff (CEOs and middle managers). Furthermore, we conducted a documentary analysis of statutes of the SCIC, reports of strategic projects, and communication materials (such as flyers and the website). We also held five in-depth interviews in 2021 to deeply understand the processes of MES. The interviewees included the CEO and co-founder of MES, the director and co-founder of MES, the first craft entrepreneur who used the dedicated space, a volunteer who develops activities in the circular economy sector, and a social entrepreneur who benefits from MES' support.

We analysed data following Miles et al. (2019) to highlight the processes by which MES involves and maintains dissimilar organisations in the co-creation of sustainability activities at the territorial level.

Advantages and drawbacks of MSMO to answer sustainability issues for, through, and on the territory

Negotiation of common goals between actors and territorial issues

MES' aim is centred on the needs of the territory. Specifically, since the beginning, the ambition of MES has been to 'answer the needs of the territory, focusing on social integration of people into economic activities, making new services accessible to citizens who need jobs'[1] (director of MES). The general aim of MES is specified in several development themes related to sustainability issues on the territory as well as to economic opportunities. Initially, the field of activities concerned the employment of non-qualified people and professional training. Then, it evolved, and MES is now active in tourism, development of craft entrepreneurship, circular economy, and eco-building. Today, MES is developing a strategic project including the creation of a co-working space, several spaces to carry out circular economy activities, new services for older adults and unemployed people (e.g. digital services), and support and assistance for social entrepreneurship. The goal is to create a 'place to animate the territory' (director of MES) and 'to meet people and develop collective projects' (social entrepreneur).

These strategic projects are linked with the territory because they are based on a territorial diagnosis. This diagnosis highlighted the impact and influence of previously developed innovations and the opportunities to develop social and economic activities. This diagnosis is based on individual meetings with organisations, collective events bringing together citizens and organisations, and documentary analysis to legitimise issues identified. It is carried out and updated regularly to develop new activities based on new issues at the territorial level. For example the 'Solidarium' strategic project was developed from meetings with entrepreneurs and local authorities of rural areas who suggested that 'this space could be more known and better used' (director of MES). This link with the territory can also be observed through the 'territorial anchorage of activities' (CEO of MES), where MES aims to develop activities, services, products, skills, and jobs that are unlikely to be relocated.

MES has always worked to bring together different types of organisations to develop these activities. In particular, they facilitate meetings and cooperative activities to seek a common vision and a shared strategy for the territory and the committed organisations. The strategic projects and themes are developed in collective events and meetings with the territory's organisations and citizens and by associating with new partners from new sectors of activity.

However, the involvement of diverse stakeholders needs specific management. It is important 'to align interests and to conserve horizontality (in the decision-making process), confidence and transversality of sectors' between the committed actors (CEO of MES, director of MES). MES allows to structure and manage all stakeholder organisations and citizens in a collective organisation as well as to facilitate the development of sustainability activities at the territorial level. The SCIC structures the discussions concerning strategic projects, decision-making process, governance system, and partnerships between members. Hence, MES created specific thematic business units with autonomy regarding their human resources and management processes. The SCIC 'is a legal structure that allows integrating local authorities and companies, with several voting groups of workers, beneficiaries, local authorities, foundations and founders' (director of MES). However, citizens and organisations talk about the need to strengthen the deployment of strategic projects to make them effective. Furthermore, they are confused concerning the 'Solidarium' project's clarity, even if they believe and trust in this new strategic project.

Thus, the strategic project guides the development of social and economic activities at the territorial level. These are negotiated between organisations and are based on the diagnosis of the territory's opportunities and issues as well as experimentation with operational activities and practices. Indeed, the negotiation of common goals, considering the desires and needs of organisations and citizens, facilitates the willingness of organisations to enter and stay in the PTCE and contribute to the strategic project and activities of MES.

Activity-oriented integration of members

The negotiation of common goals is therefore directly linked to the capacity of the PTCE to involve stakeholders. This involvement is facilitated by the alignment of the strategic project and activities aiming to address territorial issues. Indeed, the organisations and citizens interviewed highlight that action, experimentation, and practice are important to confront the project with the reality of social needs and opportunities at the territorial level. Hence, organisations and citizens are involved from the beginning of the process in the creation of new activities and mutualisation practices, such as sharing space, joint activities, and missions.

We observed that the developed activities are based on experimentation and test-error processes. For example the director of MES and the volunteer in circular economy specify that volunteer activities were not developed through formal meetings and projects but in a bottom-up process. MES prefers to 'support initiatives and experimentation' initiated by volunteers (director of MES). In this way, the volunteers began with the experimentation of a Repair Cafe. The project was successful, and they extended their services to repairing clothes, couture workshops, fab-lab, shared vegetable garden, and others. These activities are developed through shared practices alongside the existing activities and services of MES. Moreover, the digital services and training workshops were developed further to MES' participation in a call for projects and its partnering with a local authority and a social centre. These opportunities and experimentations are possible 'as long as they are not in conflict with current activities' (director of MES).

Moreover, there are several ways to involve different types of actors in the activities of MES. Collective events and volunteer activities allow mobilising citizens who 'come because they need spaces, want to exchange and be supported' (director of MES). The local authorities finance the activities of PTCE at the same time helping to legitimise it. These relationships need 'time and learning' (CEO of MES). MES' team involves the companies via dedicated meetings where opportunities for participation and collaboration are presented. Organisations share services and expertise in their domain of activities. Social entrepreneurs and NGOs are also invited to share their vision of the sustainability issues at the territorial level and to lead social and economic activities.

Thus, we observe that this mobilisation of organisations and citizens is necessary during the creation, management, and evolution of the PTCE. Due to their specific skills in their field of expertise, these stakeholders' input is crucial for updating the needs' assessment at the territorial level and developing relevant solutions to the identified issues. The logic of experimentation and freedom to cooperate with current and new stakeholders facilitates the involvement of diverse stakeholders at the territorial level.

Use of internal and external communication

We finally observed that MES makes use of their communications strategy to involve and retain stakeholders. For example MES disseminates documents formalising the joint strategic project among the relevant stakeholders. They also participate in various discourses and formal events that include all members. Moreover, MES has created several communications documents and a website. They report on their activities, projects, and goals as well as on their member organisations and investors.

These documents are used as a guide for joint activities for stakeholder organisations and help develop a shared vision during general assemblies. These are also used for external communication to specify the goals of PTCE, which can then be used to respond to calls for projects and events, and to facilitate the 'knowledge of (their) practices and methods' (director of MES). With the 'Solidarium' strategic project, the director and CEO of MES also want to tell 'a story with illustrations and explanations'. Moreover, the interviewed actors highlighted that there still exist a misunderstanding and a lack of knowledge about MES' practices and its accessibility for all the citizens and organisations at the territorial level (director of MES, social entrepreneur). So, this formalisation and communication strategy could be a way to facilitate the understanding of MES' practices and activities for all the actors (CEO of MES).

MES also regularly organises events to communicate about its projects and gain insights from the stakeholder organisations and citizens concerning their understanding of the PTCE and its current goals. These events also allow MES to improve their visibility. MES' team considers that the 'Solidarium' strategic project will need a lot of meetings or events to facilitate the understanding of the Third Place and the project and to show to all the organisations and citizens that the MES can be a good place to develop their collaborative initiatives.

Thus, communication is an important strategy for the PTCE in that it allows to address both the external audiences (the territory, investors, and other networks) and the internal ones (stakeholder organisations of the PTCE). This communication allows to enhance members' cohesion, involve members by action, and attract new members.

MSMOs for the development of territorial sustainability and social activities

The case study of MES highlights the role of MSMOs in the development of social and economic activities to solve sustainability issues at the territorial level. This is possible because of the involvement of organisations and citizens in strategic projects of the MSMO. We also analyse the processes by which this MSMO retains and renews dissimilar organisations operating on the territory and involves them in the co-creation of sustainability activities for the territory. These processes are related to:

- The negotiation of common goals between diverse organisations and citizens, based on the analysis of social and environmental issues on a territory,
- The activity-oriented integration of members, e.g., the importance of creating economic and social cooperation between organisations before their integration in the MSMO, and
- The use of communication to enhance members' cohesion, involve members by action, and attract new members.

Furthermore, we also suggest that this collective organisational form can be a way to address sustainability issues as well as to facilitate the co-creation and co-development of social and economic activities among diverse organisations at the territorial level. Hence, we suggest the relevance of using the meta-organisational approach to study trans-sectoral organised clusters for sustainability.

The role of MSMOs in addressing sustainability issues

Our analysis highlights the role of a geographically embedded collective organisation in facilitating the understanding and sharing of sustainability issues among a variety of stakeholders as well as in co-creating new solutions to these (Westman et al., 2019). More particularly, the stakeholders – organisations and citizens – participated in the diagnosis of the territorial issues to be addressed, contributed their resources, and collaborated to ensure the efficiency of joint activities. Indeed, compared to cluster literature, we highlight that the MSMO approach facilitates the integration of a variety of members in clusters for sustainability as well as their collaboration and collective contributions to solving local issues.

Moreover, the MSMO framework allows the stakeholders to question the collective goals and prioritise actions related to the sustainability issues diagnosed. This is possible due to regular discussions between stakeholders as well as experimentation and communication about the activities of the MSMO. This goes in line with the principle of communicative constitution of organisational identity and actorhood (Dobusch & Schoeneborn, 2015; Schoeneborn et al., 2019).

MSMO to facilitate social and shared innovation activities

Geographically embedded MSMOs can be seen as a lever facilitating social innovation by supporting the creation and provision of services and products addressing sustainability issues (Alvord et al., 2004; Defourny & Nyssens, 2017). Thus, social innovation is seen as a pluri-organisational and socio-territorial approach, necessitating the involvement of multiple and diverse types of organisations and citizens.

More specifically, this research demonstrates that social innovation can be seen as a lever for mobilising relevant stakeholders and engaging them in collaboration based on opportunities present in their environment (Patzelt & Shepherd, 2011). The political meetings, governance, and decision-making processes allow communication regarding the members' joint activities. This is possible because the MSMO allows for the involvement of stakeholders both in activities and in decision-making processes. Hence, it allows to involve, maintain, and renew a large variety of stakeholders, whose input is needed for solving sustainability issues.

Conclusion

The chapter contributes to analysing the advantages and drawbacks of MSMOs to answer sustainability issues for, through, and on the territory. We show that the practices of integration, retention, and renewal of organisations allow for the creation of solutions for sustainability issues. This is possible due to convergence between various stakeholders' activities and their resource-sharing practices. Our study also highlights, for the cluster literature, the potential of using the MSMO framework to help address sustainability issues. More specifically, using this framework for organised clusters can help broaden the scope of actors involved and bring together a variety of organisations and citizens, regardless of their type, nature, and sector, in addressing sustainability issues. The MSMO framework allows organisations participating in collaborative activities to maintain their individual skills while sharing them at the MSMO level to co-organise activities.

Finally, we contribute to the discussion of the role of MSMOs and organised clusters in addressing territorial sustainability issues through collective action. In particular, the chapter highlights the importance of negotiation of common goals between a variety of actors taking into account the territorial issues, the importance of activity-oriented integration of members and the use of communication within and outside the MSMO to involve new members, retain the existing ones, and renew their involvement in developing social innovation in multiple industries and sectors on a given territory.

Note

1 Quotes are translated by the authors.

References

Ahrne, G., & Brunsson, N. (2005). Organizations and meta-organizations. *Scandinavian Journal of Management*, *21*(4), 429–449. https://doi.org/10.1016/j.scaman.2005.09.005

Ahrne, G., & Brunsson, N. (2008). *Meta-organizations*. Edward Elgar Publishing. www.e-elgar.com/shop/gbp/meta-organizations-9781847209504.html

Ahrne, G., & Brunsson, N. (2011). Organization outside organizations: The significance of partial organization. *Organization*, *18*(1), 83–104. https://doi.org/10.1177/1350508410376256

Alvord, S. H., Brown, L. D., & Letts, C. W. (2004). Social entrepreneurship and societal transformation: An exploratory study. *The Journal of Applied Behavioral Science, 40*(3), 260–282. https://doi.org/10.1177/0021886304266847

Battaglia, M., Bianchi, L., Frey, M., & Iraldo, F. (2010). An innovative model to promote CSR among SMEs operating in industrial clusters: Evidence from an EU project. *Corporate Social Responsibility and Environmental Management, 17*(3), 133–141. https://doi.org/10.1002/csr.224

Berkowitz, H. (2016). *Les méta-organisations rendent-elles performatif le développement durable? Stratégies collectives dans le secteur pétrolier [Sciences de Gestion*. Univesité Paris-Saclay.

Berkowitz, H. (2018). Meta-organizing firms' capabilities for sustainable innovation: A conceptual framework. *Journal of Cleaner Production, 175*, 420–430. https://doi.org/10.1016/j.jclepro.2017.12.028

Berkowitz, H., & Bor, S. (2018). Why meta-organizations matter: A response to Lawton et al. and Spillman. *Journal of Management Inquiry, 27*(2), 204–211. https://doi.org/10.1177/1056492617712895

Berkowitz, H., Bucheli, M., & Dumez, H. (2017). Collectively designing CSR through meta-organizations: A case study of the oil and gas industry. *Journal of Business Ethics, 143*(4), 753–769. https://doi.org/10.1007/s10551-016-3073-2

Berkowitz, H., Crowder, L. B., & Brooks, C. M. (2020). Organizational perspectives on sustainable ocean governance: A multi-stakeholder, meta-organization model of collective action. *Marine Policy, 118*, 104026. https://doi.org/10.1016/j.marpol.2020.104026

Berkowitz, H., & Dumez, H. (2015). La dynamique des dispositifs d'action collective entre firmes: Le cas des méta-organisations dans le secteur pétrolier. *L'Annee sociologique, 65*(2), 333–356.

Berkowitz, H., & Gadille, M. (this volume). Meta-organizing clusters as agents of transformative change through "responsible actorhood". In E. Lupova-Henry & N. F. Dotti (Eds.), *Clusters and sustainable regional development: A meta-organisational approach*. Routledge.

Borrás, S., & Tsagdis, D. (2008). *Cluster policies in Europe*. Edward Elgar Publishing.

Bourbousson, C., & Richez-Battesti, N. (2017). Caractériser les PTCE par l'analyse processuelle: Une application en région Provence-Alpes-Côte d'Azur. *Revue internationale de l'économie sociale: Recma, 343*, 57–72. https://doi.org/10.7202/1038780ar

Brenner, T., & Mühlig, A. (2013). Factors and mechanisms causing the emergence of local industrial clusters: A summary of 159 cases. *Regional Studies, 47*(4), 480–507. https://doi.org/10.1080/00343404.2012.701730

Carmagnac, L., & Carbone, V. (2019). Making supply networks more sustainable "together": The role of meta-organisations. *Supply Chain Forum: An International Journal, 20*(1), 56–67. https://doi.org/10.1080/16258312.2018.1554163

Ceschin, F., & Gaziulusoy, I. (2016). Evolution of design for sustainability: From product design to design for system innovations and transitions. *Design Studies, 47*, 118–163. https://doi.org/10.1016/j.destud.2016.09.002

Coenen, L., Benneworth, P., & Truffer, B. (2012). Toward a spatial perspective on sustainability transitions. *Research Policy, 41*(6), 968–979. https://doi.org/10.1016/j.respol.2012.02.014

Cropper, S., & Bor, S. (2018). (Un)bounding the meta-organization: Co-evolution and compositional dynamics of a health partnership. *Administrative Sciences, 8*(3), 42. https://doi.org/10.3390/admsci8030042

Davies, A. R. (2013). Cleantech clusters: Transformational assemblages for a just, green economy or just business as usual? *Global Environmental Change, 23*(5), 1285–1295. https://doi.org/10.1016/j.gloenvcha.2013.07.010

Defourny, J., & Nyssens, M. (2017). *Économie sociale et solidaire: Socioéconomie du 3e secteur.* De Boeck.

Dobusch, L., & Schoeneborn, D. (2015). Fluidity, identity, and organizationality: The communicative constitution of anonymous. *Journal of Management Studies, 52*(8), 1005–1035. https://doi.org/10.1111/joms.12139

Fayyaz, A., Lund-Thomsen, P., & Lindgreen, A. (2017). Industrial clusters and CSR in developing countries: The role of international donor funding. *Journal of Business Ethics, 146*(3), 619–637. https://doi.org/10.1007/s10551-015-2940-6

Loorbach, D., Frantzeskaki, N., & Avelino, F. (2017). Sustainability transitions research: Transforming science and practice for societal change. *Annual Review of Environment and Resources, 42*(1), 599–626. https://doi.org/10.1146/annurev-environ-102014-021340

Lupova-Henry, E., Blili, S., & Dal Zotto, C. (2021a). Clusters as institutional entrepreneurs: Lessons from Russia. *Journal of Innovation and Entrepreneurship, 10*(1), 7. https://doi.org/10.1186/s13731-021-00149-5

Lupova-Henry, E., Blili, S., & Dal Zotto, C. (2021b). Designing organised clusters as social actors: A meta-organisational approach. *Journal of Organization Design, 10*(1), 35–54. https://doi.org/10.1007/s41469-021-00092-5

Lupova-Henry, E., & Dotti, N. F. (2019). Governance of sustainable innovation: Moving beyond the hierarchy-market-network trichotomy? A systematic literature review using the "who-how-what" framework. *Journal of Cleaner Production, 210*, 738–748. https://doi.org/10.1016/j.jclepro.2018.11.068

Lupova-Henry, E., & Dotti, N. F. (this volume). Clusters as collective actors and agents of change for (new) sustainable path development. In E. Lupova-Henry & N. F. Dotti (Eds.), *Clusters and sustainable regional development: A meta-organisational approach*. Routledge.

Miles, M. B., Huberman, A. M., & Saldana, J. (2019). *Qualitative data analysis: A methods sourcebook*. SAGE Publications.

Patzelt, H., & Shepherd, D. A. (2011). Recognizing opportunities for sustainable development. *Entrepreneurship Theory and Practice, 35*(4), 631–652. https://doi.org/10.1111/j.1540-6520.2010.00386.x

Porter, M. E. (2000). Location, competition, and economic development: Local clusters in a global economy. *Economic Development Quarterly, 14*(1), 15–34. https://doi.org/10.1177/089124240001400105

Raulet-Croset, N. (2008). La dimension territoriale des situations de gestion. *Revue francaise de gestion, 184*(4), 137–150.

Raulet-Croset, N. (2014). Le territoire comme objet de gestion. *Annales des Mines – Responsabilite et environnement, 74*(2), 48–52.

Saniossian, J. (2020). Le processus de création des méta-organisations multi-parties prenantes. In *Le cas des Pôles Territoriaux de Coopération Economique [Sciences de Gestion]*. Université de Lille.

Schoeneborn, D., Kuhn, T. R., & Kärreman, D. (2019). The communicative constitution of organization, organizing, and organizationality. *Organization Studies, 40*(4), 475–496. https://doi.org/10.1177/0170840618782284

Tvedt, H. L. (2019). The formation and structure of cleantech clusters: Insights from San Diego, Dublin, and Graz. *Norsk Geografisk Tidsskrift-Norwegian Journal of Geography, 73*(1), 53–64.

Valente, M., & Oliver, C. (2018). Meta-organization formation and sustainability in Sub-Saharan Africa. *Organization Science, 29*(4), 678–701. https://doi.org/10.1287/orsc.2017.1191

Viachka, A., & Duprat, L. (this volume). We are all in this together: The significance of meta-organisations for cluster policy. In E. Lupova-Henry & N. F. Dotti (Eds.), *Designing and managing clusters for sustainability*. Routledge.

Vifell, Å. C., & Thedvall, R. (2012). Organising for social sustainability: Governance through bureaucratization in meta-organisations. *Sustainability: Science, Practice, and Policy, 8*(1), 50–58. https://doi.org/10.1080/15487733.2012.11908084

Voegtlin, C., & Scherer, A. G. (2017). Responsible Innovation and the Innovation of responsibility: Governing sustainable development in a globalized world. *Journal of Business Ethics, 143*(2), 227–243. https://doi.org/10.1007/s10551-015-2769-z

von Weltzien Høivik, H., & Shankar, D. (2011). How can SMEs in a cluster respond to global demands for corporate responsibility? *Journal of Business Ethics, 101*(2), 175–195. https://doi.org/10.1007/s10551-010-0708-6

Westman, L., Luederitz, C., Kundurpi, A., Mercado, A. J., Weber, O., & Burch, S. L. (2019). Conceptualizing businesses as social actors: A framework for understanding sustainability actions in small- and medium-sized enterprises. *Business Strategy and the Environment, 28*(2), 388–402. https://doi.org/10.1002/bse.2256

Yin, R. K. (2009). *Case study research: Design and methods*. SAGE.

Zardet, V., & Noguera, F. (2013). Quelle contribution du management au développement de la dynamique territoriale? Expérimentation d'outils de contractualisation sur trois territoires. *Gestion et Management Public, 2*, 5–31. https://doi.org/10.3917/gmp.022.0005

7 Are North American clusters transitioning to clean technologies?

Francesco CAPPELLANO and Nico CALAVITA

Introduction

Research on economic clusters has gained a global resonance in several knowledge domains (Lazzeretti et al., 2019), including economic geography and regional planning. While clusters have been extensively discussed as an economic development mechanism, little has been said in cluster theory and policy about 'directionality' in cluster evolution (Sjøtun & Njøs, 2019) and, notably, about the orientation of innovation towards addressing societal challenges (Cappellano et al., 2021; Fagerberg & Hutschenreiter, 2019; Schot & Steinmueller, 2018).

However, recognising and analysing cluster 'directionality' become even more important given that the multiple societal and environmental challenges need urgent action. Transitioning to clean technologies has been heralded as one of the most common moves of achieving environmental sustainability (Cooke, 2008). Indeed, it has been suggested that clusters specialising in the clean technologies sector can become cost-effective solutions to comply with environmental needs and secure economic goals at the time of austerity in the aftermath of the financial crisis (Gray & Caprotti, 2011; McCauley & Stephens, 2012).

Cleantech clusters have been discussed in both European and North American contexts to step up the pace of transition towards more sustainable regional economies (Tvedt, 2019). Clusters often have a critical mass and, in some cases, political power that can make them relevant actors in shaping the industrial development paths in their regions and nations. So, understanding how these can be catalysts for a transition to more sustainable modes of production or cleaner technologies is a relevant and urgent question.

In this chapter, to address the question of 'directionality' in cluster evolution, we analyse clusters through the lens of the meta-organisational theory. Management scholarship defines meta-organisations as 'networks of firms or individuals not bound by authority based on employment relationships, but characterized by a system-level goal' (Gulati et al., 2012, p. 573). Moreover, scholars have suggested that certain clusters can be seen as meta-organisations or organisations of organisations (Lupova-Henry et al., 2021). Meta-organisations work as heterarchical

DOI: 10.4324/9781003215066-10

platforms where members cooperate, transfer knowledge, and negotiate business opportunities spurring innovation towards sustainable development (Berkowitz, 2018). Importantly, the meta-organisational perspective on clusters suggests that these can be seen as collective actors adopting deliberate strategies and pursuing collective goals – that is having a 'directionality' in their evolution. As mentioned by Davies (2013), cleantech clusters and meta-clusters ('clusters of clusters') can become 'transformative agents of change in dynamic economies' (p. 1287) as they provide a locus for experimentation of alternative development patterns, representing a catalyst for internationalisation, collaboration, and upscaling cluster activities.

Moreover, cluster secretariats – intermediary organisations lying between private and public stakeholders tasked to engage their members towards a collective goal – have been seen as drivers for change, facilitating and coordinating innovative activities to develop experimental technologies and social practices (Denney et al., 2021; Hatch et al., 2017; McCauley & Stephens, 2012). Consistently, our analysis focuses on cluster secretariats as promoting networking and cluster identity or feeling of belonging (Sjøtun & Njøs, 2019). We seek to expand our understanding of the role of cluster secretariats, as their rationale to orient cluster firms to sustainable development is still not clearly described. Are they driven to reach environmental targets or to prompt economic development and knowledge spillovers? In this chapter, we seek to unfold *how* cluster secretariats orient cluster members towards clean technologies and understand *why* cluster members engage with greener technologies.

However, discussing the 'directionality' of clusters and the role of cluster secretariats cannot disregard the policy backdrop in which they work. This chapter focuses specifically on the North American setting and discusses how the policy landscape has oriented cluster development towards clean technologies. Scholars have investigated how governments engendered cleantech growth at a regional scale through targeted sectoral policies (Cooke, 2008). Previous research on North American cases sheds light on a diverse set of policy tools pursuing the development of robust cleantech sectors at the regional and state levels (Hess & Sudibjo, 2018). This research has highlighted the need to set up intermediary business organisations to orchestrate the cleantech network. In line with this research stream, the authors investigate the role of cleantech clusters in orienting their members towards green technologies. The analysis is based on primary data collected through online interviews with representatives from cluster organisations. Clusters were selected as being meta-organisations oriented to tackle clean technologies while targeting regional and national geographical outputs.

The chapter is designed as follows: a literature section discusses the cluster concept, its policy implications, and the role of cluster organisations in guiding their members towards clean technologies. The research design section focuses on the methodology adopted, the topics addressed through the data collection, and the cluster selection process. The fourth section illustrates the main findings of the empirical research. Finally, conclusions are drawn regarding the role of cleantech cluster organisations in spurring sustainable transitions in North America.

Literature review

The meta-organisational perspective on clusters and the role of cluster secretariats

Since the seminal work of Michael Porter (1990), who coined the concept of clusters, scholars hailed the idea that co-location of companies would favour interaction among cluster actors for mutual learning, knowledge exchange, and research cooperation (Bathelt et al., 2004). The Porterian analytical concept quickly became a widely adopted public policy tool for regional economic development and improving local competitiveness (Martin & Sunley, 2003). Later, the cluster life cycle model emerged in the literature (Pronestì, 2019), capturing the idea that a cluster – as a 'composite system of entities' (Martin & Sunley, 2003, p. 1303) – is not static but evolves over time (see also Martin & Sunley, 2011). Finally, the concept of clusters has evolved from a 'geographical agglomeration' perspective, as the idea of clusters acquired an organisational facet. Indeed, the network perspective on clusters emerged (Saxenian, 1994), suggesting that clusters capitalise on the close cooperation between diverse stakeholders. These ideas were later captured by the Triple Helix (Etzkowitz & Leydesdorff, 2000) and 'Quadruple' or 'Quintuple' Helix models (Carayannis et al., 2012). These suggest that the cooperation between various stakeholders – governmental, societal, industrial, and academic – is conducive to innovation-led economic development (Cooke, 2001). A recent development in cluster studies takes the idea of organisationality even further, suggesting that these diverse stakeholders cooperate in an organised setting and act as a single entity, a meta-organisation, or organisation of organisations (Gulati et al., 2012).

Furthermore, in cluster management discussions, cluster actors and, in particular, cluster secretariats have been gradually acquiring more importance. The latter are typically set to orchestrate cluster activities, acting as brokers among the cluster actors (Coletti, 2010) and devising development plans to increase local competitiveness. Cluster secretariats deliver a number of services (Glaser, 2013), including the Foreign Direct Investments attraction (Burger et al., 2015), facilitating open innovation by engendering inter-firms knowledge spillovers within and beyond the cluster (Vlaisavljevic et al., 2020).

Being embedded in evolutionary economic narratives, the research around cluster policy has failed to detect 'orientation' in cluster development: that is the direction in which businesses collectively progress over time (Sjøtun & Njøs, 2019). However, the questions of 'directionality' have become increasingly important as the societal perception of organisations has been shifting towards a view of organisations as societal actors that are expected to adopt more responsible behaviours and practices (Bromley & Sharkey, 2015).

To address the questions of 'directionality' in cluster evolution, we build upon the meta-organisational perspective on clusters that suggests that these serve as 'meta-governance' platforms, promoting common values through their members and influencing their choices (Garaudel, 2020). Further description of the meta-organisational 'responsible actorhood' is discussed in another chapter of this book (see Berkowitz & Gadille, this volume) as a crucial condition for clusters to act as local agents of transformative change.

The role of cleantech clusters in sustainability transitions

Clean technologies have been perceived as a key element in the transition towards more sustainable development. While there is no clear-cut definition of clean technologies, scholars include a broad range of interconnected industry sectors believed to diminish planetary pollution (see Cooke, 2008). Quantitative studies (e.g. Marra et al., 2017) substantiate the spread of start-ups and nascent businesses in diversified yet related cleantech sectors, which might pave the way for long-term innovation with significant implications in sustainable transitions.

Studies on the role of the intermediaries in cleantech networks illustrate how these organisations work to intermediate, facilitate, and legitimise activities contributing to green and sustainable industrial development (Hermelin & Rämö, 2017). Further examples demonstrate that cluster organisations, set up by private and public stakeholders, can effectively tackle the need for waste management through a circular economy approach (Baldassarre et al., 2019). Our work seeks to expand these findings sizing the role and rationale of cluster secretariats. We thus seek to answer the following question: *how* do cluster secretariats orient their members towards clean technologies, and *why* do they do it?

An additional layer of research discusses why members adhere to those cluster organisations. In this regard, Ahrne and Brunsson (2005) provide insight into the rationale of individual organisations to become members of meta-organisations. Such affiliation can facilitate cooperation with other members, help reap the benefits of lobbying and public campaigns the meta-organisations engage in, and accrue the member 'social status'. Thus, there is a need to investigate whether these also apply to businesses joining the cluster meta-organizations promoting clean technologies. In fact, membership to a cluster is reported to positively affect the brand reputation as it helps express companies' engagement with environmental and social justice topics (von Weltzien Høivik & Shankar, 2011). Therefore, we want to examine *why* cluster members affiliate with clean technologies cluster meta-organisations.

Answering these questions is not possible without consideration for the policy climate in which these cluster secretariats operate. Despite the common perception of the 'laissez-faire' approach to economic development in North America, there are tangible cases of successful public-funded cluster initiatives, including the textbook examples of Silicon Valley in California; Route 128 in Massachusetts; the Research Triangle in North Carolina; and urban clusters in Austin, Texas, and Akron, Ohio (Baily & Montalbano, 2018). Research on cleantech clusters has brought insight into the policy tools adopted both in Canada and the United States, where state and provincial governments funded 1) R&D activities pursuing technological invention; 2) the market-oriented commercialisation and business incubation phases; and 3) intermediary organisations enhancing networking, mentoring, information sharing, and matchmaking across business needs and academic curricula (Hess & Sudibjo, 2018).

Recently, the Canadian National Government sought to stimulate the knowledge-intensive economy through a national policy initiative – termed 'Canada Superclusters' – around specific activities, such as digital technology, protein industries, advanced manufacturing, scale artificial intelligence, and oceans (Doloreux & Frigon, 2022). While this initiative is primarily geared to prompt economic impacts and commercial results, it can also help tackle persistent challenges such as ocean pollution or radical shift in the food sector.

Moreover, preliminary literature analysis, although very small in size, showcases how intermediary actors – such as Écotech in Montreal (Canada) that since 2008 has been promoting clean technologies development and commercialisation in Quebec – can function to help shift economic growth in more sustainable directions (McCauley & Stephens, 2012). Formed by three entrepreneurs, this organisation received government funding and managed to develop a strategic vision for the Montreal cluster (Hatch et al., 2017). Another example comes from the U.S. North-East, where the Institute for Energy and Sustainability (IES) was set in 2009 to promote and develop the clean technology cluster initiative leveraged by the state government of Massachusetts and the support of two local universities (McCauley & Stephens, 2012).

In what follows, we analyse the policy climate influencing the green orientation of clusters in North America and the rationale and role of cluster secretariats in orienting the meta-organisations' members as well as the members' rationale for joining these meta-organisations.

Research design

The data was collected through online interviews with cluster secretariat representatives through a semi-structured questionnaire which allowed for greater flexibility in exploring the peculiarities of each cluster organisation. The authors held interviews with five organisations. Each interview lasted approximately 30 minutes, and the authors transcribed the contents that the interviewee validated. The respondents were high-level representatives from cluster secretariats, including senior managers or accountants.

The questionnaire was built around three sets of questions addressing the policy climate, the rationale of cluster secretariats to orient the meta-organisations' members towards clean technologies, and their role in 'directing' the cluster towards more sustainable practices.

The first set of questions addressed the policy climate to identify how the multi-scalar institutional framework supported the spread of clean technologies. This group of questions inspected the roles of Federal, State, and local governments in supporting the transition towards cleaner and greener technology. Furthermore, each interviewee was asked about how the political events in the last 3 years influenced the policy climate.

The second group of questions focused on the rationale of cluster secretariats to orient the meta-organisations' members towards clean technologies. Other questions inspected the rationale of cluster companies to adhere to cleantech-oriented cluster meta-organisations. More specifically, the questions addressed: i) the economic rationale to adopt new technologies; ii) the brand reputation implications; and iii) the possibility to participate in – and eventually influence – the law-making process.

The third group of questions addressed the role of cluster organisations. Building on the study by Denney et al. (2021) that focused on agents responsible for cluster change and the 'meta-organisational approach' (Lupova-Henry et al., 2021), we explored how collective decisions have been made by the cluster actors regarding membership, hierarchy, common targets to reach, and monitoring protocols.

Cluster organisations surveyed

The organisations were selected based on their nature, scope, and geographical outreach. The authors picked only the clusters that could be considered as 'organisations of organisations' with a clear focus on clean technologies and regional activities. Only the Canadian organisation has a national scope, although their main activities are located in the Atlantic Ocean Canadian provinces.

Thus, all surveyed actors are meta-organisations focused on clean technologies. They differ in their targeting of local, regional, national, and international geographic contexts. They include:

- The CleanTech Alliance represents over 1,100 member organisations spanning ten U.S. states and three Canadian provinces. Founded in 2007 by business and cleantech leaders, the Alliance facilitates the generation and growth of cleantech companies and jobs. Relying on multiple committees, the secretariat promotes collective action to advocate for business interests, organise networking events, and prompt commercialising new clean technologies.
- The Northeast Clean Energy Council (NECEC) brings together business leaders and public stakeholders to influence policy regulations and strategies throughout the Northeast. Since 2006, NECEC has been working to support start-ups and companies through business match-making initiatives while tailoring grants with federal and state stakeholders for the cleantech industry. NECEC participated at the UN COP21 to enact knowledge transfer at the global scale.
- The Environmental & Energy Technology Council of Maine (E2Tech) works to promote clean technology business and economic development organisations. E2Tech facilitates networking opportunities for its members, partners, and the public. It helps businesses benefit from funding opportunities, mentorship activities, and strategic partnerships with public

stakeholders. E2tech also serves to increase the proficiency of its members through specific capacity-building activities.

- Founded in 2008, the Colorado Cleantech Industry Association (CCIA) gathers almost 100 public, private, and non-profit stakeholders. CCIA works to drive the expansion of a cleaner, cheaper, more efficient, and secure energy economy. CCIA assists its members in advocacy activities towards the state government, organises networking events, facilitates access to and supports the search for funding opportunities. It helps companies interpret market trends and needs and train members' employees.
- Established in 2017, as part of the 'Canadian Supercluster' initiative, Canada's Ocean Supercluster (ORCA) is an industry-led transformative cluster model pursuing cross-sectoral collaboration, accelerating innovation, and growing Canada's ocean economy. It works to attract private and public funding to secure financial support to its 400+ members, mainly start-ups and SMEs. Boosting innovation, the ORCA promotes a sustainable approach towards the ocean economy.

Findings

Policy support from different levels of governments in the North American context

Our analysis shows that the 'geography' of support towards clean technologies in Canada and the United States is somewhat 'fuzzy'. The support measures are scattered across different levels of government – federal or national, state or province, and local – and have changed significantly over time. In fact, the clean technologies – as part of environmental concerns – have been a reason for tensions across the last three U.S. federal administrations.

According to the Executive Director of a cluster association,

> the last [U.S. federal] Administration was a disaster for clean technologies. Under the current Administration, we are having a lot more money going towards clean technologies. Although we have not received any funds yet, they are promised to each state and should be available shortly. We are very optimistic on the policy climate, in particular, the infrastructure and stimulus funds that have been promised by President Biden.

The president of a cluster organization confirms that after the last U.S. presidential elections, the shift of political orientation at the federal level of government is 'straightforward'.

Above the 49th parallel border, the Canadian National Government is reported to be very active in driving the transition towards sustainable development. It is strongly supporting the adoption of green technologies. The political support varies across provinces where coastal ones – most notably British

Columbia and Nova Scotia – are more concerned with sustainability issues than the inner provinces.

While the U.S. federal government policies are dependent on the political orientation of the leading party, the subnational levels are very diverse in regard to clean technologies and sustainable development. As reported by Bird & Clevenger (2019) we can observe how the two coasts predominantly offer a solid engagement to de-carbonise their economy before 2050. The majority of those states are ruled by Democrats, while a surging number of Southern and Central states have been issuing new mandates/executive orders to ensure a clean energy transition.

Our interviewees report a consistent picture, although there are differences within single states and at different institutional levels, including political support at the local level but not at state levels. In fact, cluster secretariats need to navigate this diverse policy landscape adapting to un-supportive policy contexts. These meta-organisations are well situated to guide their members when the policy climate supports cleantech business. This is the case of Washington State in the Pacific North-West as the Seattle local policy climate is very supportive of the adoption and the spread of clean technologies. Overall, Washington State also prompts energy transition, having established a Clean Energy Fund that will provide USD 40 million every year. Those public financial resources help the commercialisation of new clean energy products. Therefore, cluster secretariats are called to support public institutions sorting effective projects to be funded.

On the other hand, more significant public funding available to support clean technologies attracts more investors and businesses to become potential members or partners of cluster secretariats. State governments have been pushing clean technologies also by setting measurable emission thresholds. This is the case in Massachusetts. The state government had set targets concerning CO_2 emission in 2020 and has recently established the target for 2030 and the net-zero target for 2050 that is set as a binding document. As a vice-president of cluster organization commented, 'New York and Rhode Island also have aggressive laws to reduce the polluting emissions. In general, all the Northeast is very supportive of clean energy'. This helps the cluster meta-organisations orient a higher number of businesses that are required to adopt cleaner technologies to comply with regulations.

Also, in the Western non-coastal State of Colorado, the state is working on a policy framework conducive to the spread of clean technologies. The State of Colorado and the Denver city government support the cluster meta-organisations financially through subsidies and patronage. The interviewee commented that this policy climate helps them to work across business and public stakeholders including the 'National Renewable Energy Laboratory' (nrel.gov), which is a federal entity, located in Colorado. This institution helps to promote a lot of government–private sector collaboration that supports the transition through 'providing funding opportunities, grants, and helping with commercialisation'.

As further discussed, the secretariats work to disseminate public funding opportunities across their members, and – in especially supportive policy contexts – they serve at the 'front-end' to support their members with filing funding applications. In more conservative states, such as Idaho, where there is no significant interest to push towards clean technologies adoption, cluster secretariats work with local public institutions (e.g. city governments) and grass-roots organisations to help mitigate business' environmental footprint.

The rationale of cluster secretariats for leading their members towards clean technologies

As discussed in the literature, the reasons for cluster members' transition to more sustainable forms of energy production are not clearly understood. While several U.S. states and Canadian provinces pledged to take action against global warming, there is an additional reason explaining the spread of clean technologies businesses. The president of a cluster organization reported that the local politicians support green cluster meta-organisations as '[sustainable] economic development also means job development. High-tech means well-paid job positions that are pursued by local politicians. Therefore, they are interested to support the spread of new green technologies'. An interviewee clarified how the birth of their cluster organisation reflects the mentality in North America. As a vice-president of a cluster organization pointed out,

> originally, our organisation was founded upon the concern of global warming. Founding members were businessmen. They saw business opportunities to move towards sustainability. Many of our organisations are for-profit; just a few are non-profit organisations. The economic rationale was very clear from the beginning. It is a matter of mentality. Money talks, so it worked to create better jobs in green growth.

The rationale of cluster members to adhere to clean technologies meta-organisations

As discussed in the literature, membership in meta-organisations can result from multiple different rationales. They include economic convenience, authentic concern for global warming, and a marketing choice to enhance the companies' brand reputation.

An interviewee reported that the cluster members – mainly private companies – initially were driven by a specific goal: preventing or mitigating climate change. This was even more true in specific parts of the United States, as values and ethos that focus on respecting natural resources are widespread in the Pacific Northwest. Furthermore, the interviewees outlined how several companies are genuinely and seriously engaged with this topic. Other surveyed executives acknowledged 'a wide social responsibility and growing acceptance that sustainability is important. Actors feel responsible for lowering pollutants in the oceans'.

On the other hand, there is a purely economic interest as green technologies allow savings in production processes. Furthermore, the cost of green technologies is reported to have become lower or equal to traditional technologies dependent on fossil fuels. This may eventually allow smoother market entry for clean technologies. In a Canadian case, the economic convenience was based on the incentives provided by the national government to stimulate transition.

The members' brand reputation is definitely part of the picture. Most notably, multinational companies are joining cleantech clusters to enhance their brand reputation and participate in the policy advocacy activities the cluster secretariats lead. As a vice-president of a cluster organization admitted, 'at the beginning, some of the companies understood that if they took leadership, this could also benefit their brand reputation. Now, if the companies don't show any commitment, they get damaged'. In fact, the perceived company engagement in sustainability is reported to be also appreciated by financial markets. As an interviewee pointed out,

> following the example of Tesla, many smaller companies have reaped the benefits of entering into the stock market with a green technology-based business. The equity markets have opened up an additional avenue for green business financing. Because of the value to their brand reputation, we have a lot of companies investing in green technologies that have not really done so before. For instance, banks and investment funds are increasing their investments in green technologies-based companies. Additionally, we see increased venture capital and social impact capital flowing into cleaner and greener companies.

The lobbying activities organised by the meta-organisations lure many companies to become members. Indeed, the cluster secretariats promote collective interests within the law-making process. In fact, specific industry sectors are extremely sensitive to clean energy regulations. This is the case of 'utilities firms [which] are switching from resisting against clean energy changes to aligning their needs with environmental policy goals', as claimed by a vice-president of a cluster organization. Moreover, 'some businesses are favourable to more stringent environmental regulations' as a cluster organisation representative reported. Airline companies also engage with clean technologies cluster meta-organisations, as the air-mobility sector is very impactful to the environment. The airline company, a member of a cluster organisation surveyed, has been reported to explore alternatives to polluting jet fuels while, at the same time, advocating against environmental policies perceived as harmful to their industry sector.

The role of cluster secretariats and cluster governance in promoting clean technologies

The role of cluster organisations lies at the intersection between public governments and businesses. Through cluster policies, legislators can create market opportunities or impose penalties. The cluster organisations lobby all government levels to align public and private interests. At the same time, cluster organisations provide support for public decision-makers by giving feedback on law proposals. The close interaction with public institutions emerges when cluster organisations are called to champion the project proposals concerning clean technologies to get funded.

Although most cluster organisations do not have financial or technical resources to prompt research and development activities on their own, they do support technological innovation across their cluster members through a number of activities. First, they promote networking activities within the cluster. Those activities can either facilitate businesses teaming up or matchmaking with investors. As a cluster secretariat representative admitted:

> We help to connect partners. For instance, one insect-farming company is working to produce a less water-intensive food product. This company is cooperating with a data centre, to use the heat produced by the data centre to help the insect farming process.

Consistently, other cluster secretariats reported that networking is crucial in the clean technologies sector. Their organisations act as brokers to connect funders, mentors, and entrepreneurs. In fact, according to a cluster CEO, 'a wide number of opportunities develop behind the scenes, where businessmen mentor each other. In Seattle, there is a strong business network, where the collaborative culture is quite shared. Members help each other'.

Moreover, along with facilitating networking, several cluster organisations support their members to file grant applications. Sometimes, they work in cooperation with public agencies. This is the case of Massachusetts, where an interviewed organisation acted as a 'convener', inviting its members to file applications through the agency funding clean technologies projects. Other organisations work to scan tenders and advertise projects through their clusters to facilitate companies to get funding. As the Executive Director of a cluster organization pointed out, 'we work as a cheerleader: any time we see any interesting project, we send information to our members'.

Furthermore, the cluster organisations build their networks beyond the state or regional borders. Some acknowledged that they recognise the global challenge of climate change, therefore while acting locally, they want to share data with other peers to influence the global move towards sustainable development. Another cluster organisation teamed up with a foreign high education institution to establish the 'Blue Technology Barometer': a benchmarking tool designed to assess 50 coastal countries and territories globally and ranking them based on technologies and solutions developed and implemented to clean up the oceans, reduce sea-related carbon emissions, and enhance sustainability in maritime industries.

Several representatives of cluster organisations mentioned that they do not set any compulsory thresholds or objectives for their members concerning the implementation of clean technologies. Although cluster organisations are committed to encouraging their members not to engage in 'green-washing' practices, there is no monitoring system on clean technologies' deployment. This is not surprising as the nature of clustering is collaborative and voluntary.

The focus of cluster organisations has been expanding the reach of cleaner technologies and clean energy through commercialisation and adoption. But things might change in a short time as public funding is expected to increase sharply to the benefit of the cleantech and clean energy sector. Thus, according to an Executive Director of cluster association,

> there might be more competition as the clean technologies are cross-sectoral and there won't be money for all the sectors. As there will be more money, competition will determine winners. As competition increases, we will start seeing more compulsory demands and minimums thresholds that we haven't seen before.

Discussion and conclusions

This work links two research streams. On the one hand, we built upon the evolutionary economic geography perspective to investigate whether clusters in the North American context follow a 'direction' towards addressing societal challenges. On the other hand, we applied the meta-organisational theory to discuss the agency of clusters.

Adopting a meta-organisational perspective, this analysis attempts to shed light on cluster secretariats' role in the transition towards clean technologies. Our findings show that they do act as agents for change, in line with the literature discussed (cf. Denney et al., 2021; Hatch et al., 2017; McCauley & Stephens, 2012). Moreover, in line with meta-organisational literature (Berkowitz, 2018; Garaudel, 2020), cluster secretariats are found to work at the intersection between public and private sectors, favouring communication in both directions: influencing law-making processes and sharing funding opportunities with private stakeholders. Furthermore, they act as brokers to favour business opportunities among their members. In fact, cooperation among members usually works as an inducement to join a meta-organisation (Ahrne & Brunsson, 2005). Although we observed a clear 'directionality' in clusters' orientation towards clean technologies, our research shows that it is not based on any compulsory thresholds or targets that cluster members must meet but relies on collaboration and voluntary engagement. However, as public funding for clean technologies is expected to grow in the short term in the United States, competition among firms may increase, leading to a more robust monitoring system of clean technology deployment.

Our study also found that in the North American policy context, public and organisational support for clean technologies is present mainly at state levels in the United States and the national level in Canada, although it differs across territories and within provinces or states. The rationale of public sector support seems to be more related to the economic impacts of clean technologies on the local job market. Consistently, the cluster secretariats are driving the transition towards more sustainable and clean technologies mainly because of the economic implications for their territories.

Finally, our chapter explored why companies and firms join cluster meta-organisations focused on clean technologies. We found their motivations resulting from both the economic convenience of deploying new technologies and efforts to enhance their brands' reputation as well as the possibility to influence the law-making process through the lobbying activities of the cluster organisations.

It is expected that, as the perils of global warming become painfully clear, the move to clean technologies will accelerate accordingly. Hopefully, the results of this research will help understand the role of certain cluster organisations in guiding the transition to a cleaner future.

References

Ahrne, G., & Brunsson, N. (2005). Organizations and meta-organizations. *Scandinavian Journal of Management*, *21*(4), 429–449. https://doi.org/10.1016/j.scaman.2005.09.005

Baily, M. N., & Montalbano, N. (2018). *Clusters and innovation districts: Lessons from the United States experience*. Economic Studies at Brookings Institutions.

Baldassarre, B., Schepers, M., Bocken, N., Cuppen, E., Korevaar, G., & Calabretta, G. (2019). Industrial symbiosis: Towards a design process for eco-industrial clusters by integrating circular economy and industrial ecology perspectives. *Journal of Cleaner Production*, *216*, 446–460. https://doi.org/10.1016/j.jclepro.2019.01.091

Bathelt, H., Malmberg, A., & Maskell, P. (2004). Clusters and knowledge: Local buzz, global pipelines and the process of knowledge creation. *Progress in Human Geography*, *28*(1), 31–56. https://doi.org/10.1191/0309132504ph469oa

Berkowitz, H. (2018). Meta-organizing firms' capabilities for sustainable innovation: A conceptual framework. *Journal of Cleaner Production*, *175*, 420–430. https://doi.org/10.1016/j.jclepro.2017.12.028

Berkowitz, H., & Gadille, M. (this volume). Meta-organizing clusters as agents of transformative change through "responsible actorhood". In E. Lupova-Henry & N. F. Dotti (Eds.), *Clusters and sustainable regional development: A meta-organisational approach*. Routledge.

Bird, L., & Clevenger, T. (2019, December 20). 2019 was a watershed year for clean energy commitments from U.S. states and utilities. *World Resources Institute*. www.wri.org/insights/2019-was-watershed-year-clean-energy-commitments-us-states-and-utilities

Bromley, P., & Sharkey, A. J. (2015). Casting call: The expansion of actorhood in US firms, 1960–2010. *Academy of Management Proceedings*, 15743.

Burger, M. J., Karreman, B., & Eenennam, F. (2015). The competitive advantage of clusters: Cluster organisations and greenfield FDI in the European life science industry. *Geoforum*, 179–191.

Cappellano, F., Makkonen, T., Dotti, N. F., Morisson, A., & Rizzo, A. (2021). Where innovation meets directionality: An index to measure regional readiness to deal with societal challenges. *European Planning Studies*, *30*(8), 1549-1576. https://doi.org/10.1080/09654313.2021.1976114

Carayannis, E. G., Barth, T. D., & Campbell, D. F. (2012). The Quintuple Helix innovation model: Global warming as a challenge and driver for innovation. *Journal of Innovation and Entrepreneurship*, *1*(1), 1–12.

Coletti, M. (2010). Technology and industrial clusters: How different are they to manage? *Science and Public Policy*, *37*(9), 679–688. https://doi.org/10.3152/030234210X12778118264413

Cooke, P. (2001). Regional innovation systems, clusters, and the knowledge economy. *Industrial and Corporate Change*, *10*(4), 945–974.

Cooke, P. (2008). Cleantech and an analysis of the platform nature of life sciences: Further reflections upon platform policies. *European Planning Studies*, *16*(3), 375–393.

Davies, A. R. (2013). Cleantech clusters: Transformational assemblages for a just, green economy or just business as usual? *Global Environmental Change*, *23*(5), 1285–1295. https://doi.org/10.1016/j.gloenvcha.2013.07.010

Denney, S., Southin, T., & Wolfe, D. A. (2021). Entrepreneurs and cluster evolution: The transformation of Toronto's ICT cluster. *Regional Studies*, *55*(2), 196–207.

Doloreux, D., & Frigon, A. (2022). The innovation superclusters initiative in Canada: A new policy strategy? *Science and Public Policy*, *49*(1), 148–158. https://doi.org/10.1093/scipol/scab071

Etzkowitz, H., & Leydesdorff, L. (2000). The dynamics of innovation: From National Systems and "Mode 2" to a Triple Helix of university – industry – government relations. *Research Policy*, *29*(2), 109–123.

Fagerberg, J., & Hutschenreiter, G. (2019). Coping with societal challenges: Lessons for innovation policy governance. *Journal of Industry, Competition and Trade*, 1–27.

Garaudel, P. (2020). Exploring meta-organizations' diversity and agency: A meta-organizational perspective on global union federations. *Scandinavian Journal of Management*, *36*(1), 101094. https://doi.org/10.1016/j.scaman.2020.101094

Glaser, A. (2013). The role of cluster organisations in the constructions of collaborative R&D projects: The case of the ICT & Health Clusters in the Paris region. *35th DRUID Celebration Conference 2013*.

Gray, M., & Caprotti, F. (2011). Cleantech clusters and the promotion of the low carbon transition: Criteria for success and evidence from Copenhagen, Masdar and online platforms. *Carbon Management*, *2*(5), 529–538.

Gulati, R., Wohlgezogen, F., & Zhelyazkov, P. (2012). The two facets of collaboration: Cooperation and coordination in strategic alliances. *Academy of Management Annals*, *6*(1), 531–583. https://doi.org/10.5465/19416520.2012.691646

Hatch, C. J., Tremblay, D.-G., & Cazabon-Sansfaçon, L. (2017). The role of social actors in advancing a green transition: The case of Québec's cleantech cluster. *Journal of Innovation Economics Management*, *n° 24*(3), 63–87.

Hermelin, B., & Rämö, H. (2017). Intermediary activities and agendas of regional cleantech networks in Sweden. *Environment and Planning C: Politics and Space*, *35*(1), 130–146. https://doi.org/10.1177/0263774X16644256

Hess, D. J., & Sudibjo, M. N. (2018). Supporting regional cleantech sectors in North America. *Sustainability: Science, Practice and Policy*, *14*(1), 22–30.

Lazzeretti, L., Capone, F., Caloffi, A., & Sedita, S. R. (2019). Rethinking clusters: Towards a new research agenda for cluster research. *European Planning Studies*, *27*(10), 1879-1903.

Lupova-Henry, E., Blili, S., & Dal Zotto, C. (2021). Designing organised clusters as social actors: A meta-organisational approach. *Journal of Organization Design*, *10*(1), 35–54. https://doi.org/10.1007/s41469-021-00092-5

Marra, A., Antonelli, P., & Pozzi, C. (2017). Emerging green-tech specializations and clusters: A network analysis on technological innovation at the metropolitan level. *Renewable and Sustainable Energy Reviews*, *67*, 1037–1046.

Martin, R., & Sunley, P. (2003). Deconstructing clusters: Chaotic concept or policy panacea? *Journal of Economic Geography*, *3*(1), 5–35.

Martin, R., & Sunley, P. (2011). Conceptualizing cluster evolution: Beyond the life cycle model? *Regional Studies*, *45*(10), 1299–1318. https://doi.org/10.1080/00343404.2011.622263

McCauley, S. M., & Stephens, J. C. (2012). Green energy clusters and socio-technical transitions: Analysis of a sustainable energy cluster for regional economic development in Central Massachusetts, USA. *Sustainability Science*, 7(2), 213–225. https://doi.org/10.1007/s11625-012-0164-6

Porter, M. (1990). The competitive advantage of nations. *Harvard Business Review*, 73–93.

Pronestì, G. (2019). *Life cycle of clusters in designing smart specialization policies*. Springer International Publishing.

Saxenian, A. (1994). *Regional advantage: Culture and competition in silicon valley and route 128*. Harvard University Press.

Schot, J., & Steinmueller, W. E. (2018). Three frames for innovation policy: R&D, systems of innovation and transformative change. *Research Policy*, *47*(9), 1554–1567. https://doi.org/10.1016/j.respol.2018.08.011

Sjøtun, S. G., & Njøs, R. (2019). Green reorientation of clusters and the role of policy: The normative and the neutral route. *European Planning Studies*, *27*(12), 2411–2430.

Tvedt, H. L. (2019). The formation and structure of cleantech clusters: Insights from San Diego, Dublin, and Graz. *Norsk Geografisk Tidsskrift-Norwegian Journal of Geography*, *73*(1), 53–64.

Vlaisavljevic, V., Medina, C. C., & Van Looy, B. (2020). The role of policies and the contribution of cluster agency in the development of biotech open innovation ecosystem. *Technological Forecasting and Social Change*, *155*(119987), 1–15.

von Weltzien Høivik, H., & Shankar, D. (2011). How can SMEs in a cluster respond to global demands for corporate responsibility? *Journal of Business Ethics*, *101*(2), 175–195. https://doi.org/10.1007/s10551-010-0708-6

8 Clean technology clusters

Meta-organising firms for sustainability

Assia VIACHKA

Introduction

To contribute to sustainability, organisations must invest in the development and implementation of cleaner technologies. These can be understood as products, techniques, and processes with reduced environmental footprint and ensuring more efficient and responsible use of natural resources, raw materials, and energy (Kemp et al., 1992). The long-term benefits of sustainability are not difficult to recognise. However, in the short run, individual organisations might have difficulties combining sustainability and profitability goals. Indeed, becoming a sustainable business requires investment, operational adjustments, and changes to business practices. Therefore, sustainability is a complex pursuit that necessitates the formation of inter-organisational constellations for strategic collaboration. One such constellation is the 'cleantech' or green cluster.

Cleantech clusters have been described as organised intermediate entities facilitating interaction, networking, and collaboration between organisations (Tvedt, 2019). They represent a form of cooperation strategy for developing and adopting clean technologies (Tanţău & Chinie, 2013). Green clusters appear to be oriented towards creating knowledge and collaboration between actors instead of focusing on production systems and value chains (Tvedt, 2019). These actors are not necessarily located in close geographic proximity to each other; Gray and Caprotti (2011) mention virtual green clusters or online communities of geographically dispersed cleantech organisations. Clusters are, however, understood in the literature as geographic concentrations of industrially related organisations. Therefore, it is still unclear to what extent the practice of establishing green clusters is informed by mainstream industrial cluster theory. At the same time, it has been argued that green clusters can potentially accelerate sustainability transitions (Gray & Caprotti, 2011; McCauley & Stephens, 2012). Thus, supporting these entities with theoretical knowledge and adequate policies is important to achieving sustainability.

This chapter aims to investigate the use of the cluster concept in mobilising organisations to collectively seek a path to a greener economy. The chapter studies 34 green clusters and shows that these are meta-organised entities (Ahrne & Brunsson, 2005, 2008) made up of independent and formally linked

DOI: 10.4324/9781003215066-11

organisations. These entities use the cluster concept to create an organisational space (Yeung, 2005) in which the collectives can prosper. This organisational space is as much a geographic as it is an abstract space, constructed of the different social, institutional, and cultural dimensions that constrain economic action. Therefore, this study considers the modes of organising of the cleantech clusters, their geographical scope, and the linkages between the cluster firms. The results show that green clusters resemble geographical clusters: 'geographic concentrations of interconnected companies, specialised suppliers, service providers, firms in related industries, and associated institutions' (Porter, 2000, p. 15). However, they also deviate from theory in ways that suggest misconceptions of the role of geographic proximity and industrial competition in the outcome of economic clustering. Thus, the chapter argues that there is a gap between theory and practice in the conceptualisation of clusters. To mitigate this theory–practice gap, it addresses the link between meta-organising and geographic proximity: the latter being the combination of physical, cognitive, organisational, social, and institutional distances between actors. The different dimensions of proximity were suggested to be equally important in information sharing and collaboration between organisations (Boschma, 2005).

The chapter is structured as follows. First, it explains the link between clean technologies, clusters, and meta-organising and then presents the empirical study. The discussion focuses on how the entities included in the study used the cluster concept to frame their collectives. Then, the chapter explains why green clusters deviating from mainstream geographical cluster theory are a source of concern. Finally, it suggests that it is important to address the relationship between meta-organising and geographic proximity if theory and practice are to be reconciled.

Clean technologies, clusters, and meta-organisations

Clean technologies are, in broad terms, innovations that contribute to the development of a more sustainable economy and should be understood not as an industry but as a wide range of tools that promote the development of products and services with low environmental impact. Cleantech intensive industries include renewable energy, green transportation, green buildings, recycling, and grey water but are not limited to these. Recent contributions to the literature highlight the tendency for cleantech actors to be organised into complex socio-spatial formations called 'clusters'. Cleantech clusters are seen to be a strategy for fostering cleantech innovation and transforming regions into sustainable hotspots (Cooke, 2015; Davies, 2013; McCauley & Stephens, 2012; Tvedt, 2019). Cleantech clusters have been established close to large cities such as San Diego, Graz, and Dublin (for a structural analysis of the clusters, see Tvedt, 2019). The goal of cleantech clustering is to integrate key regional actors' efforts and foster innovation. This strategy is implemented at the regional level and the national and transnational scale with the establishment of large clusters and meta-clusters (i.e. partnerships of cleantech clusters). Meta-clusters act as gateways that connect cleantech companies, capital, decision-makers, and other actors across the globe; cleantech clusters, therefore, are complex formations involving actors from the public, private, and civil society sectors (Davies, 2013). Their hybrid composition and different geographical foci have prompted authors to question the extent to which mainstream industrial cluster theory can explain the nature of the interactions taking place in cleantech clusters (Cooke, 2015; Davies, 2013; Tvedt, 2019).

The literature on geographical clusters (for an overview, see Vorley, 2008) suggests that the spatial concentration of industrial firms generates positive externalities. Firms benefit from the economic and innovation activities of their neighbouring firms; clusters become self-reinforcing systems in which cooperation and competition between firms promote the creation of knowledge, innovation, and other advantages that are inaccessible to outsiders. Therefore, identifying and supporting clusters are considered crucial to the competitiveness of nations (Porter, 2000). Lindqvist et al. (2013) show that initiatives have been implemented in many sectors to strengthen and support clusters. These endeavours are organised to move a sector towards 'ideal features of a cluster in terms of a specialised, competitive, collaborative and collectively innovative' industries (Fromhold-Eisebith & Eisebith, 2005, p. 1252). These initiatives aim to correct any market imperfections that could prevent the emergence of externalities and the growth of geographical clusters. They also promote a new social order of collaboration and organised collective action within the cluster (Ketels, 2013).

Cluster initiatives vary between regions partly due to the concept of the cluster being adopted differently across institutional contexts (Sternberg et al., 2010). It is also due to differences in the rationales of the initiatives, which are shaped by academic ideas as well as political preferences (Uyarra & Ramlogan, 2017). This diversity makes the connection between the practice of establishing cluster initiatives and the theory of economic clustering questionable. The presence of a theory–practice gap in the understanding of the cluster concept is suggested by the cleantech meta-clusters mentioned before. The benefits associated with clustering are derived through the spontaneous co-location of firms and industries. Economic clustering theory, for example, suggests a link between geographic proximity and organisations collaborating and sharing knowledge. This is explained by the establishment of social conventions and informal networks, which form over time and via repeated interactions (e.g. Camagni, 2009). By intentionally grouping organisations into clusters, practitioners create opportunities for interaction, facilitating inter-organisational collaboration and information sharing. The newly-formed clusters are, however, formally organised and goal-oriented entities. Geographical clusters are clusters in which 'independent and informally linked companies and institutions represent a robust organisational form' (Porter, 1998, p. 80). Therefore, geographical clusters are not formal entities and do not presuppose governance. The theory is not only less relevant when actors are not co-located but also provides knowledge that is not directly applicable to organised cluster entities.

Understanding the formation, structure, and governance of organised clusters has been given some attention in the literature. Some studies have distinguished between spontaneous (or bottom-up) and policy-driven (or top-down) clusters (Fromhold-Eisebith & Eisebith, 2005; Su & Hung, 2009). This literature suggests that governance regimes differ depending on the influence of the actors involved. Other studies (e.g. Calignano et al., 2018; Ingstrup, 2013) have addressed the role of the individuals or organisations central to the cluster-organising process (often called cluster managers or facilitators). However, the literature often confuses 'cases of spontaneous or organic cluster emergence with organised efforts to stimulate and manage clusters' (Uyarra & Ramlogan, 2017, p. 40). This chapter contributes to this stream of literature by studying the practice of organising cleantech actors into clusters. The overarching aim of the chapter is to investigate the usage of the cluster concept in the deliberate creation of organisational spaces in the cleantech domain. Yeung (2005) argues that organisations often configure their relationships across physical space so that they effectively produce 'organisational space': 'a spatial configuration or area constituted by ongoing relations within and between organisations' (Yeung, 2005, p. 220). Organisations consciously create these spaces to exclude competitors and shape an economic space in which they can prosper. Actors form and join clusters in the cleantech domain to influence development trajectories (Davies, 2013). This chapter focuses on understanding how cleantech clusters are organised and to what extent they resemble geographical clusters.

Cleantech cluster studies (e.g., Tvedt, 2019) often describe participating companies as cluster members (Lindqvist et al., 2013). In their extensive research on organised clusters, Lindqvist et al. (2013) highlight that cluster companies were linked in a membership-based structure in 73 per cent of cases studied. This finding suggests that the entities could, in some cases, be meta-organised (Ahrne & Brunsson, 2005, 2008). Meta-organisations are formally organised entities formed by autonomous organisations. Joining a meta-organisation is voluntary, and members continue to be autonomous organisations. They must, however, comply with the rules set by the collective. Therefore, the first question addressed is whether cleantech clusters were meta-organised. Meta-organising could be assumed if 1) the cleantech cluster entities were established legally as independent organisations, 2) the cluster entities had formal organisational structures, 3) their members were easily identified as independent organisations, and 4) restrictions to membership were present. Meta-organisations also usually have clear criteria for membership (i.e. regarding the attributes members must have), restricting which organisations can be granted membership and, at the same time, defining the degree of member similarity.

The second question is whether cleantech clusters have a geographical anchor or exist solely as an abstract space of relationships. Recent evidence has indicated that cleantech activities concentrate in larger urban centres (Marra et al., 2017). However, the boundaries of cleantech clusters seem to extend far beyond those traditionally associated with a cluster (often expressed in terms of regional and sectoral codes). The study considered the geographical scope of the cleantech entities, the types of actors involved in the cluster, and the linkages between the member firms. However, the goal is not to determine whether the organised clusters displayed agglomeration economies or industrial specialisation. Instead, the research focused on understanding whether the collectives were formed by organisations that were 1) co-located, 2) provided similar products or services, and 3) had industrial linkages (inter-firm interdependences). Another important research objective was to learn more about the inter-organisational dynamics of the collective: firms in geographical clusters are often competitors, but they also collaborate (Porter, 1998).

Finally, this research also sought to gain insights into practitioners' understandings of the cluster concept. A cluster entity is organised and governed following practitioners' beliefs regarding the attributes of a cluster. These beliefs influence the choice of involved organisations and collective activities. Therefore, it is essential to understand the relationship between theory and practice. Is the practice of establishing cleantech clusters aligned with the theory of economic clustering?

The remainder of this chapter will focus on the relevance of the results to theory and practice. The goal of the analysis is twofold. First, the objective is to examine cleantech clusters' organisational, geographic, and relational characteristics. The second objective is to determine whether research on clusters should be advanced through endeavouring to understand the geographic implications of organising business collaborations in different socio-spatial formations.

Cleantech clusters study: methodology and results

The first stage consisted of an extensive Internet search for cluster initiatives in the European cleantech domain. In the second stage of the research project (2013–14), information was collected using an online survey. The survey was descriptive and contained questions about the history and operations of the initiative. A descriptive survey is a predefined and structured method for obtaining respondents' perspectives on and experiences with a specific subject. Potential participants were first contacted via social media, email, or phone, and the scope and structure of the study were explained to them. The survey was then sent to those involved with the management of the initiative (cluster managers). Each contacted person was also asked about other European cleantech initiatives known to them to allow the identification of as many clusters as possible. Sixty-seven organisations answered the survey. However, only those organisations in which collective organising could be identified were included in the study. Several public agencies or private companies used the cluster concept solely to legitimise their operations (e.g. the sale of services, implementation of policy), and thus they were excluded. These organisations did interact with cleantech actors, but there was no evidence of the actors interacting with each other in an organised way. Cleantech collectives that did not use the cluster concept in their operations were excluded from this search. The initiatives included in the study were revisited 7 years later, in 2021, to ensure the cases included in the results represented cases of stable organising. Cases in which collective organising no longer took place (four in total) were excluded from the main analysis. Additional data (analyses of documents, press, official websites) was also collected and used. The 34 analysed cases are spread across Europe (6 in central, 10 in eastern, 4 in northern, 8 in southern, and 6 in western Europe; many (25) entities use the term 'cluster' in their official name or communication (e.g. 'we are a cluster', 'we support a cluster')).

Table 8.1 Analysed cluster initiatives

	Association	*Consortium*	*Facility*
Descriptive statistics			
Cases (count)	19	10	5
Officially a 'cluster'(count)	16	9	0
Narrow industrial focus (count)	11	8	2
Age (median)	5 years	4 years	18 years
Size in the number of employees:			
≥ 5 / 6–25 / 26–50 / ≤ 51 (count)	9 / 7 / 1 / 2	6 / 3 / 0 / 1	0 / 1 / 2 / 2
Size in number of companies:			
≥ 9 / 10–29 / 30–79 / 80–199 / ≤ 200 (count)	0 / 6 / 5 / 2 / 6	2 / 5 / 2 / 1 / 0	0 / 0 / 1 / 2 / 1
Organising			
Financing sources	public + fees + other	mostly public	public + sales of services
Mode of organising	membership	partnership	lodging
Q1. Restrictive membership (mean)	2.88	3.2	2.25
Cluster manager operational focus	network	technology	location
Cluster companies			
Geographical scope (count): city/regional/national/transnational	2 / 10 / 7 / 0	1 / 8 / 1 / 0	1 / 2 / 2 / 0
Q2. Collaboration (mean) (Alpha 0.741)	2.91	2.54	2.60
Q3. Competition (mean)	2.94	3.50	3.50
Q4. Similarities (mean)			
Products/Markets (Alpha 0.812)	2.92	3.65	3.87
Technology	3.00	2.90	3.50
Q5. Industrial linkages (mean):			
Manufacturing (plants, processes)	1.89	1.20	1.75
Inputs (materials)	2.18	2.00	1.75
Products (assembled, used together)	2.39	3.00	2.00
Distribution (channels, services)	1.94	2.33	2.50
Spearman's test	*Q6. Inputs – Manufacturing (.421*)*		
Significant correlations	*Manufacturing – Distribution (.438*)*		
*** at 0.01*	*Products – Distribution (.570**)*		
** at 0.05*	*Inputs – Distribution (.594**)*		
	*Inputs – Products (.581**)*		

All scales are 1 to 5 Likert scales.

Meta-organised entities?

All the clusters considered are managed by independent organisations with at least one employee. These are responsible for selecting members and organising collective activities and have been divided into three main types based on their role and organisational structure (presented later). The objective is to highlight crucial differences in how the collectives were organised, not to develop a classification.

The members were usually listed on the organisation's website, most of the participating organisations being companies (usually producers or suppliers), public bodies, academic institutions (research bodies, universities), or other actors (e.g. unions, consumer associations, venture capitalists). The consortium model was, on average, the most restrictive in accepting new company members.

Association

Associations are cluster entities that were legally established and could be identified as meta-organisations. The meta-organisation actively promoted the recruitment of more members by communicating the initiative's purpose and benefits. The websites of all associations had a section only accessible by members. The associations used different membership categories (e.g. full or associated member), and were often financed in different ways (e.g. membership fees and private funds). They were, however, primarily dependent on public funds. The cluster managers were focused on expanding the network '*to connect companies, R&D representatives, service providers, . . . investors and (public) funding institutions . . .* ', as reported by a managing director (respondent n. 17). They also aim to '*create a community of experts and organisations that will work together*' towards sustainability (managing director, respondent n. 29). The cluster entity served as a platform for members to access funds, projects, contacts, and information that would otherwise be more difficult to access. The activities of the associations benefited the members in diverse ways, such as organising events and meetings, providing training programs, disseminating know-how, marketing products). In two cases, the association acted as a gateway to the region, promoting the arrival of members who fit the cleantech criteria. Some associations even held competitions, also open to non-members, awarding prizes for contributions to the cleantech domain.

Consortium

The consortiums are cluster entities that generally function as partnerships. The consortium members were always clearly stated, although how to join was not always specified. A clear distinction was usually made between members and other partners that work with the consortium. The consortiums were legally established organisations and could also be identified as meta-organisations. They were primarily publicly funded and served as an interface that members could use to exchange expertise, find partners, collaborate, and present themselves as a group. The consortiums were all structured around developing specific technologies and products, cluster managers often taking a direct role in projects. The meta-organisation could, for example, be driving forward a 'program developed by the [the members] with a cluster purpose' (general manager, respondent n. 15), support the innovation process (both the technical and managerial sides), and work on creating visibility for developed products. The cluster manager was, in two cases, even responsible for the development of a common technology, which was only made available to the members (e.g. cloud software for the evaluation of sustainability in buildings).

Facility

Facility cluster entities were managed by a research centre or a scientific park. These organisations provided physical facilities (e.g. laboratories, office space, aulas) and were funded by public financing and sales of services. They conducted research, collaborated scientifically with companies, organised projects, hosted events (e.g. technology fairs, congresses, conferences), and disseminated knowledge (e.g. scientific papers, research data). The facilities' scientific activities and physical infrastructure generated centripetal forces, drawing cleantech organisations to their locations. Typically, the locations were of many square metres that provided equipped space and a campus with shared areas and open access research facilities. The cluster entities were described by referring not only to the facility tenants but also to organisations located out of their premises. The cluster entities were not linked in a membership structure and, thus, were not considered to be meta-organisations. The facilities could, however, impose rules on companies renting space or participating in projects at the facility. At least three facilities were accredited and could provide certification services to cleantech companies (e.g. product quality stamps or sustainability labels).

Geographical cluster dimensions

The geographical scope of many initiatives (24) was narrow, with most participating cleantech companies located within the same city or region. The national cluster entities did not consider distance to be a significant barrier to collaboration (mean 2.11 on a 1–5 Likert scale). Most of the entities reported that they either operated in several sectors (eight) or had no sectoral focus (five). Thus, organisations were included based on projects or their overall fit with the cluster's technological and business direction. A president of one of the associations even explained that cleantech was, in their view, '*a quality factor relevant for each sector/industry*' (respondent n. 28). Many of the clusters (ten) focused primarily on producing and distributing clean and renewable energy, alternative fuels, green transportation, and other energy-efficient solutions. However, a small number (six) sought to provide environmentally friendly solutions to traditional sectors (e.g. textiles, automotive, wood, agriculture). Other areas of cluster expertise were pollution prevention, waste management, water efficiency, green buildings, and biotech. However, the cluster managers considered the products and market segments of the companies to be somewhat similar. They also considered the industrial linkages between the companies to be low, though the positive correlations indicate value chain integration in at least some of the clusters.

Overall, the cluster members collaborate predominately in research and development (mean 3.66). The associations collaborated on average more than the other clusters in product marketing (3.06) and human capital development (2.80), achieving a higher average collaboration score. Competition was also present within the collectives.

What is a 'cluster'?

The cluster managers were asked to confirm whether they agreed with a suggested list of statements about cluster companies, which was compiled based on the cluster framework of Porter (2000), widely used in policymaking. Almost all respondents agreed that cluster companies must collaborate and share information. Many did not, however, agree that cluster companies should be competitors. From the correlations between the statements, some cluster managers understood clusters to be geographical concentrations of competing companies. However, the more popular view was to see clusters as communities of collaborating companies with strong connections to public and academic institutions. Industrial linkages (mean 4) showed no correlations with other dimensions. A consortium director explained that companies in a cluster '*share a common interest*' (respondent n. 10), while the project manager of a cluster association stated that their companies '*are willing to work for the common good*' (respondent n. 11). In almost all cases, companies were expected to contribute financially to the cluster (mean 3.10 11 on a 1–5 Likert scale) and to provide knowledge and expertise (mean 3.55).

Discussion: meta-organisational space

The cleantech clusters included in this study provide evidence that clusters are understood as business collectives, made up of organisations that work together driven by shared goals and interests. The clusters were often coordinated by identifiable and financially autonomous meta-organisations, acting as hubs of the organising process. Associations and consortiums established organisational boundaries and asserted member rights and obligations by linking the cleantech actors within a membership structure. Both associations and consortiums can be seen as meta-organisations

Table 8.2 Significant correlations

Variables	*Mean*	*A*	*B*	*C*	*D*	*E*	*F*	*G*
A. Located in the same geographical area		4.03						
B. Collaborating/ working together			4.43					
C. Sharing information/interacting			.710**	4.50				
D. Competing against each other		.529**			3.23			
E. A community				.590**		4.00		
F. Connected to the research world						.472**	4.03	
G. Connected to the public sector			.398*	.525**		.493**	.622**	3.57

Spearman's test, significant at 0.01(**) and at 0.05(*)

facilitating interaction between members; the two, however, function differently. Associations openly welcomed new members and were less concerned about the type of companies, based on the belief that the bigger the membership base is, the more financially stable (due to the increasing amount of fees) and influential the meta-organisation would be. Therefore, it was not surprising to find that many associations had a national focus, this broader geographic scope leading to a higher number of potential members. However, while members can be seen as assets, they also can pose constraints (Ahrne & Brunsson, 2005). While larger collective may benefit from the pooling of the resources of more organisations, the coordination costs, the potential for conflicts, and the risk of collaboration failure also increase with the number of members. Using more specific membership criteria can help a meta-organisation avoid becoming dependent on having many members. Most consortiums applied this strategy, the cluster entities often operating in one industry (narrow industrial focus in Table 8.1), restricting the number of potential new members. A meta-organisation has a dual nature (Garaudel, 2020): it is not only a collective, but also an individual organisation trying to fulfil its own organisational purpose. The consortiums were publicly funded technology development initiatives, whereas a meta-organisation partners with its members, ensuring collaboration to deliver results (e.g. technologies, products). Rigid organisational boundaries promote stability and help the meta-organisation maintain and facilitate relations. In contrast, the associations focused on expanding their organisational boundaries to achieve legitimacy and recognition by external organisations and, thus, be able to deliver more benefits to their members (e.g. larger network or more projects). The meta-organisations, therefore, organise cluster entities differently, depending on the purpose for establishing a collective.

Ahrne and Brunsson (2008) observed that meta-organisations seem to find it difficult to describe themselves and therefore use a myriad of terms such as associations, commissions, and networks. Why do they also use the term cluster? Binding a social collective together requires boundaries and the continuous demarcation of organisational identity (Dobusch & Schoeneborn, 2015). Any organisation with a voluntary membership must find a similarity and a common purpose that can motivate members to associate. A meta-organisation cannot exist without an identity. The cluster label provides a category that is specific and, yet broad enough, to accommodate different situations. The cleantech collectives studied were, for example, often formed by quite different organisations (e.g. a range of firms, universities, even banks). However, the cluster concept connects these 'geographically proximate groups of interconnected companies and associated institutions' in a structure defined by their 'commonalities and complementarities' (Porter, 2000, p. 16). Neither the cleantech nor the cluster are, however, well-established organisational categories. Listing their members, therefore, allows the meta-organisations to assert an organisational identity, the identity being dependent on those of the associated organisations (Ahrne & Brunsson, 2005).

Despite not being membership-based structures, the facilities showed some degree of meta-organisational design (Gulati et al., 2012). The facilities are property owners (they own physical infrastructure). Therefore, they have clear boundaries (both geographical and organisational) and a hierarchical position that allows them, to some extent, to organise their tenants. They present themselves as meta-organisations by referring to their tenants. Listing their tenants helps the facilities attract organisations in the same organisational category and become recognised as collective entities. At the same time, recognising the facilities as places for science and research means that they do not need the cluster label to establish identity. Instead, they used the cluster concept to organise beyond their organisational boundaries: connecting the facility and its tenants to organisations located somewhere else. When used in this way, cluster concept refers to more fluid social arrangements brought together through a network of projects.

All organisations face an uncertain environment outside their organisational boundaries. Therefore, establishing meta-organisations creates a common organisational space that allows organisations to collectively control the surrounding environment. As discussed in this chapter, the cleantech clusters were expected to become communities of companies and institutions (e.g. universities and public agencies) willing to contribute cognitively and financially to the development of cleantech. The cluster concept appears to support the establishment of a social order that promotes unity and the search for common ground, even where a meta-organisation is absent. The facilities control their network (at least to some extent) without formally organising, so nurturing the idea of a cluster entity. At the same time, the green clusters devised strategies to expand their organisational space – for instance by allowing organisations to associate with the collective without being members (e.g. cluster partners, associates, or partial members). Through arranging competitions and awarding prizes, associations attempt to spread common values and encourage joint actions in the cleantech domain. Facilities test and certify cleantech products, thereby also influencing the cleantech domain to some degree.

Cleantech is, however, a guiding principle for innovation, not an industry. The companies' primary activities were rarely related (industrial linkages being most relevant in the consortium). Some cluster entities have geographically distant members, suggesting that the cluster label can sometimes be misleading. Cluster externalities are related in the literature to geographical concentration (e.g. more diverse and cheaper services, better suppliers, bigger pool of skilled labour), industrial specialisation (e.g. economies of scale, reduced transaction costs, cost reduction in areas such as marketing, R&D, and financing), social capital development (e.g. non-opportunistic behaviour, trust, collaboration), and knowledge development (e.g. technological spillovers, information sharing, access to tacit and codified knowledge). The externalities in geographical clusters can differ. Organised clusters may have different goals, depending on their business environment. The cleantech clusters included in this study collaborated primarily in research and development with involved companies expected to share their knowledge and expertise with the collective. However, knowledge externalities in clusters emerge from the co-location of similar economic activities that apply similar technologies, geographic proximity promoting interaction and knowledge exchange. Organised collectives that are not geographical clusters might, therefore, not show cluster externalities.

However, formal organisations can handle complexities, take decisions, and coordinate activities over large distances. It remains to be investigated whether meta-organising can lead to externalities in non-geographical clusters. The meta-organisations studied brought people together in meetings and events (e.g. conferences), with daily interaction at the facilities also being possible. Knowledge externalities also require some degree of similarity between organisations if learning and innovation are to occur (Boschma, 2005). Geographic proximity has more dimensions than just the distance between economic actors. Organisations may be geographically close but still very distant in technological, social, and organisational terms, making collaboration difficult. Meta-organisations are, however, established based on similarity, and membership is open to a defined category of organisations. The cleantech entities, for example, included companies considered to be similar in terms of economic activity (products, services) and the technology they use. Meta-organisations can, therefore, help increase the proximity between organisations, supporting the collectives in their movement towards becoming self-sustaining systems. Their formal dimension allowed the green clusters to create closed information systems, with technology and knowledge only available to the members. Meta-organisations can, however, also become exclusive and powerful agents. The effect of this on cluster externalities is yet unknown. For example two of the studied associations helped cleantech organisations locate in a region. These associations had the power to decide which organisation was considered 'cleantech', potentially leading to quite different co-location patterns than where a meta-organisation is not established.

The study results confirm that the practice of establishing cleantech clusters is not always aligned with theory in the understanding of the cluster concept. The studied cleantech clusters strived to build business collectives that resemble geographical clusters. Important theoretical dimensions may, however, have been overlooked. For example most cluster managers believe that cluster companies should not compete with each other in the market. However, competition and collaboration are equally crucial to innovation (Porter, 2000). It is therefore essential to understand how practice and theory can be reconciled. This chapter identifies the studied cleantech clusters as meta-organised entities that resemble but do not entirely correspond to geographical clusters. It is believed that the link between meta-organising and geographic proximity should therefore be investigated further to understand better how practitioners can be better supported in their use of the cluster concept.

Limitations

This study has limitations, which should be considered when reading the results. The method and sample size did not allow questions to be statistically tested; thus, this chapter cannot claim results to be generalisable. Most of the cluster entities studied were meta-organisations. How often cluster initiatives are meta-organised, however, remains to be determined. A typology of meta-organised clusters also remains to be constructed. Our interest in this study was in understanding how the cluster concept was used to organise cleantech actors. The cleantech entities were divided into three groups to show the differences in how the collectives were organised and not to formulate a typology. Furthermore, the analysis was based on self-reported data (survey answers, documentation produced by clusters), while secondary data on companies (e.g. actual location) were not collected. Measures were taken to ensure that the cluster manager did answer the survey, though the online survey design could not certify the respondent's identity. The research finally did not investigate how the cleantech clusters take decisions. Meta-organisations have a decided social order (Ahrne & Brunsson, 2008) maintained by a central authority, often represented by a board or a similar organisational unit. Hence, hierarchy and decision-making should also be considered.

Appendix

Table 8.3 Survey questions[1] included in Table 8.1

ID	*Questions text*	*Likert scale*	
Q1	Are there restrictions as to which companies can join your initiative/organisation/projects?	1–5	Not at all – Very much
Q2	Most of the cluster companies we support are located within . . .		
Q3	Over the last 3 years, how much did the companies engage in joint activities?	1–5	Not at all – Very much
	1. Purchasing; 2. Branding; 3. Human capital development; 4. Business environment development; 5. R&D		
Q4	How intense is the competition between the companies?	1–5	Not at all – Very much
Q5	On average, how similar are the companies in terms of:	1–5	Not at all – Extremely
	1. Products/services; 2. Market segment(s); 3. Technology		
Q6	Approximately how many of the companies share:	1–5	None – All (3 is "Half of the companies")
	1. Manufacturing; 2. Inputs/ materials 3. Products (must be assembled and/or used together); 3. Distribution channels		
Q7	What do you consider to be a 'cluster'? Companies in a cluster are . . .	1–5	Disagree strongly – Agree strongly

1 The questions are abbreviated. The table does not contain the explanatory text which ensured the respondents understood the meaning of the questions. Question 1 to 5 were formulated based on Lindqvist et al. (2013). All questions had a free-text choice option.

References

Ahrne, G., & Brunsson, N. (2005). Organizations and meta-organizations. *Scandinavian Journal of Management*, *21*(4), 429–449. https://doi.org/10.1016/j.scaman.2005.09.005

Ahrne, G., & Brunsson, N. (2008). *Meta-organizations*. Edward Elgar Publishing. www.e-elgar.com/shop/gbp/meta-organizations-9781847209504.html

Boschma, R. (2005). Proximity and innovation: A critical assessment. *Regional Studies*, *39*(1), 61–74.

Calignano, G., Fitjar, R. D., & Kogler, D. F. (2018). The core in the periphery? The cluster organization as the central node in the Apulian aerospace district. *Regional Studies*, *52*(11), 1490–1501.

Camagni, R. (2009). Territorial capital and regional development. In *Handbook of regional growth and development theories* (pp. 118–132). Edward Elgar Publishing.

Cooke, P. (2015). Green governance and green clusters: Regional & national policies for the climate change challenge of Central & Eastern Europe. *Journal of Open Innovation: Technology, Market, and Complexity*, *1*(1), 1. https://doi.org/10.1186/s40852-015-0002-z

Davies, A. R. (2013). Cleantech clusters: Transformational assemblages for a just, green economy or just business as usual? *Global Environmental Change*, *23*(5), 1285–1295. https://doi.org/10.1016/j.gloenvcha.2013.07.010

Dobusch, L., & Schoeneborn, D. (2015). Fluidity, identity, and organizationality: The communicative constitution of anonymous. *Journal of Management Studies*, *52*(8), 1005–1035. https://doi.org/10.1111/joms.12139

Fromhold-Eisebith, M., & Eisebith, G. (2005). How to institutionalize innovative clusters? Comparing explicit top-down and implicit bottom-up approaches. *Research Policy*, *34*(8), 1250–1268.

Garaudel, P. (2020). Exploring meta-organizations' diversity and agency: A meta-organizational perspective on global union federations. *Scandinavian Journal of Management*, *36*(1), 101094. https://doi.org/10.1016/j.scaman.2020.101094

Gray, M., & Caprotti, F. (2011). Cleantech clusters and the promotion of the low carbon transition: Criteria for success and evidence from Copenhagen, Masdar and online platforms. *Carbon Management*, *2*(5), 529–538.

Gulati, R., Wohlgezogen, F., & Zhelyazkov, P. (2012). The two facets of collaboration: Cooperation and coordination in strategic alliances. *Academy of Management Annals*, *6*(1), 531–583. https://doi.org/10.5465/19416520.2012.691646

Ingstrup, M. B. (2013). Facilitating different types of clusters. *Management Revue*, *24*(2), 133–150.

Kemp, R., Olsthoorn, X., Oosterhuis, F., & Verbruggen, H. (1992). Supply and demand factors of Cleaner technologies: Some empirical evidence. *Environmental and Resource Economics*, *2*(6), 615–634. https://doi.org/10.1007/BF00330287

Ketels, C. (2013). Recent research on competitiveness and clusters: What are the implications for regional policy? *Cambridge Journal of Regions, Economy and Society*, *6*(2), 269–284. https://doi.org/10.1093/cjres/rst008

Lindqvist, G., Ketels, C., & Sölvell, Ö. (2013). *The cluster initiative greenbook 2.0*. Ivory Tower Publishers.

Marra, A., Antonelli, P., & Pozzi, C. (2017). Emerging green-tech specializations and clusters: A network analysis on technological innovation at the metropolitan level. *Renewable and Sustainable Energy Reviews*, *67*, 1037–1046.

McCauley, S. M., & Stephens, J. C. (2012). Green energy clusters and socio-technical transitions: Analysis of a sustainable energy cluster for regional economic development in Central Massachusetts, USA. *Sustainability Science*, 7(2), 213–225. https://doi.org/10.1007/s11625-012-0164-6

Porter, M. E. (1998, November 1). Clusters and the new economics of competition. *Harvard Business Review*. https://hbr.org/1998/11/clusters-and-the-new-economics-of-competition

Porter, M. E. (2000). Location, competition, and economic development: Local clusters in a global economy. *Economic Development Quarterly*, *14*(1), 15–34. https://doi.org/10.1177/089124240001400105

Sternberg, R., Kiese, M., & Stockinger, D. (2010). Cluster policies in the US and Germany: Varieties of capitalism perspective on two high-tech states. *Environment and Planning C: Government and Policy*, *28*(6), 1063–1082.

Su, Y.-S., & Hung, L.-C. (2009). Spontaneous vs. policy-driven: The origin and evolution of the biotechnology cluster. *Technological Forecasting and Social Change*, *76*(5), 608–619.

Tanțău, A. D., & Chinie, A. (2013). Green clusters as new cooperation strategy for cleantech companies. In A. R. Thomas, N. A. Pop, & C. Bratianu (Eds.), *The changing business landscape of Romania: Lessons for and from transition economies* (pp. 189–208). Springer. https://doi.org/10.1007/978-1-4614-6865-3_11

Tvedt, H. L. (2019). The formation and structure of cleantech clusters: Insights from San Diego, Dublin, and Graz. *Norsk Geografisk Tidsskrift-Norwegian Journal of Geography*, *73*(1), 53–64.

Uyarra, E., & Ramlogan, R. (2017). Cluster policy in an evolutionary world? Rationales, instruments and policy learning. In *The life cycle of clusters*. Edward Elgar Publishing.

Vorley, T. (2008). The geographic cluster: A historical review. *Geography Compass*, *2*(3), 790–813.

Yeung, H. W. (2005). Organizational space: A new frontier in international business strategy? *Critical Perspectives on International Business*.

Part 3

Clusters as meta-organisations in a broader context

9 The roles of meta-organisations in transitions

Analysing the food packaging cluster in Finland

Sanne BOR and Greg O'SHEA

Introduction

Sustainability transitions are complex change processes that demand both technological and social changes. Sustainability transitions can be defined as 'major, non-linear changes in societal cultures, structures and practices . . . that arise from the coevolution between economy, society and ecology' (Loorbach & Wijsman, 2013, p. 22). Multi-stakeholder collaboration is seen as being vital in solving complex sustainability issues, and organisations collaborate in many ways to anticipate or prepare for and to cope with or organise for the changes unfolding in their environment (Gray & Purdy, 2018). From the literature on meta-organisation (e.g. Ahrne & Brunsson, 2008; Berkowitz & Bor, 2018), as well as multi-actor alliances (e.g. Lavie et al., 2007) and clusters (e.g. Lupova-Henry et al., 2021), we know that organisations utilise collaboration to increase the sharing of information and sharing risks in the development of new industry standards or sharing the costs for R&D to develop innovative solutions. Also, transition management literature acknowledges the importance of collaboration, as in coalition and network building, and collective visioning between stakeholders (Kivimaa et al., 2019; Loorbach et al., 2010).

However, little is known about the roles played by meta-organisations, organisations of which other organisations are members (Ahrne & Brunsson, 2008), in sustainability transitions. There have been calls for more empirical and conceptual research to understand how meta-organisations potentially facilitate the transition to sustainability (Berkowitz et al., 2020; Ferraro et al., 2015). From a recent typology of intermediates such as industry associations (i.e. meta-organisations) by Kivimaa and colleagues (2019), we know that regime-based intermediaries may be given a mandate from the dominant regime actors to facilitate and push for change. Meta-organisations can, thus, act as vehicles helping their members deal with insecurity in their collective environment (Ahrne & Brunsson, 2008). They can also help organisations manage challenges from their environment through decision-making, sharing of information, and lobbying (Berkowitz & Bor, 2018; Berkowitz & Dumez, 2016), thereby reducing costs and risks.

Clusters have been traditionally seen as 'geographic concentrations of interconnected companies and institutions in a particular field' (Porter, 1998,

DOI: 10.4324/9781003215066-13

p. 78). Recent work has recognised that these interconnected companies and institutions can begin to organise as meta-organisations (Gadille et al., 2013; Lupova-Henry et al., 2021). However, the meta-organising of interconnected companies and institutions may remain partial (as highlighted by Berkowitz & Bor, this volume), drawing only on some organising elements. In addition, the interconnected companies and institutions can also meta-organise into several partially overlapping meta-organisations instead of a single one. In cases where multiple (meta-)organisations with divergent goals and orientations are present in a geographical cluster, the latter may have difficulties transitioning towards sustainability.

This is the situation that we are interested in this chapter. In particular, we focus on the case of the food packaging cluster in Finland (see also Bor et al., 2021; Sonck-Rautio et al., 2022), whereby multiple meta-organisations try to organise (part of) the cluster. This differs from some other clusters discussed in this volume (see, e.g. Cappellano & Calavita, this volume; Viachka & Duprat, this volume), as the food packaging cluster discussed in this chapter is being organised through multiple, somewhat overlapping meta-organisations which do not form one overarching meta-organisation (with a collective direction or goal). The questions arising then are what role these meta-organisations play and how do they adjust to one another, and what does this mean in terms of their ability to facilitate a transition towards a more sustainable future.

The food packaging cluster in Finland is particularly interesting, as it has faced multiple pressures to change towards more sustainable packaging in recent years (Hakala et al., 2021; Sonck-Rautio et al., 2022; Sundqvist-Andberg & Åkerman, 2021). These multiple pressures are not one-directional and can even be contradictory in terms of the solutions they demand. For example food packaging has been pressured to improve the prevention of food waste and the high carbon footprint of food. This often has meant that solutions were sought in different types of plastic layers to better protect the food and ensure a longer shelf-life of products. However, the food industry has also been pressured to prevent the negative impacts of food packaging, particularly of plastics, on the environment, specifically in relation to marine litter (Bor et al., 2022). This has meant the introduction of 'producer responsibility' for recycling the packaging they place in the market and new regulations around single-use plastics. In addition to these pressures, some food companies are also committed to fighting against climate change. This has all meant that food companies are eagerly searching for new solutions in materials and in packaging design to cope with these challenges (Bor et al., 2022). As there is strong pressure for change, the questions we therefore explore are: what are the roles the different meta-organisations involved in the food packaging cluster (for material, packaging, food, retail, and producer recycling responsibilities) currently take on? And, what do they think should be done in the future to help the firms involved better cope with the sustainability pressures?

This chapter is organised such that we first discuss roles that meta-organisations may play in transitions. We draw thereby on the existing literature on the purposes or goals of meta-organisations. Thereafter, we present our data included in the chapter and the data gathering and analysis processes and discuss the results.

Potential roles played by meta-organisations in transitions

While extant literature has not discussed meta-organisations' roles explicitly, it has discussed the various purposes meta-organisations can have (Ahrne & Brunsson, 2008; Berkowitz & Bor, 2018; Garaudel, 2020). On the one hand, meta-organisations may act to protect their members from their environment (Ahrne & Brunsson, 2008) – for example by acting as a voice for all (Frandsen & Johansen, 2018) or ensuring stable structures through regulating a field – that is through setting standards (Lawton et al., 2018). This means that meta-organisations can aim to maintain the status quo. From a transition studies perspective, meta-organisations thus could be understood as supporting and protecting the regime players (those players in power and central in the current system) from landscape pressures – that is changing norms, values and expectations, and from disruptive innovations introduced by niche players (Geels, 2002; Geels & Kemp, 2007). On the other hand, meta-organisations have been studied as vehicles aiming at change, working towards a more sustainable world, socially or environmentally (Berkowitz et al., 2017, 2020; Carmagnac & Carbone, 2019; Chaudhury et al., 2016; Karlberg & Jacobsson, 2015; Vifell & Thedvall, 2012). This is also the focus of this edited book (see also Lupova-Henry & Dotti, this volume), whereby meta-organisations are conceptualised as agents of transformative change (see Berkowitz & Gadille, this volume), as drivers of sustainability in the tourism sector (see Nadegger & Dobusch, this volume), driving innovation and transformation in the food sector (see Gebhardt, this volume). Whether industry protecting or change-oriented, meta-organisations can focus on performing outward functions (Garaudel, 2020); that is they may aim to influence actors or opinions outside the meta-organisation. Likewise, meta-organisations may focus on inward functions (Garaudel, 2020); that is they may influence or support their own members. We combine both the inward–outward orientation with the change protection–change-promoting orientations into a four-field typology of purpose orientation in meta-organisation (see Berkowitz & Bor, this volume). Thus, we identify four meta-organisational roles in transitions: two regime-protecting roles – Member Harmoniser and Change Protector – and two change- promoting roles – Innovation Supporter and Change Facilitator. These are explained as follows in the next paragraph.

The Member Harmoniser role of meta-organisations (as identified in Table 9.1) is inward-bound and focused on regime maintenance. That is the meta-organisation takes as its role to ensure members create and maintain a collective identity (Ahrne & Brunsson, 2008) through socialisation (Garaudel, 2020). Important thereby is also the collective reputation (i.e. an industry's reputation) which is influenced by the actions of members. Meta-organisations aim to protect the reputation – for example through the development of standards and standardised practices (Ahrne & Brunsson, 2008) and by reinforcing compliance with these (König et al., 2012). The other regime-maintaining role identified in Table 9.1 is that of the Change Protector, which is outward-bound and aims not to change the (actions of) members but the perceptions,

Table 9.1 Types of purpose orientation – meta-organisational roles in transitions

	Inward bound	*Outward bound*
Regime-maintaining orientation	Member harmoniser 'The preservation of sectoral commons (such as reputation)' (Berkowitz & Bor, 2018, p. 206); 'provide an opportunity for socialization' (Garaudel, 2020, p. 7); 'enable coopetition among member-organisations' (Berkowitz et al., 2020, p. 2); 'allow to build synergies and economies of scale' (Berkowitz et al., 2020, p. 3); 'to reinforce compliance through activities such as training personnel of member organisations as well as monitoring and sanctioning members' (König et al., 2012, p. 1327)	Change protector 'To influence other legitimating institutions (different from governments) in order to have their principles and values as the common ones accepted by other actors in the institutional field' (Berkowitz et al., 2017, p. 754); 'to protect their member organisations and the industry' (Frandsen & Johansen, 2018, p. 104); 'to defend the industry's interests (in the case of trade associations) or the interests of the activity sector to which they belong' (Laurent et al., 2020, p. 24)
Change/transition orientation	Innovation Supporter 'Facilitates knowledge transfers and collective learning' (Berkowitz, 2018, p. 423); 'Produces reporting mechanisms and enhances social responsibility' (Berkowitz, 2018, p. 423); 'tackling sustainability issues by allowing members to collectively develop responses to social or environmental challenge' (Berkowitz & Bor, 2018, p. 206); 'creating a collective playing field' (Berkowitz & Bor, 2018, p. 206); 'to develop innovative tools that change the status quo' (Berkowitz et al., 2017, p. 758); 'coordinating action where there is commitment from interested parties' (Cropper & Bor, 2018, p. 9); 'push their members to develop certain practices or adopt certain structures at the company level' (Garaudel, 2020, p. 7); 'to exchange information and knowledge' (Karlberg, 2019, p. 67).	Change Facilitator 'Working towards some general interest' (Ahrne & Brunsson, 2008, p. 69); 'an inter-organisational space for dialogue' (Berkowitz et al., 2020, p. 2); 'co-constructed a new regulatory frame' (Berkowitz & Souchaud, 2019, p. 962); 'preceded and shaped the new market' (Berkowitz & Souchaud, 2019, p. 961); 'develop strategic planning advice with commissioners for development and deployment' (Cropper & Bor, 2018, p. 8); 'influencing the behaviour of external decision- makers' (Garaudel, 2020, p. 7); 'to achieve external influence' (Ahrne & Brunsson, 2005, p. 434)

ideas, policy suggestions, and other aspects of the external environment. In this role, the meta-organisation tries to act as a boundary, an obstacle to change in a field, aiming to create a stable and favourable environment for its members (Ahrne & Brunsson, 2008). Lobbying, promotional work, and communication to different external constituencies are central tasks of meta-organisations in this role.

Besides the two regime-protecting roles described before, meta-organisations can also have two change-promoting roles. The meta-organisation in the Innovation Supporter role aims to support members to innovate and helps find novel solutions or practices for members to cope with or preferably function better in the changing environment. Central to this is that members exchange and co-develop knowledge (Berkowitz, 2018), which will help them find ways to improve and collaboratively work on challenges they face (Berkowitz & Bor, 2018). Through recommendations, rewards, and other tools, meta-organisations may also steer or push their members into a particular direction (Garaudel, 2020). And finally, meta-organisations can also take the Change Facilitator role. This means that the meta-organisation aims to facilitate change that involves other actors besides its members. These meta-organisations thus work towards a general interest (Ahrne & Brunsson, 2008) by bringing the relevant stakeholders together for dialogue (Berkowitz et al., 2020), that is on regulation (Berkowitz & Souchaud, 2019) or strategic planning (Cropper & Bor, 2018) or by influencing stakeholders to take steps to accommodate a change (Garaudel, 2020; Karlberg & Jacobsson, 2015).

While meta-organisation literature has not had much explicit discussion on the roles meta-organisations play in transitions, we can construct, through the analysis of the purposes of meta-organisations described in the literature, a set of roles that meta-organisations may play (as described before). In the transition literature, we identify an explicit discussion about intermediaries or types of actors that aim to advance transitions (de Haan & Rotmans, 2018; Fischer & Guy, 2009; Gliedt et al., 2018; Kivimaa et al., 2019; Parag & Janda, 2014; Wittmayer et al., 2017). For example Kivimaa et al. (2019), in their analysis of the literature, highlight five types of intermediaries:

"(1) A ***systemic intermediary*** *operating on all levels (niche, regime, landscape), promoting an explicit transition agenda and taking the lead in aiming for change on the whole system level.*

(2) A ***regime-based transition intermediary*** *that is tied through, for example, institutional arrangements or interests to the prevailing socio-technical regime but has a specific mandate or goal to promote transition and, thus, interacts (often) with a range of niches or the whole system.*

(3) A ***niche intermediary*** *typically working to experiment and advance activities of a particular niche and trying to influence the prevailing socio-technical system for that niche's benefit.*

(4) A ***process intermediary*** *that facilitates a change process or a niche project rather than broader niche (or TIS) level; often without explicit individual agency or*

agenda, but in support of context-specific (project-based or spatially located) and/ or external (niche, regime) priorities set by other actors.

(5) *A **user intermediary** translating new niche technologies to users and user preferences to developers and regime actors, qualifying the value of technology offers available."*

(Kivimaa et al., 2019, pp. 1068 and 1070, emphasis our own).

These different intermediary types can be connected to the identified roles of meta-organisations with a change orientation. However, these intermediaries may take on an Innovation Supporter or change-facilitator role for diverse groups of actors that need mediation within the transition. They may take on both roles, as is particularly clearly highlighted in the description of the niche intermediary type. The transition literature also has a rather limited discussion on roles. A notable exception is a study by Wittmayer and colleagues (2017), who highlight the relevance of the concept of roles in transition research and suggest that future empirical research may bring deeper insight into the concept. This is exactly what the remainder of this chapter will seek to do.

Methodology

The research from which we draw our insights is a multidisciplinary study of different actors (companies, ministries, NGOs, consumers) and their actions involved in the transition to a sustainable food packaging industry. There are four different industries involved in this transition: the food industry, the materials industry, the packaging industry, and the waste industry (see also Figure 9.1). In this chapter, we draw on the data collected from seven meta-organisations that play a role in this transition and represent (parts) of these industries.

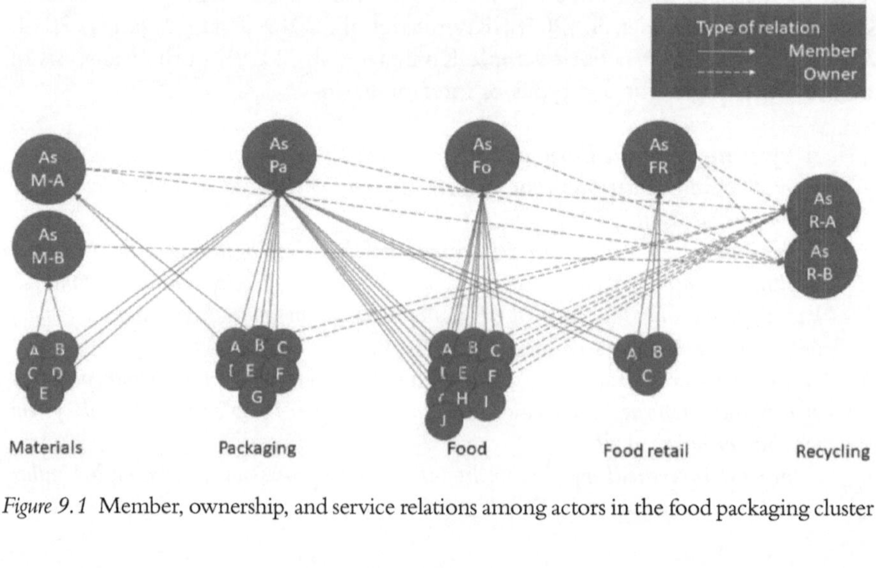

Figure 9.1 Member, ownership, and service relations among actors in the food packaging cluster

The food packaging cluster in Finland includes firms along the supply chain from packaging materials to the recycling of food packaging. Various meta-organisations represent these firms in the food packaging cluster: one for each type of material producers (e.g. plastics, cardboard, glass, metal), one for packaging producers (for different materials and applications), one for food producers (each with their own challenge regarding the preservation of food, such as meat, nuts, flour, snacks), one for food retailers, and different producer responsibility organisations (one for each type of material, e.g. glass, fibre, plastic, metal).

Of all these meta-organisations, we focused on those meta-organisations that the interviewed companies identified as central in the transition towards sustainable food packaging. Five of the meta-organisations identified were industry associations from different industries such as plastics (material or packaging MO), forest (material or packaging MO), packaging (material or packaging MO), food and drinks (food or food retail MO), and grocery trade (food or food retail MO). In addition, they identified two producer responsibility meta-organisations, one for fibre (paper/cardboard) material and one for plastics material (both recycling MOs). The material and the food meta-organisations were more restrictive in their membership, only accepting members that work in the industry. The packaging association is different as it includes packaging industry companies as well as the actors along the supply chain (upstream the material companies and downstream the consumer companies, from among other food and consumer goods). Importantly, some of the firms in the cluster are members of several meta-organisations simultaneously; this is especially true for the larger and more established food producers and food retail firms. In addition, the Waste Act of Finland requires companies to handle the waste management of the products they import or manufacture, including their packaging (Minister of Environment of Finland, 2011). This has resulted in multiple meta-organisations aiming at finding a cost-efficient solution for packaging waste management by taking care of the legal obligation for member companies. Currently, there are five different producer responsibility organisations, one for each type of material. We interviewed the one for fibre packaging and the one for plastic packaging.

In total, we conducted 12 interviews with these seven meta-organisations; five of the seven meta-organisations were interviewed twice, where possible, using the same interviewee (only in one case this was not possible). An initial interview was conducted in spring 2020 and focused broadly on the transition and its governance. The follow-up interviews in 2021 focused more specifically on the meta-organisations' roles in the transition, both in relation to their members and their environment. The interviews were held online through MS Teams and lasted between 45 and 60 minutes. They were recorded and transcribed (see Table 9.2 for an overview). The transcripts comprise 126 pages of data. We have anonymised the responses in the interviews with the meta-organisations by grouping meta-organisations into three groups: material or packaging, food or food retail, and material recycling.

Table 9.2 Overview of interviews

Case nr.	*Interviews, dates*	*Total no of words*	*Type of industry*
11	Two interviews: 3.3.2020, 25.3.2021	17 575	Material or packaging MO
13	Two interviews: 23.3.2020, 25.3.2021	13 774	Food or food retail MO
15	Two interviews: 26.3.2020; 31.3.2021	12 740	Food or food retail MO
32	Two interviews: 1.6.2020; 16.4.2021	12 035	Material recycling MO
33	Two interviews: 22.6.2020; 1.4.2021	13 052	Material or packaging MO
39	One interview: 9.3.2021	7 246	Material or packaging MO
44	One interview, two representatives: 7.4.2021	5 662	Material recycling MO

The meta-organisations analysed provide useful and powerful examples rather than a representative sample (Siggelkow, 2007). In each case, we interviewed a manager of the meta-organisation who was our key informant and had good overall knowledge of the meta-organisation. We borrow the basic assumption from Gioia et al. (2013) that the people constructing their organisational realities are 'knowledgeable agents', namely people in organisations who know what they are trying to do and can explain their thoughts, intentions, and actions.

The analysis procedure was abductive, reflecting the process of creative inferencing from the data, double-checking these inferences with more data, while moving back and forth between data and theory iteratively (Timmermans & Tavory, 2012). First, we read interview accounts from the original transcripts to identify excerpts relating to what could be interpreted as roles and assigned keywords to the selected excerpts. This first level of interpretation gathered these excerpts, or quotes, alongside initial findings, which were coming from the literature review. From the 12 interviews, 102 pieces of text were extracted as being relevant to understanding the roles of meta-organisations in sustainability transitions. As the research progressed, we started to see similarities and differences among the many categories, and we grouped these under specific labels or phrasal descriptors. We did this second-level analysis alongside the development of the categories through the literature review in an abductive process. The second researcher reperformed the whole analysis process, making comparisons with the first reviewer's extracts and groupings. The groupings were then agreed upon and merged to form the third-level analysis. The latter focused on developing the final framework consisting of four descriptors or labels for purposeful actions or roles. These were framed as MO-identified roles for maintaining the status quo (two roles) and MO-identified roles for promoting change (two roles). We further clustered MOs into three groups representing the three industrial systems involved in the overall food packaging transition and the recycling industry.

Findings and analysis

Our analysis aimed at better understanding the roles played by the different meta-organisations in the transition of the food packaging cluster to sustainability. We focused on the four roles identified. First, we analysed the roles aimed at maintaining the status quo: the member harmoniser role with an inward focus and the change protector role with an outward focus. Second, we focused on the roles aimed at facilitating the transition: the Innovation Supporter with an inward focus and the Change Facilitator with an outward focus. In total, we coded 102 quotes as relevant to these roles. Note that this also includes statements that highlighted the need for these roles and not just the existence of these roles alone.

As highlighted in Table 9.3, 65 per cent of these quotes had a regime-maintaining orientation, while 35 per cent of the quotes discussed a change orientation. In contrast, 41 per cent of the quotes highlighted an inward focus and 59 per cent an outward focus. The change protector role was discussed most frequently by the interviewees.

After this initial role analysis, we focused on the differences among the meta-organisations involved in the transition. Our analysis shows (see Table 9.4) that the material and packaging meta-organisations, as well as the recycling meta-organisations, place more emphasis on the regime-maintaining roles (74 per cent and 86 per cent), while the food and retail meta-organisations are more oriented towards change (52 per cent).

The Member Harmoniser role seeks to ensure that the regime stays in place by influencing the members of the meta-organisation through identity creation and enforcing compliance with agreed practices. We coded 23 quotations to

Table 9.3 Number of quotes coded for each role

	Inward focus	*Outward focus*
Regime-maintaining orientation	Member Harmoniser 23 quotes coded (23%)	Change Protector 43 quotes coded (42%)
Change orientation	Innovation Supporter 18 quotes coded (18%)	Change Facilitator 18 quotes coded (18%)

Table 9.4 Number of quotes coded for each role per group of associations

	Member harmoniser	*Change protector*	*Innovation supporter*	*Change facilitator*	*Total*
Food or food retail	4 (11%)	14 (37%)	10 (26 %)	10 (26%)	38 (100%)
Material or packaging	15 (26%)	27 (48%)	7 (12%)	8 (14%)	57 (100%)
Recycling	4 (57%)	2 (29%)	1 (14%)	0 (0%)	7 (100%)
Total	23 (23%)	43 (42%)	18 (18%)	18 (18%)	102 (100%)

this role (23 per cent of the total codes). Most belonged to the materials and/or packaging associations (15 of 23) that see their prime roles as being information providers and ensuring the prosperity of their members: 'This means we actually have a role of information provider [for our members], somehow setting the stage and trying to create circumstances, an environment where the whole packaging value chain prosper and profit'.

The recycling meta-organisations are also working to keep the status quo (57 per cent of total codes for these associations). This is less in the case of the food or retail associations, with only 11 per cent of their total of 38 codes.

The Change protector role (43 codes) focuses on affecting the members' environment to make it more predictable and stable. For the Material and/or Packaging associations, 27 codes from a total of 57 (48 per cent) related to this 'protection role', making it their prime concern. This is also important for the food or retail associations with 14 of 38 codes (or 37 per cent): 'It is our job to promote the member companies, the operating conditions. Making the field known and so on'.

This role is less important for the recycling associations (two codes) that focus more on implementing existing policies than lobbying on behalf of their members to change such policies.

The Innovation Supporter role concentrates on helping member organisations adjust to change or motivating them to change and supporting them. We allocated 18 codes or 18 per cent of the total codes to this role. In contrast to the 'maintenance' roles, we see the food or retail associations discussing the support of innovation more (10 codes of the 18 codes or 56 per cent): 'They [other industry associations] have a much stronger role to play, advising and training their own membership. So, we have such a role as well, small'.

Also, the material and/or packaging associations do see a role for themselves as being supporters or catalysts for their members' innovation efforts to be actively oriented towards more sustainable packaging. Indeed, they have already started taking on this role: 'So, we hired what we called the recycling trainer, a personal trainer for companies, . . . to go to companies and discuss . . . to put flames on the process'.

One interesting aspect highlighted in relation to this role is the challenges presented by the heterogeneity of members. We observed this in both the food/retail and the material/packaging associations. Membership heterogeneity creates barriers to this role, as change and innovation will affect some of the members more than others and, thus, may cause the balance of power among members to shift. The material or packaging associations were very wary of the need to remain 'neutral' in this respect: 'We have a terribly wide and heterogeneous [membership] . . . and have to be careful what we say so as not to affect competition between materials, for example'.

The Change Facilitator role focuses on facilitating and motivating the external environment to change. Our analysis has shown that the food and retail associations are again much more focused on these roles, with 10 of the codes from the total of 18 codes for this role descriptor (56 per cent). Moreover, they clearly understand that solutions will need to be found from cooperation with other associations: 'It's kind of obvious you have to co-operate with other associations, particularly when we're talking about climate change goals'.

On the other hand, the material or packaging associations think less about the need for collaboration to find innovative solutions. However, they do recognise that common, cross association, and cross-industry R&D will be needed: 'We would invite people from different universities, universities of applied sciences, and institutes, and create a forum for research and development people and also invite people from companies to join'.

One of the key insights from this analysis is that there is a clear wish or a need for this role. However, the different associations do not see themselves taking on this role on their own. They do highlight the development of an agreement among some of the associations and different ministries, the so-called Matsit. This would facilitate the commitment to material efficiency in the food sector:

> Now we are in the process of defining goals for the next period, and we have been thinking together . . . we would set goals for these two things in Matsit: recyclability of all packaging and then decreasing plastics content in packaging.

Discussion

This chapter provides insights into the transition of clusters towards sustainability and the role of the organisation of clusters therein. Recent cluster studies propose seeing these as organised entities or meta-organisations (see Lupova-Henry et al., 2021). The chapters by Cappellano and Calavita as well as Viachka and Duprat in this volume provide further examples of such clusters and discuss their role in sustainability transitions. These meta-organisations make deliberate efforts to promote the transition towards sustainability. In this chapter, we explored a cluster that includes multiple meta-organisations which are not organised at the 'meta-level', that is these meta-organisations do not come together in one meta-meta-organisation but remain more of a geographic agglomeration on a national scale (also see Gebhardt, this volume). Our analysis of the food packaging cluster in Finland highlighted that while there is some interaction and coordination, the field still lacks a meta-organisation bringing the cluster together – that is a meta-meta-organisation (a possibility highlighted by Nadegger & Dobusch, this volume).

The meta-organisations interviewed highlighted the need for a common vision and goals as well as more active change facilitation, though they do not see themselves taking on such a role. Change facilitation role in the Finnish food packaging cluster is thus seen as being too weak to push this cross-industry transition successfully. More interaction among the various sectors is needed to manage and implement the transition in food packaging. In particular, actors involved need to envision the future together and agree on the pathways through which to travel to such a future (Köhler et al., 2019). Our study shows how the conflicting interests of the meta-organisations involved in the cluster and a fundamentally 'geographical' view of the cluster, as opposed to a meta-organisational one (cf. Nadegger & Dobusch, this volume), limit the development of system-level goals needed for a whole industry to transition to sustainability.

The chapter also contributes to the literature on meta-organisations by developing a theoretical framework that identifies four distinct roles that meta-organisations can play in transitions and identifies some of the reasons for meta-organisations to take on one role as opposed to another. We noted that while affecting the food and food retail industry, the transition affects the material and packaging industries more severely. The meta-organisations in these industries seek to harmonise and protect members by trying to slow down and prevent change where possible. One of the key issues in this context is that the power relations among members in the material and packaging industries are shifting, as some materials (wood fibre) start replacing others (plastics) (Sonck-Rautio et al., 2022). This shift in power relations creates competitive pressures among the different members of these meta-organisations. For these meta-organisations, it is therefore important to ensure that the members remain committed and keep together. Without a collective commitment, they will be unable to influence the environment that creates these tensions, nor will they be able to find innovative solutions to ensure a future for all members. Thus, transitions can create internal tensions within a meta-organisation, and, when this happens, such meta-organisations will focus more on trying to maintain the status quo to keep the members on board.

In addition to the focus on maintaining the status quo in the materials and packaging associations, we noted that the food and retail associations are much more focused on change. This can be explained by the type of pressure experienced by companies in this industry to change (e.g. from customer demands or regulation). While this pressure is not equal towards all food companies, they all experience it and are all forced in the same direction towards reduced use of materials and plastics. Furthermore, as part of a green deal with the ministry, they already have committed to enhancing material efficiency to prevent food loss or unnecessary packaging. They are further stimulated by regulation (producer responsibility) which makes their members feel the costs of unsustainable packaging solutions. This means that the members are focused on finding ways to change and fulfil their commitments. However, food and retail associations do not wish to focus on helping their members find collective solutions to transition to more sustainable packaging because the sustainability of packaging creates a competitive edge; it is one of the ways in which food companies compete with one another. For this reason, they fear that collective action in relation to sustainable packaging could lead to competition law violations and related lawsuits.

Another interesting aspect of the case is that the large food and retail companies are members of multiple meta-organisations. In our case, these include a food or retail meta-organisation, the packaging meta-organisation, and one or more recycling meta-organisations. Membership in multiple meta-organisations allows some companies to influence different sides. While we have not analysed this aspect specifically, we know that these member organisations may, through their membership in different meta-organisations involved in the transition, also help create and force connections between the different meta-organisations. While this study did not focus on this phenomenon, we think this is a promising area for future research that could deepen our understanding of clusters' transitions to sustainability (Lupova-Henry & Dotti, 2019).

Finally, this chapter also provides insights for transition studies. The analysis of the roles played by meta-organisations shows that they are significant players in transitions. As similarly concluded by Berkowitz and Gadille (this volume), the transition literature has focused on the central role of niche actors in the transition while it has much neglected the role played by meta-organisations. As noted, the materials and packaging meta-organisations in the Finnish food packaging cluster focus on maintaining the status quo. Therefore, the niche players in these industries may be pressured to fall in line to do what incumbents are doing. Thus, we see high potential in future studies of how meta-organisations focused on maintaining the status quo affect the niche innovation process and the adoption of niche innovations. On the other hand, the studied meta-organisations were collaborating – for example through agreements with one another supporting the change, and thus the collective steps they take in promoting the transition are also worthy of further study.

Conclusion

Transition studies have indicated the need to co-create solutions across multiple sectors – that is in this case, the whole cluster, at the same time (Andersen & Markard, 2020; Bor et al., 2022; Papachristos et al., 2013). Meta-organisations can play a central role in this. However, when multiple meta-organisations are involved, and none can take on the facilitation role across different industries, barriers to collective action may arise. Thus, there is a need to organise among these meta-organisations. This meta-meta-organising, even if only partial, for example by formulating and promoting action towards reaching system-level goals, is necessary for a successful transition towards sustainability.

References

Ahrne, G., & Brunsson, N. (2005). Organizations and meta-organizations. *Scandinavian Journal of Management, 21*(4), 429–449. https://doi.org/10.1016/j.scaman.2005.09.005

Ahrne, G., & Brunsson, N. (2008). *Meta-organizations*. Edward Elgar Publishing.

Andersen, A. D., & Markard, J. (2020). Multi-technology interaction in socio-technical transitions: How recent dynamics in HVDC technology can inform transition theories. *Technological Forecasting and Social Change, 151*(February), 119802. https://doi.org/10.1016/j.techfore.2019.119802

Berkowitz, H. (2018). Meta-organizing firms' capabilities for sustainable innovation: A conceptual framework. *Journal of Cleaner Production, 175*, 420–430. https://doi.org/10.1016/j.jclepro.2017.12.028

Berkowitz, H., & Bor, S. (2018). Why meta-organizations matter: A response to Lawton et al. and Spillman. *Journal of Management Inquiry*, *27*(2), 204–211. https://doi.org/10.1177/1056492617712895

Berkowitz, H., & Bor, S. (this volume). Meta-organisation as partial organisation: An integrated framework of organisationality and decisionality. In E. Lupova-Henry & N. F. Dotti (Eds.), *Clusters and sustainable regional development: A meta-organisational approach*. Routledge.

Berkowitz, H., Bucheli, M., & Dumez, H. (2017). Collectively designing CSR through meta-organizations: A case study of the oil and gas industry. *Journal of Business Ethics*, *143*(4), 753–769. https://doi.org/10.1007/s10551-016-3073-2

Berkowitz, H., Crowder, L. B., & Brooks, C. M. (2020). Organizational perspectives on sustainable ocean governance: A multi-stakeholder, meta-organization model of collective action. *Marine Policy*, *118*(May). https://doi.org/10.1016/j.marpol.2020.104026

Berkowitz, H., & Dumez, H. (2016). The concept of meta-organization: Issues for management studies. *European Management Review*, *13*(2), 149–156. https://doi.org/10.1111/emre.12076

Berkowitz, H., & Gadille, M. (this volume). Meta-organizing clusters as agents of transformative change through "responsible actorhood". In E. Lupova-Henry & N. F. Dotti (Eds.), *Clusters and sustainable regional development: A meta-organisational approach*. Routledge.

Berkowitz, H., & Souchaud, A. (2019). (Self-)regulation of sharing economy platforms through partial meta-organizing. *Journal of Business Ethics*, *159*(4), 961–976. https://doi.org/10.1007/s10551-019-04206-8

Bor, S., O'Shea, G., Sundqvist-Andberg, H., & Åkerman, M. (2021). Moving to sustainable food packaging: The actions of the food industry. In *Proceedings of the 35th Annual Conference of the British Academy of Management* (p. 539). British Academy of Management.

Cappellano, F., & Calavita, N. (this volume). Are North American clusters transitioning to clean technologies? In E. Lupova-Henry & N. F. Dotti (Eds.), *Designing and managing clusters for sustainability*. Routledge.

Carmagnac, L., & Carbone, V. (2019). Making supply networks more sustainable "together": The role of meta-organisations. *Supply Chain Forum: An International Journal*, *20*(1), 56–67. https://doi.org/10.1080/16258312.2018.1554163

Chaudhury, A. S., Ventresca, M. J., Thornton, T. F., Helfgott, A., Sova, C., Baral, P., Rasheed, T., & Ligthart, J. (2016). Emerging meta-organisations and adaptation to global climate change: Evidence from implementing adaptation in Nepal, Pakistan and Ghana. *Global Environmental Change*, *38*, 243–257. https://doi.org/10.1016/j.gloenvcha.2016.03.011

Cropper, S., & Bor, S. (2018). (Un)bounding the meta-organization: Co-evolution and compositional dynamics of a health partnership. *Administrative Sciences*, *8*(3), 42. https://doi.org/10.3390/admsci8030042

de Haan, F. J., & Rotmans, J. (2018). A proposed theoretical framework for actors in transformative change. *Technological Forecasting and Social Change*, *128*, 275–286. https://doi.org/10.1016/j.techfore.2017.12.017

Ferraro, F., Etzion, D., & Gehman, J. (2015). Tackling grand challenges pragmatically: Robust action revisited. *Organization Studies*, *36*(3), 363–390. https://doi.org/10.1177/0170840614563742

Fischer, J., & Guy, S. (2009). Re-interpreting regulations: Architects as intermediaries for low-carbon buildings. *Urban Studies*, *46*(12), 2577–2594. https://doi.org/10.1177/0042098009344228

Frandsen, F., & Johansen, W. (2018). Voices in conflict? The crisis communication of meta-organisations. *Management Communication Quarterly*, *32*(1), 90–120. https://doi.org/10.1177/0893318917705734

Gadille, M., Tremblay, D.-G., & Vion, A. (2013). La méta-organisation territorialisée, moteur d'apprentissages collectifs. *Revue Interventions économiques. Papers in Political Economy, 48*, Article 48. https://journals.openedition.org/interventionseconomiques/2156

Garaudel, P. (2020). Exploring meta-organizations' diversity and agency: A meta-organizational perspective on global union federations. *Scandinavian Journal of Management, 36*(1), 101094. https://doi.org/10.1016/j.scaman.2020.101094

Gebhardt, C. (this volume). What governance for regional innovation clusters? Meta-organisational analysis of the German innovation cluster "physics for food". In E. Lupova-Henry & N. F. Dotti (Eds.), *Designing and managing clusters for sustainability*. Routledge.

Geels, F. W. (2002). Technological transitions as evolutionary reconfiguration processes: A multi-level perspective and a case-study. *Research Policy, 31*(8), 1257–1274. https://doi.org/10.1016/S0048-7333(02)00062-8

Geels, F. W., & Kemp, R. (2007). Dynamics in socio-technical systems: Typology of change processes and contrasting case studies. *Technology in Society, 29*(4), 441–455. https://doi.org/10.1016/j.techsoc.2007.08.009

Gioia, D. A., Corley, K. G., & Hamilton, A. L. (2013). Seeking qualitative rigor in inductive research: Notes on the Gioia methodology. *Organisational Research Methods, 16*(1), 15–31. https://doi.org/10.1177/1094428112452151

Gliedt, T., Hoicka, C. E., & Jackson, N. (2018). Innovation intermediaries accelerating environmental sustainability transitions. *Journal of Cleaner Production, 174*, 1247–1261. https://doi.org/10.1016/j.jclepro.2017.11.054

Gray, B., & Purdy, J. (2018). *Collaborating for our future: Multistakeholder partnerships for solving complex problems*. Oxford University Press. https://doi.org/10.1093/oso/9780198782841.001.0001

Hakala, H., Harlin, A., Katajajuuri, J.-M., Leinonen, I., Sonck-Rautio, K., Tynkkynen, N., Viitala, E.-J., & Viitanen, J. (2021). *Towards sustainable food packaging: Six sustainability criteria developed by Package-Heroes* (M. Åkerman & H. Sundqvist-Andberg, Eds.). Package-Heroes. www.packageheroes.fi/en/2021/04/14/sustainability-criteria/

Karlberg, E. (2019). *Organizing the voice of women: A study of the Polish and Swedish women's movements' adaptation to international structures* [Södertörns högskola]. http://urn.kb.se/resolve?urn=urn:nbn:se:sh:diva-39332

Karlberg, E., & Jacobsson, K. (2015). A meta-organisational perspective on the Europeanization of civil society: The case of the Swedish women's lobby. *Voluntas, 26*(4), 1438–1459. https://doi.org/10.1007/s11266-014-9463-0

Kivimaa, P., Boon, W., Hyysalo, S., & Klerkx, L. (2019). Towards a typology of intermediaries in sustainability transitions: A systematic review and a research agenda. *Research Policy, 48*(4), 1062–1075. https://doi.org/10.1016/j.respol.2018.10.006

Köhler, J., Geels, F. W., Kern, F., Markard, J., Onsongo, E., Wieczorek, A., Alkemade, F., Avelino, F., Bergek, A., Boons, F., Fünfschilling, L., Hess, D., Holtz, G., Hyysalo, S., Jenkins, K., Kivimaa, P., Martiskainen, M., McMeekin, A., Mühlemeier, M. S., . . . Wells, P. (2019). An agenda for sustainability transitions research: State of the art and future directions. *Environmental Innovation and Societal Transitions, 31*, 1–32. https://doi.org/10.1016/j.eist.2019.01.004

König, A., Schulte, M., & Enders, A. (2012). Inertia in response to non-paradigmatic change: The case of meta-organisations. *Research Policy, 41*(8), 1325–1343. https://doi.org/10.1016/j.respol.2012.03.006

Laurent, A., Garaudel, P., Schmidt, G., & Eynaud, P. (2020). Civil society meta-organisations and legitimating processes: The case of the addiction field in France. *VOLUNTAS: International Journal of Voluntary and Nonprofit Organisations, 31*(1), 19–38. https://doi.org/10.1007/s11266-019-00094-8

Lavie, D., Lechner, C., & Singh, H. (2007). The performance implications of timing of entry and involvement in multipartner alliances. *Academy of Management Journal, 50*(3), 578–604. https://doi.org/10.5465/amj.2007.25525906

Lawton, T. C., Rajwani, T., & Minto, A. (2018). Why trade associations matter: Exploring function, meaning, and influence. *Journal of Management Inquiry, 27*(1), 5–9. https://doi.org/10.1177/1056492616688853

Loorbach, D., Bakel, J. C., Whiteman, G., & Rotmans, J. (2010). Business strategies for transitions towards sustainable systems. *Business Strategy and the Environment, 19*(2), 133–146. https://doi.org/10.1002/bse.645

Loorbach, D., & Wijsman, K. (2013). Business transition management: Exploring a new role for business in sustainability transitions. *Journal of Cleaner Production, 45*, 20–28. https://doi.org/10.1016/j.jclepro.2012.11.002

Lupova-Henry, E., Blili, S., & Dal Zotto, C. (2021). Designing organised clusters as social actors: A meta-organisational approach. *Journal of Organization Design, 10*(1), 35–54. https://doi.org/10.1007/s41469-021-00092-5

Lupova-Henry, E., & Dotti, N. F. (2019). Governance of sustainable innovation: Moving beyond the hierarchy-market-network trichotomy? A systematic literature review using the "who-how-what" framework. *Journal of Cleaner Production, 210*, 738–748. https://doi.org/10.1016/j.jclepro.2018.11.068

Lupova-Henry, E., & Dotti, N. F. (this volume). Clusters as collective actors and agents of change for (new) sustainable path development. In E. Lupova-Henry & N. F. Dotti (Eds.), *Clusters and sustainable regional development: A meta-organisational approach*. Routledge.

Minister of Environment of Finland. (2011). *Waste act (646/2011)* (No. 646/2011). Finland's Minister of Environment. https://finlex.fi/fi/laki/kaannokset/2011/en20110646_20140528.pdf

Nadegger, M., & Dobusch, L. (this volume). Meta-organisations as drivers for sustainability across tourism clusters in the Alps: A case study of "Alpine Pearls". In E. Lupova-Henry & N. F. Dotti (Eds.), *Designing and managing clusters for sustainability*. Routledge.

Papachristos, G., Sofianos, A., & Adamides, E. (2013). System interactions in socio-technical transitions: Extending the multi-level perspective. *Environmental Innovation and Societal Transitions*, 7, 53–69. https://doi.org/10.1016/j.eist.2013.03.002

Parag, Y., & Janda, K. B. (2014). More than filler: Middle actors and socio-technical change in the energy system from the "middle-out". *Energy Research and Social Science, 3*(C), 102–112. https://doi.org/10.1016/j.erss.2014.07.011

Porter, M. E. (1998, November 1). Clusters and the new economics of competition. *Harvard Business Review*. https://hbr.org/1998/11/clusters-and-the-new-economics-of-competition

Siggelkow, N. (2007). Persuasion with case studies. *Academy of Management Journal, 50*(1), 20–24. https://doi.org/10.5465/amj.2007.24160882

Sonck-Rautio, K., Bor, S., O'Shea, G., Tynkkynen, N., Varho, V., & Åkerman, M. (2022). Power and responsibility in transition to sustainable food packaging. In V. Pál (Ed.), *Social and cultural aspects of the circular economy*. Routledge. https://doi.org/10.4324/9781003255246-7

Sundqvist-Andberg, H., & Åkerman, M. (2021). Sustainability governance and contested plastic food packaging: An integrative review. *Journal of Cleaner Production, 306*, 127111. https://doi.org/10.1016/j.jclepro.2021.127111

Timmermans, S., & Tavory, I. (2012). Theory construction in qualitative research: From grounded theory to abductive analysis. *Sociological Theory, 30*(3), 167–186. https://doi.org/10.1177/0735275112457914

Viachka, A., & Duprat, L. (this volume). We are all in this together: The significance of meta-organisations for cluster policy. In E. Lupova-Henry & N. F. Dotti (Eds.), *Designing and managing clusters for sustainability*. Routledge.

Vifell, Å. C., & Thedvall, R. (2012). Organising for social sustainability: Governance through bureaucratization in meta-organisations. *Sustainability: Science, Practice, and Policy*, *8*(1), 50–58. https://doi.org/10.1080/15487733.2012.11908084

Wittmayer, J. M., Avelino, F., Steenbergen, F., & Loorbach, D. (2017). Actor roles in transition: Insights from sociological perspectives. *Environmental Innovation and Societal Transitions*, *24*, 45–56. https://doi.org/10.1016/j.eist.2016.10.003

10 Meta-organisations as drivers for sustainability across tourism clusters in the Alps

A case study of 'Alpine Pearls'

Monica NADEGGER and Leonhard DOBUSCH

Introduction

The tourism industry currently discusses the urgency to change tourism development towards economic, ecological, and social sustainability. Scholars like Ruhanen et al. (2015) discuss a wide range of sustainability topics within tourism research, from sustainable tourism practices and development to more specific fields like rural or heritage tourism. However, implementing sustainable changes requires 'a commitment to move beyond steady-state tourism, the redefinition of spatio-temporal system boundaries, an appreciation of complex socio-ecological systems and the accommodation of global environmental forces' (Higham & Miller, 2018, p. 4). Realising the need to better understand collaborative intra-destination approaches for sustainable development, tourism researchers have explored the concept of clusters (Pearce, 2014; Porter, 1998). The concepts of tourism destinations and clusters show distinctive overlaps. Tourism destinations, similarly to clusters, are characterised as an array of simultaneously competing and collaborating actors and businesses in a distinct geographical location (Beritelli et al., 2014; Buhalis, 2000; Saraniemi & Kylänen, 2011). In tourism destinations, collective effort is needed to implement (sustainable) innovation and development along the customer journey. Thus, the cluster perspective offers the possibility to evaluate destinations as 'a conglomeration of activities and facilities . . . where tourism production and consumption occur simultaneously' (Pearce, 2014, p. 143). Destinations can display dynamics similar to clusters where heterogeneous actors collaborate and compete to provide services to travellers along the value chain in a distinct territory (García-Villaverde et al., 2020; Lee et al., 2020). Although cluster approaches can account for intra-destination innovation through collaborative and competitive, that is 'coopetitive', dynamics and local ties along the supply chain (Fundeanu, 2015; Lee et al., 2020; Novelli et al., 2006), they fail to explain how to organise change beyond a destination's geographical boundaries and how to collectively address the grand challenges of sustainable tourism development in the long term.

Questioning sustainable innovation as a task of isolated tourism clusters in a fixed, given territory (Beritelli et al., 2014), a meta-organisational perspective

DOI: 10.4324/9781003215066-14

can help to understand both the potential and challenges for sustainability (Berkowitz, 2018; Berkowitz & Dumez, 2016) in the tourism industry beyond predefined destination boundaries. Meta-organisations can facilitate long-term collective action and the creation of legitimacy and accountability among member organisations by introducing (at least partially or temporarily) organisational characteristics like common goals, shared values, and 'soft' approaches to monitoring and sanctioning (Ahrne, Brunsson, & Seidl, 2016; Ahrne & Brunsson, 2005, 2011; Berkowitz, 2018). The aim of this chapter is thus to investigate how 'coopetitive' intra-destination cluster dynamics and meta-organisational inter-destination management can be combined to facilitate sustainable development in the tourism industry. The study investigates this research question with an illustrative example of the Alpine Pearls, an association of several tourism destinations which develop green mobility across the Alps.

The following chapter is structured as follows. First, the literature review focuses on the concept of the tourism cluster, its peculiarities and implications for sustainable intra-destination development. Then, the chapter introduces the theoretical lens on meta-organisations for collectively organising sustainable development across destinations. In the following, the case study of the Alpine Pearls illustrates three meta-organisational characteristics which facilitate sustainable development: rationale for collective action, membership, and decision-making and structure. The chapter outlines the opportunities and challenges for organising sustainable development by combining cluster and meta-organisational collaboration in tourism destinations.

Literature review: destinations as tourism clusters

Tourism destinations are defined as an 'amalgam of tourism products, offering an integrated experience to consumers within a geographically well-defined area' (Buhalis, 2000, p. 97). Within these areas, multiple firms in diverse sectors, such as hospitality, infrastructure, or public institutions, provide services central to tourists' travel experiences (Beritelli et al., 2014; Fundeanu, 2015; Laing & Lewis, 2017). However, suppose a destination is merely considered a loosely connected agglomeration of individual business firms in a specific place. In that case, one fails 'to uncover the engine that powers destination and the dynamic process between context-bound interconnected actors' (Saraniemi & Kylänen, 2011, p. 136). These territories or their geographical boundaries are usually set by public organisations like 'Destination Management Organisations' (DMOs) (Grimstad, 2011), which, at the same time, assist in the coordination of inter-firm relations (Jackson & Murphy, 2002, 2006). With DMOs, tourism clusters can become (at least partially) organised (Ahrne & Brunsson, 2005). A DMO can deploy resources, finance specific initiatives in a given region, and assist in the identity development of a destination (Beritelli et al., 2014). It provides 'a political and legislative framework for tourism marketing' (Buhalis, 2000, p. 98). However, the link between different firms and service providers is crucial to creating value along the customer journey and a holistic tourism experience to be advertised by the DMO. To understand how these businesses co-exist as rivals in the same sector and partners along the value chain, the approach of tourism clustering has emerged to conceptualise the complexity, interdependence, and coopetition in tourism destinations (Jackson & Murphy, 2006; Laing & Lewis, 2017).

Porter (1998) defines clusters as 'geographic concentrations of interconnected companies, specialised suppliers, service providers, firms in related industries, and associated institutions (for example, universities, standards agencies and trade associations) in particular fields that compete but also cooperate' (Porter, 1998, p. 197). While the geographical boundaries can shift over time (Beritelli et al., 2014), the role of territory and local resources is crucial for a successful exchange of services between the supply (i.e. destination) and the demand (i.e. tourist) sides (Kádár & Gede, 2021). In contrast to horizontal clusters with multiple manufacturing businesses from the same sector, tourism clusters are considered diagonal. They include interdependent, complementary, and heterogeneous firms that supply a wide range of products and services linked through consumer experiences (Fundeanu, 2015; García-Villaverde et al., 2020; Laing & Lewis, 2017; Michael, 2003). To collectively create value and services, organisations in tourism clusters must cooperate while competing: the product or service (i.e. a holistic travel experience) can only be created through partnerships between multiple companies, institutions, and authorities (Fundeanu, 2015). If an organisation within a destination fails to cooperate and merely competes, the destination cannot offer a holistic travel experience.

With geographical proximity at the core of its definition, the concept of a tourism cluster is especially helpful in describing and understanding regional development within destinations (Fyall et al., 2012; Novelli et al., 2006). To leverage these coopetitive dynamics successfully, firms within destinations exploit territorial resources and benefit from geographic concentration and proximity (Pearce, 2014). Once the relations between firms are established, tourism clusters pioneer and drive innovation, creativity, and development (García-Villaverde et al., 2020; Żemła, 2014) through the reduction of transaction costs, systematic learning, and access to specialised services, investments, and funding, synergies, availability of knowledge and information, as well as benchmarking of performances among firms within the cluster (Lee et al., 2020; Rodríguez-Victoria et al., 2017). All these benefits occur due to the simultaneous competition and cooperation between co-located firms in the cluster's immediate area (on a local level) to increase (global) competitiveness (Erkuş-Öztürk, 2009; Gardiner & Scott, 2014; Lee et al., 2020; Novelli et al., 2006). Once again, (geographical) proximity is critical, as Porter (Porter, 1998) outlines: 'Competitive advantages in a global economy lie in local things – knowledge and relationships that distant rivals cannot match' (Porter, 1998, p. 77). Local, territorial uniqueness is crucial to the functioning of tourism clusters (Pearce, 2014), allowing to channel economic advantages and stay competitive beyond the local context (Laing & Lewis, 2017; Novelli et al., 2006). With their case of UNESCO heritage cities in Spain, García-Villaverde et al. (2020) exemplify how firms can be the first 'to offer new products and services to provide attractive experiences' leveraging their 'deep knowledge of the territory based on close ties with agents of the cluster, with the ability to identify changes in preferences of customers through diverse ties and with enough financial resources' (García-Villaverde et al., 2020, p. 11). The goal of (organised) tourism clustering is thus to strengthen competitiveness in a global market by increasing economic growth, productivity, and efficiency through cooperative advantages like economies of scale (Gardiner & Scott, 2014; McLennan et al., 2016). The relationship among clusters is, thus, a competitive one, where the profits of one cluster (e.g. a customer deciding to choose a specific destination) depend on the losses of another cluster (i.e. a customer not visiting another destination) (Jarillo, 2013).

Development within tourism clusters has mainly been discussed from an economic perspective. As Derlukiewicz et al. (2020) highlight, tourism clusters can also strengthen, promote, and ensure sustainable development among members through coopetition. However, research on tourism clusters focuses on how inter-firm relations in the destination are managed but not in what context or with what goals in mind (except for economic growth) these clusters operate (Pearce, 2014). It fails to acknowledge joint management structures and collaborative efforts beyond geographic proximity or discuss how inter-destination collaboration can help address shared problems or grand challenges requiring joint solutions (Fyall et al., 2012; Żemła, 2014). Sharpley (2020) urges rethinking how to 'rebalance tourism on a global basis' and highlights the need for 'research into how the necessary institutional, structural and behavioural transformation might be achieved' (Sharpley, 2020, p. 1942). If the focus is on sustainability as a shared (global) problem with the need for collaboration on a larger scale, the required mediated inter-destination development and innovations cannot be grasped by cluster theory linking innovation and development solely to ties within destination boundaries. Fyall et al. (2012) argue that the 'inter-destination collaboration requires a clarity of purpose . . . with the emphasis on system value creation' (Fyall et al., 2012, p. 22).

Consequently, to reach ambitious sustainability goals and face 'super-wicked' problems like climate change (Wright & Nyberg, 2017), inter-destination collaboration must be organised around long-term collective goals to tackle grand challenges (George et al., 2016). While tourism clusters can face some of these challenges and fuel innovation through coopetitive dynamics within a particular territory, the collaborative efforts beyond these geographical boundaries remain unclear. Collective efforts on an inter-destination level have to be organised differently. Thus, this chapter focuses on the concept of meta-organisations (Ahrne & Brunsson, 2005, 2011) to theoretically frame this joint endeavour for sustainable development across destination boundaries.

Theoretical background: meta-organisational approaches for inter-destination collaboration

While organisations in tourism clusters are bound through co-location in a shared territory, meta-organisations have other organisations (from various sectors or industries) as formal members. Ahrne and Brunsson (2005, 2008) define the characteristics that distinguish meta-organisations from organisations or firms with individuals as members. With organisations as members, meta-organisations face not only different challenges but also opportunities. They usually have better access to resources and are able to leverage more organised forms of collective action (compared to individuals) (Ahrne et al., 2016; Ahrne et al., 2016; Ahrne & Brunsson, 2005). While individuals' membership in organisations depends on their free will and incentives through economic benefits (e.g. salary), members in meta-organisations are united by sharing a common goal (Ahrne & Brunsson, 2005). As Jarillo (2013) points out, their relationship can be regarded as a cooperative one with a non-zero-sum outcome in mind: each member believes 'there will be more to share (and will be shared fairly) by cooperating' (Jarillo, 2013, p. 131). In the case of sustainable tourism and the protection of environmental resources through strategic cooperation, the net gain (i.e. an intact environment and a liveable planet) benefits all tourism clusters without inflicting any losses on competitors.

Without formal authority (like an institution or government) (Chaudhury et al., 2016; Gulati et al., 2012), membership in meta-organisations is often voluntary and linked to the member organisations' strive for a system-level goal such as sustainability (Ahrne & Brunsson, 2005; Berkowitz & Bor, 2018; Valente & Oliver, 2018). As member organisations are independent, autonomous actors, who have decision-making power and resources themselves, meta-organisations often cannot exercise organisational strategies like sanctioning or monitoring (Ahrne et al., 2016; Ahrne & Brunsson, 2005, 2011; Berkowitz, 2018; Berkowitz & Bor, 2018). Decisions in meta-organisations are often made by member organisations collectively following heterarchical structures and 'producing soft laws through decision-making by consensus' (Carmagnac & Carbone, 2019, p. 58). With autonomous organisations as members, meta-organisations are often 'reluctant to accept too much organisation' (Ahrne et al., 2016, p. 97). Thus, meta-organisations can be seen as partial organisations, exhibiting only some of the elements of complete, formal organisations (Ahrne & Brunsson, 2011; Schoeneborn & Dobusch, 2019).

Tourism clusters and meta-organisations both unite various organisations as their members to foster innovation and collective action in a more or less organised way. Although these aspects are similar and overlap in both concepts, there are three differences leading up to the collective action worth exploring (see Table 10.1). First, tourism clusters create collective action, development, and innovation through coopetition within local ties and draw their resources and advantages from their geographical proximity and their striving for economic competitiveness. Meta-organisations channel collective action through shared identity, accountability, and legitimacy linked to a shared vision, not shared territory (Berkowitz & Bor, 2018; Berkowitz & Dumez, 2016; Carmagnac & Carbone, 2019). However, as Viachka and Duprat (this volume) show, some meta-organisations inherit spatial dimensions of clusters and are anchored in their territories, contributing to their social sustainability. Bound by a collective identity, meta-organisations as associations or networks of organisations can be especially

Table 10.1 Comparing tourism clusters and meta-organisations as different ways of collective action

	Tourism clusters	*Meta-organisations*
Rationale for action	• Exploitation of territorial resources through coopetition. • Increasing efficiency and productivity.	• Guiding members through a shared, common goal (e.g. sustainable tourism).
Member organisations	• Firms situated diagonally along the customer chain. • Geographically proximate actors.	• Organisations that fulfil the membership criteria. • Voluntarily contribution to a shared vision.
Decision-making	• Cooperation and competition among individual firms along the value chain. • No formalised decision-making mechanism. • Rationale for decision: local innovation and global competition.	• Heterarchical through consensus, standards, and 'soft' laws. • Members can be sanctioned via exclusion.

effective at knowledge management across firms or geographical boundaries. As Dyer and Nobeoka (2000) emphasise with their case study of knowledge-sharing networks at Toyota, 'the effectiveness of collaboration increases when stakeholders "have a shared purpose"' (Dyer & Nobeoka, 2000, p. 351).

Second, tourism clusters link (member) organisations to provide services guided by customer experiences (diagonality) and create economic and competitive advantages within territorial boundaries (Fundeanu, 2015; García-Villaverde et al., 2020; Laing & Lewis, 2017; Michael, 2003). Meta-organisations, however, select their members according to more or less formalised membership criteria and align their actions through soft rules and standards or the so-called informal or social forms of control and governance (Dyer & Singh, 1998).

Third, tourism clusters emerge without a specific structure or hierarchy. Dominant organisations can leverage existing business opportunities, while smaller firms with weaker ties struggle to collaborate and be included in the territorial value chain (Fundeanu, 2015). There are no defined paths or rationales for collective decision-making in tourism clusters. These processes are rarely formalised as they emerge from localised ties between firms. From a tourism cluster perspective, decisions to become more sustainable are thus situated in values within the individual firms (Grimstad, 2011) but are not guided by shared vision spanning these organisations. In meta-organisations, decision-making is often heterarchical and based on consensus, with the voices of all members being included (Carmagnac & Carbone, 2019). While this allows all members to participate in the decision-making process, some actors can still have more influence than others.

While cluster theory can explain intra-destination collaboration as well as innovative capabilities and efficiency within destinations (Erkuş-Öztürk, 2009; Novelli et al., 2006; Porter, 1998), meta-organisations can extend the power of collaboration beyond geographical limits and govern inter-destination collaboration guided by a shared vision, working towards sustainability as a system-level goal (Berkowitz & Bor, 2018). Thus, in this chapter, we argue that the combined intra- and inter-destination collaboration striving for sustainable development should be understood through the complementary perspectives of tourism clusters and meta-organisations as two paths leading to collective action on different levels.

Illustrative case study: Alpine Pearls – destinations striving for green mobility & sustainable travel

With an illustrative case study of the 'Alpine Pearls', a meta-organisation in the European Alps, this chapter explores how meta-organisations can help to foster sustainable tourism development across destinations. Alpine Pearls considers itself an umbrella organisation for sustainable tourism and soft mobility. The meta-organisation was founded in 2006 with 17 member destinations as a follow-up to two projects funded by the European Union (Alp Mobility I + II). Fifteen years later, members include 19 destinations ('member pearls') in Alpine regions spreading across five countries: Austria (Werfenweng, Mallnitz, Weissensee, Hinterstoder), Germany (Bad Reichenhall, Berchtesgaden), Slovenia (Bled, Bohinj), Switzerland (Disentis/Mustér), and Italy (Ceresole Reale, Chamois-Le Magdeleine, Cogne, Forni di Sopra, Limone Piemonte, Moena, Moos im Passeiertal, Taschings, Villnöss, Alpe Cimbra). Additionally, more than 90 accommodation businesses (hotels, bed and breakfasts, apartments) in the designated destinations are included as affiliated hosts. All these destinations share some commonalities in terms of their destination territory. They offer 'spectacular mountain views, breath-taking beauty, and authentic Alpine customs' (Alpine Pearls, 2022) and are similar in their destination structure, being community-based Alpine areas with family-led and small businesses (Flagestad & Hope, 2001). With a focus on car-free holidays and green mobility, the goal of Alpine Pearls is to protect the environment while maintaining a smooth and trouble-free service experience for travellers.

The Alpine Pearls serves as an insightful case of meta-organising in the context of tourism clusters for two main reasons. First, the members of the Alpine Pearls span several different types of organisations (private, single firms like accommodation businesses and public organisations like DMOs or municipalities). Second, although they focus on a specific destination type (alpine, rural areas), they go beyond individual destination borders and span five countries with varying governmental structures. Figure 10.1 illustrates the meta-organisation of Alpine Pearls as extending the localised, intra-destination ties of tourism clusters to inter-destination, transnational collaboration, united by the goal of sustainable tourism development.

The following section will outline three main differences between tourism clusters and meta-organisations (see Table 10.1) with an illustrative case study to explore how meta-organisations like the Alpine Pearls build upon or extend the ability for sustainable development across destinations.

Rationale for collective action

Member destinations of the Alpine Pearls share a common goal. The members want to foster sustainable, soft, and gentle tourism through the means of green mobility. Five overarching guidelines specify the vision of the meta-organisation and its members: (1) environmentally friendly mobility, (2) environmental protection and renewable energy, (3) conservation and biodiversity, (4) preservation of local heritage, and (5) supporting local businesses and local food suppliers. To implement these goals, Alpine Pearls encourages all destinations to engage in the collective production of knowledge (e.g. through conferences and annual meetings in one of the destinations), product development on a local (e.g. establishing localised supply chains for affiliated hotel businesses), and transnational level (e.g. through shared marketing and branding campaigns with public transport or other public institutions). Alpine Pearls, as a meta-organisation, understands its mission in the linkage of the destinations and the establishment of core principles and values guiding (and uniting) all destinations. By bundling up destination resources all over the Alps, Alpine Pearls coordinates and secures the funding of projects together with the European Union (e.g. the INTERREG project for alpine areas).

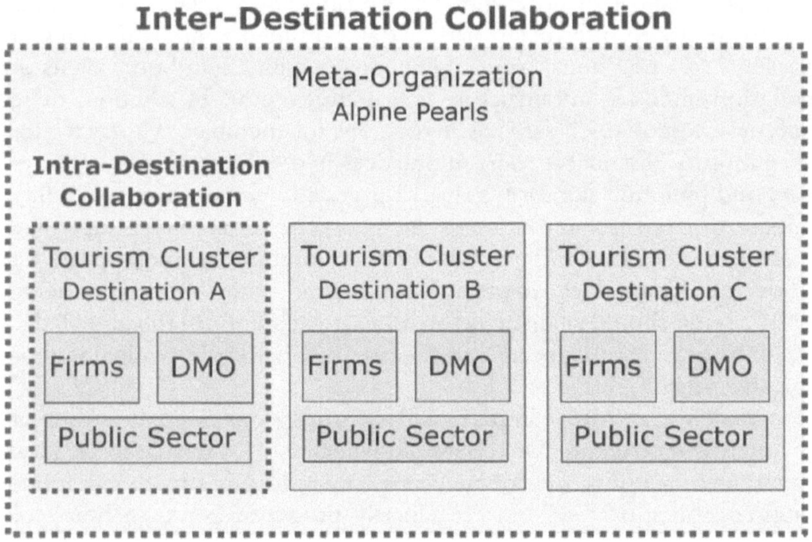

Figure 10.1 The Alpine Pearls as a meta-organisation that spans across destination borders and localised tourism clustering

Similar to the coopetitive rationale in tourism clusters (Erkuş-Öztürk, 2009; Lee et al., 2020; Rodríguez-Victoria et al., 2017), the vision and strategic goal of the Alpine Pearls are to offer a holistic and sustainable travel experience for the consumers too. However, the economic profit and efficiency inherent in competitive cluster dynamics are not the guiding principles. The Alpine Pearls encourages members to act sustainably: to secure tourism travel's long-term viability, preserve the region's unique character, and gain a competitive advantage over other destinations with a different (non-sustainable) focus.

Membership

Members of Alpine Pearls feature various types of organisations such as municipalities or destination management organisations (which represent associations of multiple municipalities in geographically connected regions). The destination has to be represented by a legal entity with an organisational structure (e.g. a designated spokesperson or a CEO). Further, the municipality or destination has to agree with the principles of sustainable development with a written resolution. In addition, tourism has to be a central part of its economy, manifested in a 3-year-median of overnight stays or the overnight stays per inhabitant. The tourism intensity sets the annual membership fee, dividing members into four categories with annual fees ranging from 12,000 to 25,000 Euros. All members have to commit to the membership criteria before being admitted. Each of the guidelines mentioned before (environmentally friendly mobility, environmental protection and renewable energies, conservation and biodiversity, preservation of local heritage, and supporting local business and local food suppliers) entails mandatory criteria that all members must meet. For example the town centre has to offer pedestrian or traffic-calmed zones and represent some elements of a traditional, rural alpine village with no industry plants or other pollution-intensive infrastructure (e.g. transit roads). In addition, there are premium criteria, which serve as suggestions for members who strive for the proliferation of sustainable tourism practices in a specific area. The list of mandatory and premium standards spans 12 pages and ranges from e-mobility requirements for citizens and tourists to the use of the Alpine Pearls logo on a destination's website. There is the possibility of becoming a 'candidate pearl' for 3 years if the destination does not meet the mandatory criteria yet. Introducing the candidate status should facilitate destinations to benefit from the knowledge and the resources of member pearls and the meta-organisations while developing sustainable tourism services.

Like tourism clusters, Alpine Pearls includes organisations along the customer journey: hotels, infrastructure, DMOs, or municipalities. Compared to the local ties within tourism clusters, the Alpine Pearls only indirectly strengthens intra-destination collaboration (e.g. fostering locally produced goods in hotels or developing new e-mobility transportation offers). Alpine Pearls presumes that these local ties exist with the prerequisites for an already functioning inter-firm destination network with tourism as a core economic sector in the respective regions. Their goal is to unite tourism clusters and guide their individual efforts towards sustainable development.

The Alpine Pearls as a meta-organisation is distinct from tourism clusters in two more ways. First, membership in the Alpine Pearls is voluntary. Organisations or destinations, which focus on sustainable travel, can become a part of it, but they also have other options. In contrast, some tourism clusters and DMO networks (e.g. in Austria) require mandatory participation in the activities of destinations (e.g. through mandatory tourism taxes). However, this participation cannot be considered membership per se but is rather an allocation to a legislative territory on the basis of the firms' geographical location. Second, membership in the Alpine Pearls meta-organisation is only partly limited to a geographical area. Member destinations have to be situated in an alpine context but are not limited to a specific country, district, or governmental destination boundary. They can consist of multiple clusters or only parts of the tourism cluster. The members are not united by their geographical context within a particular area but by facing similar challenges in their common quest for sustainable development. With a focus on small and community-structured destinations as members (Flagestad & Hope, 2001; Gajdošík et al., 2017), Alpine Pearls offers the possibility to share knowledge and establish solutions helpful for various clusters across destination borders.

Decision-making and structure

Although the membership is formalised (through annual fees, prerequisites for membership, and mandatory and premium admission criteria), the Alpine Pearls structure is rather heterarchical. All members make strategic decisions about future steps, the admission of new members, the evaluation of the requirements, and planned activities in an annual general assembly. When it comes to monitoring, each member is individually responsible for evaluating the extent to which they meet the prerequisites. In addition, an independent, external team (currently integrated into a student project at an Austrian University of Applied Sciences) is visiting a designated pearl each year to check on the criteria and the progress of the destination. If some members do not meet all requirements, weak spots are discussed in the assembly, and the meta-organisation provides suggestions for improvement in these areas. The only possibility for sanctions is the exclusion of the respective member or voluntary resignation from the meta-organisation.

The monitoring requirements in the Alpine Pearls meta-organisation focus on its members' accountability, trust, and reflexivity. This is typical for 'softer' approaches to administrative laws, rules, and standards and draws upon the accountability of the destinations to meet the collectively established values (Berkowitz, 2018; Berkowitz & Bor, 2018). The association-like structure ensures that every member can vote and participate in the decision-making concerning all members. Although the tourism clusters within the Alpine Pearls, their individual firms, and organisations can be guided by this shared vision, trust, and reflexivity, they still mainly situate their collaboration in intra-destination ties. Collaborating through localised ties and proximity does not mean that tourism clusters cannot or will not evolve towards more sustainable businesses. However, the path towards sustainability is not guided by a formalised decision-making process as it is in meta-organisations, but the decisions to collaborate emerge out of geographical proximity and localised business ties.

Discussion: opportunities and challenges for sustainable development through intra- and inter-destination collaboration

By focusing on the rationale for participation, the type of members, and decision-making processes, Alpine Pearls as a meta-organisation unites tourism clusters around a common goal and enables sustainable development across destination boundaries (Berkowitz & Bor, 2018; Berkowitz & Dumez, 2016; Carmagnac & Carbone, 2019; Fyall et al., 2012). Echoing Berkowitz (2018), the results show how the Alpine Pearls as a meta-organisation fosters collective action and innovation through reflexivity, accountability, and responsiveness to grand challenges and extends the innovative capabilities of tourism clusters beyond economies of scale. Meta-organisations such as Alpine Pearls can add an overarching goal to the localised ties in tourism clusters and direct the collective action towards a common goal (Grimstad, 2011; Pearce, 2014). While clustering strengthens the local initiatives and fosters innovation and collaboration by focusing on specific characteristics of a given territory, meta-organisations can guide inter-destination development towards a longer-term, macro-perspective of sustainability on a global scale. United by a shared vision, meta-organisations can direct local and global ties towards a common agenda and enable collaboration beyond short-term economic benefits and competitive advantages through economies of scale. Being part of a meta-organisation, tourism clusters can improve intra- and inter-destination development efforts by leveraging knowledge from other meta-organisational members and their striving for sustainability without neglecting their territorial resources and competitive advantages (Fundeanu, 2015; García-Villaverde et al., 2020; Laing & Lewis, 2017; Michael, 2003) .

In our case, the members are pre-selected through the more formalised membership criteria of Alpine Pearls that reflect the shared purpose of the meta-organisation. However, these criteria can only be established with soft monitoring and sanction rules (Ahrne & Brunsson, 2005, 2011; Carmagnac & Carbone, 2019). Referring to Berkowitz (2018) and Berkowitz and Dumez (2016), the collective strive for sustainability is guided by accountability and reflexivity rather than by 'too much organisation' (Ahrne et al., 2016, p. 97). Although soft rules and informal types of social control and governance can be as (or even more) effective than formal contracts or laws (Dyer & Singh, 1998), the partial (Ahrne & Brunsson, 2005) or varying degree (Dobusch & Schoeneborn, 2015) of organisation and the heterarchical structure can lead to difficulties in altering, extending, or changing the meta-organisational values and aligning them with the goals of member organisations. Organisations as members and meta-organisations themselves face tensions with respect to their autonomy in decision-making. As Ahrne et al. (2016) state: 'The members must be autonomous actors, although belonging to an autonomous organisation; and the meta-organisation must be an autonomous actor, even though its members are autonomous' (Ahrne et al., 2016, p. 9). This struggle for autonomy can lead to difficulties in establishing actorhood for destinations as autonomous organisations and associations as Alpine Pearls as meta-organisations (for an in-depth discussion of actorhood in relation to accountability, reflexivity, and restructuring, see the chapter by Berkowitz and Gadille in this volume). Without exercising decision-making power on a local level, the Alpine Pearls can only guide member destinations through accountability, reflexivity, and moral and ethical values and offer them shared knowledge, global partnerships, and pooled resources. This may not be enough for more powerful destinations or tourism clusters capable of leveraging such benefits independently.

While there is a need for the membership criteria and monitoring and sanctioning strategies, the shared vision, the heterarchical structure, and the common goal of all members of Alpine Pearls are central aspects of collaboration (and success) in meta-organisation. Dyer and Nobeoka (2000) highlight the importance of a shared purpose for effective collaboration, as they state:

> The "identity" of the firm is defined by the organisational boundaries which dictate who is (and who is not) a member of the organisation, by shared goals and values, and by patterns of interaction among many individuals that give rise to a common language unit and common frameworks for action.
>
> (Dyer & Nobeoka, 2000, p. 352)

These collective goals and frameworks for action, facilitated by the umbrella of the meta-organisation, can also guide intra-destination development in tourism clusters, even if formal membership criteria or decision-making structures are missing. Within Alpine Pearls, the ties among members and guiding visions (see previous subsection on membership) for the meta-organisation develop in yearly meetings and conferences, where autonomous and sometimes competing destinations meet. The destinations situate their shared identity as being alpine and sustainable rather than as being competitors for the same market (although they are). They foreground collaborative relations to create additional value through ecological travel (Jarillo, 2013). With the emphasis on a shared purpose and values as 'the glue that holds [autonomous organisations] together' (Schoeneborn & Dobusch, 2019, p. 319), future research can reflect upon the role and dynamics of shared values for inter-organisational collaboration from a meta-organisational perspective. Mainly because of the dependency on values as uniting principles and the absence of hierarchical structures and sanctioning mechanisms in meta-organisations, they may be especially valuable for reflecting upon the role of value-based management.

Conclusion

This chapter shows how a meta-organisational perspective on sustainable development can extend the understanding of inter-destination collaboration in the tourism industry with a case study of Alpine Pearls in European Alpine regions. Circling back to the redefinition of spatial boundaries, an appreciation of socio-ecological systems, and acknowledging global environmental forces as requirements for sustainable change (Higham & Miller, 2018), the combination of tourism cluster dynamics with meta-organisational approaches outlines a possible way of implementing sustainable development practices in the tourism industry.

While this is an important first step in analysing the interdependence of both concepts for intra- and inter-destination collaboration (Fyall et al., 2012), future research could explore this dynamic with longitudinal, empirical research. This chapter highlights the importance of a meta-organisational approach to inter-destination collaboration as a suitable framework for analysing other transnational tourism associations and underlines the practical relevance for meta-organisations in the tourism industry. The conclusion outlines the interplay between meta-organisations and tourism clusters as being particularly valuable for community-based tourism destinations (Flagestad & Hope, 2001) with many small and family businesses. Meta-organisations like Alpine Pearls can help these complex arrays of actors create knowledge, implement change, and strive for a more sustainable future for the tourism industry. They can help unite individual regions and destinations by channelling their innovative capabilities towards a common goal without neglecting their unique territories and the local ties within the destinations. We, thus, see meta-organisations as capable of transcending destination boundaries and fostering inter-destination collaboration without neglecting the role of geographical proximity and coopetitive dynamics within destinations.

References

Ahrne, G., & Brunsson, N. (2005). Organizations and meta-organizations. *Scandinavian Journal of Management, 21*(4), 429–449. https://doi.org/10.1016/j.scaman.2005.09.005

Ahrne, G., & Brunsson, N. (2008). *Meta-organizations*. Edward Elgar Publishing. www.e-elgar.com/shop/gbp/meta-organizations-9781847209504.html

Ahrne, G., & Brunsson, N. (2011). Organization outside organizations: The significance of partial organization. *Organization, 18*(1), 83–104. https://doi.org/10.1177/1350508410376256

Ahrne, G., Brunsson, N., & Kerwer, D. (2016). The paradox of organizing states: A meta-organization perspective on international organizations. *Journal of International Organizations Studies*, 7(1), 5–24.

Ahrne, G., Brunsson, N., & Seidl, D. (2016). Resurrecting organization by going beyond organizations. *European Management Journal, 34*(2), 93–101. https://doi.org/10.1016/j.emj.2016.02.003

Alpine Pearls. (2022). *Alpine pearls | About us*. www.alpine-pearls.com/en/about-us/alpine-pearls/

Beritelli, P., Bieger, T., & Laesser, C. (2014). The new frontiers of destination management. *Journal of Travel Research, 53*(4), 403–417. https://doi.org/10.1177/0047287513506298

Berkowitz, H. (2018). Meta-organizing firms' capabilities for sustainable innovation: A conceptual framework. *Journal of Cleaner Production, 175*, 420–430. https://doi.org/10.1016/j.jclepro.2017.12.028

Berkowitz, H., & Bor, S. (2018). Why meta-organizations matter: A response to Lawton et al. and Spillman. *Journal of Management Inquiry, 27*(2), 204–211. https://doi.org/10.1177/1056492617712895

Berkowitz, H., & Dumez, H. (2016). The concept of meta-organization: Issues for management studies. *European Management Review, 13*(2), 149–156. https://doi.org/10.1111/emre.12076

Berkowitz, H., & Gadille, M. (this volume). Meta-organizing clusters as agents of transformative change through "responsible actorhood". In E. Lupova-Henry & N. F. Dotti (Eds.), *Clusters and sustainable regional development: A meta-organisational approach*. Routledge.

Buhalis, D. (2000). Marketing the competitive destination of the future. *Tourism, Management, 21*, 97–116.

Carmagnac, L., & Carbone, V. (2019). Making supply networks more sustainable "together": The role of meta-organisations. *Supply Chain Forum: An International Journal, 20*(1), 56–67. https://doi.org/10.1080/16258312.2018.1554163

Chaudhury, A. S., Ventresca, M. J., Thornton, T. F., Helfgott, A., Sova, C., Baral, P., Rasheed, T., & Ligthart, J. (2016). Emerging meta-organisations and adaptation to global climate change: Evidence from implementing adaptation in Nepal, Pakistan and Ghana. *Global Environmental Change, 38*, 243–257. https://doi.org/10.1016/j.gloenvcha.2016.03.011

Derlukiewicz, N., Mempel-Śnieżyk, A., Mankowska, D., Dyjakon, A., Minta, S., & Pilawka, T. (2020). How do clusters Foster sustainable development? An analysis of EU policies. *Sustainability, 12*(4), 1297. https://doi.org/10.3390/su12041297

Dobusch, L., & Schoeneborn, D. (2015). Fluidity, identity, and organizationality: The communicative constitution of anonymous. *Journal of Management Studies, 52*(8), 1005–1035. https://doi.org/10.1111/joms.12139

Dyer, J. H., & Nobeoka, K. (2000). Creating and managing a high-performance knowledge-sharing network: The Toyota case. *Strategic Management Journal, 21*(3), 345–367.

Dyer, J. H., & Singh, H. (1998). The relational view: Cooperative strategy and sources of interorganisational competitive advantage. *The Academy of Management Review, 23*(4), 660–679.

Erkuş-Öztürk, H. (2009). The role of cluster types and firm size in designing the level of network relations: The experience of the Antalya tourism region. *Tourism Management, 30*(4), 589–597. https://doi.org/10.1016/j.tourman.2008.10.008

Flagestad, A., & Hope, C. A. (2001). Strategic success in winter sports destinations: A sustainable value creation perspective. *Tourism Management, 22*(5), 445–461. https://doi.org/10.1016/S0261-5177(01)00010-3

Fundeanu, D. D. (2015). Innovative regional cluster, model of tourism development. *Procedia Economics and Finance, 23*, 744–749. https://doi.org/10.1016/S2212-5671(15)00501-8

Fyall, A., Garrod, B., & Wang, Y. (2012). Destination collaboration: A critical review of theoretical approaches to a multi-dimensional phenomenon. *Journal of Destination Marketing & Management, 1*(1–2), 10–26. https://doi.org/10.1016/j.jdmm.2012.10.002

Gajdošík, T., Gajdošíková, Z., Maráková, V., & Flagestad, A. (2017). Destination structure revisited in view of the community and corporate model. *Tourism Management Perspectives, 24*, 54–63. https://doi.org/10.1016/j.tmp.2017.07.009

García-Villaverde, P. M., Elche, D., & Martínez-Pérez, Á. (2020). Understanding pioneering orientation in tourism clusters: Market dynamism and social capital. *Tourism Management, 76*, 103966. https://doi.org/10.1016/j.tourman.2019.103966

Gardiner, S., & Scott, N. (2014). Successful tourism clusters: Passion in paradise. *Annals of Tourism Research*, *46*, 171–173. https://doi.org/10.1016/j.annals.2014.01.004

George, G., Howard-Grenville, J., Joshi, A., & Tihanyi, L. (2016). Understanding and tackling societal grand challenges through management research. *Academy of Management Journal*, *59*(6), 1880–1895. https://doi.org/10.5465/amj.2016.4007

Grimstad, S. (2011). Developing a framework for examining business-driven sustainability initiatives with relevance to wine tourism clusters. *International Journal of Wine Business Research*, *23*(1), 62–82. https://doi.org/10.1108/17511061111121416

Gulati, R., Wohlgezogen, F., & Zhelyazkov, P. (2012). The two facets of collaboration: Cooperation and coordination in strategic alliances. *Academy of Management Annals*, *6*(1), 531–583. https://doi.org/10.5465/19416520.2012.691646

Higham, J., & Miller, G. (2018). Transforming societies and transforming tourism: Sustainable tourism in times of change. *Journal of Sustainable Tourism*, *26*(1), 1–8. https://doi.org/10.1080/09669582.2018.1407519

Jackson, J., & Murphy, P. (2002). Tourism destinations as clusters: Analytical experiences from the new world. *Tourism and Hospitality Research*, *4*(1), 36–52.

Jackson, J., & Murphy, P. (2006). Clusters in regional tourism an Australian case. *Annals of Tourism Research*, *33*(4), 1018–1035. https://doi.org/10.1016/j.annals.2006.04.005

Jarillo, J. C. (2013). *Strategic networks*. Routledge.

Kádár, B., & Gede, M. (2021). Tourism flows in large-scale destination systems. *Annals of Tourism Research*, *87*, 103113. https://doi.org/10.1016/j.annals.2020.103113

Laing, C., & Lewis, A. (2017). Exploring clustering as a destination development strategy for rural communities: The case of La Brea, Trinidad. *Journal of Destination Marketing & Management*, *6*(3), 184–195. https://doi.org/10.1016/j.jdmm.2016.03.006

Lee, Y.-J. A., Jang, S., & Kim, J. (2020). Tourism clusters and peer-to-peer accommodation. *Annals of Tourism Research*, *83*, 102960. https://doi.org/10.1016/j.annals.2020.102960

McLennan, C. J., Becken, S., & Watt, M. (2016). Learning through a cluster approach: Lessons from the implementation of six Australian tourism business sustainability programs. *Journal of Cleaner Production*, *111*, 348–357. https://doi.org/10.1016/j.jclepro.2015.01.085

Michael, E. J. (2003). Tourism micro-clusters. *Tourism Economics*, *9*(2), 133–145. https://doi.org/10.5367/000000003101298312

Novelli, M., Schmitz, B., & Spencer, T. (2006). Networks, clusters and innovation in tourism: A UK experience. *Tourism Management*, *27*(6), 1141–1152. https://doi.org/10.1016/j.tourman.2005.11.011

Pearce, D. G. (2014). Toward an integrative conceptual framework of destinations. *Journal of Travel Research*, *53*(2), 141–153. https://doi.org/10.1177/0047287513491334

Porter, M. E. (1998, November 1). Clusters and the new economics of competition. *Harvard Business Review*. https://hbr.org/1998/11/clusters-and-the-new-economics-of-competition

Rodríguez-Victoria, O. E., Puig, F., & González-Loureiro, M. (2017). Clustering, innovation and hotel competitiveness: Evidence from the Colombia destination. *International Journal of Contemporary Hospitality Management*, *29*(11), 2785–2806. https://doi.org/10.1108/IJCHM-03-2016-0172

Ruhanen, L., Weiler, B., Moyle, B. D., & McLennan, C. J. (2015). Trends and patterns in sustainable tourism research: A 25-year bibliometric analysis. *Journal of Sustainable Tourism*, *23*(4), 517–535. https://doi.org/10.1080/09669582.2014.978790

Saraniemi, S., & Kylänen, M. (2011). Problematizing the concept of tourism destination: An analysis of different theoretical approaches. *Journal of Travel Research*, *50*(2), 133–143. https://doi.org/10.1177/0047287510362775

Schoeneborn, D., & Dobusch, L. (2019). Alternating between partial and complete organization: The case of anonymous. In G. Ahrne & N. Brunsson (Eds.), *Organization outside organizations: The abundance of partial organization in social life* (pp. 318–333). Cambridge University Press. https://doi.org/10.1017/9781108604994.015

Sharpley, R. (2020). Tourism, sustainable development and the theoretical divide: 20 years on. *Journal of Sustainable Tourism*, *28*(11), 1932–1946. https://doi.org/10.1080/09669582.2020.1779732

Valente, M., & Oliver, C. (2018). Meta-organization formation and sustainability in Sub-Saharan Africa. *Organization Science*, *29*(4), 678–701. https://doi.org/10.1287/orsc.2017.1191

Viachka, A., & Duprat, L. (this volume). We are all in this together: The significance of meta-organisations for cluster policy. In E. Lupova-Henry & N. F. Dotti (Eds.), *Clusters and sustainable regional development: A meta-organisational approach*. Routledge.

Wright, C., & Nyberg, D. (2017). An inconvenient truth: How organisations translate climate change into business as usual. *Academy of Management Journal*, *60*(5), 1633–1661. https://doi.org/10.5465/amj.2015.0718

Żemła, M. (2014). Inter-destination cooperation: Forms, facilitators and inhibitors–the case of Poland. *Journal of Destination Marketing & Management*, *3*(4), 241–252. https://doi.org/10.1016/j.jdmm.2014.07.001

11 Urban super-cluster as a novel approach to clustering in megapolises

The case of Moscow Innovation Cluster

Evgeniy KUTSENKO, Saule ISMAGULOVA, and Ekaterina IVANOVA

Introduction

Clusters have traditionally been associated with innovation and economic growth due to agglomeration externalities, occurring among the co-located actors such as business, academia and related institutions, and networking around a specific functional niche (Andersson et al., 2004; Porter, 1998). Academic studies and practical efforts to develop territories with high-growth potential, knowledge circulation, and entrepreneurial activity have led to the formalisation of a cluster-based approach. There now exist professional associations of cluster practitioners (TCI Network, 2022), standards of cluster management excellence (ESCA, 2022), guidelines on cluster policies (Lämmer-Gamp et al., 2011), all aimed at fostering innovative scenarios of spatial economic development.

Today, the share of the urban population is growing (United Nations, 2018), as is the number of megapolises (Dobbs et al., 2011). Innovative activity is thus increasingly concentrated in urban settings hosting a large portion of high-tech businesses, knowledge centres, and advanced infrastructure. These developments require adjusting innovation policies to the city level. Such policies are expected to drive economic growth and new job creation, improve city management, and foster a sustainable and diversified urban economy (Tyurchev, 2021).

Surprisingly, cluster theory and policy grounded in agglomeration effects have brought limited insight into the difference between clusters in cities and rural areas. Few works examine the features of urban cluster initiatives (van den Berg & Braun, 2017), particularly in megapolises. Still, clusters in megapolises exist and demand closer scholarly and practical attention. This chapter focuses on the role of cluster initiatives – or 'organised' clusters – in megapolises. It challenges the existing knowledge on agglomeration economies and their relevance for urban clustering. Specifically, this chapter aims at developing a novel approach to designing and organising clusters in megapolises and proposes a framework of 'urban super-clusters' that allows to leverage some of the benefits of the urban settings while attenuating their negative effects, such as congestion and increased transaction costs. This framework is expected to be relevant for other megapolises, where the city leaders are rethinking cluster policy.

DOI: 10.4324/9781003215066-15

To develop this conceptual framework, we discuss the foundations of cluster theory in relation to the features of megapolises, which concentrate scientific knowledge, ground-breaking technologies, and entrepreneurial and creative prosperity (Boos et al., 2020). We build upon the meta-organisational framework (Ahrne & Brunsson, 2005) and discuss its potential for rethinking clusters in urban settings. We then present a case study of one of the most recent and ambitious urban cluster initiatives – the Moscow Innovation Cluster (from now on, the MIC). This research demonstrates that the MIC has gone far beyond the traditional cluster policy approaches and has much in common with meta-organisations (Berkowitz, 2018; Gulati et al., 2012; Lupova-Henry et al., 2021). We thus suggest that an organisational view on clustering, unlike the geographical one, allows for a better understanding of the dynamics and positive effects of urban super-clusters, such as the MIC. This approach facilitates collective actions among its members while tackling coordination challenges in megapolises.

This chapter is structured as follows. First, we present theoretical background for an urban super-cluster institutional design, which fits the features of megapolises into the meta-organisational framework. Then, the methodology and case description are presented. The following section summarises the findings of the case study. Finally, we discuss the research results and highlight their implications for theory and practice.

Theoretical background

Cluster policy has many theoretical underpinnings, starting with Alfred Marshall (1920) and Michael E. Porter (1998) (see a detailed discussion in Lupova-Henry & Dotti, this volume). Over the years, clusters have become central in regional research and policy practices (Cooke, 1995; Ketels, 2013). At the same time, scientific literature increasingly points to the special role of cities in innovation processes (Feldman & Audretsch, 1999; Florida et al., 2017; Hospers, 2003). Indeed, over the past decades, large cities have become places for the emergence and support of clusters (Lorenzen & Frederiksen, 2008; van den Berg et al., 2001), acting as intermediaries in facilitating knowledge generation, information transmission and firm creation (McCann, 2008). In what follows, we will discuss the features of megapolises bridging these with the meta-organisational views of clusters. We will then develop a conceptual framework for 'urban super-clusters' based on this theoretical background.

Megapolises and innovation-based economic development

Academic research has been increasingly focusing on the role of cities in innovation-based economic development. In particular, five key features of megapolises may be especially relevant in this context: a multitude of economic actors, industrial diversity, high transaction cost barriers, dependency on external interactions, and a variety of support mechanisms seen as public goods.

First, megapolises bring together a multitude of economic actors such as companies, universities, and public and non-profit organisations. The benefits of their co-location include increasing returns and higher rates of innovation, thanks to better access to specialised labour, supplier linkages, and knowledge spillovers (Beaudry & Schiffauerova, 2009). Moreover, the urbanisation process entails developing new economic activities, leading to a more diversified industrial structure, thus bringing more knowledge generation and exchange opportunities across industries (Lorenzen & Frederiksen, 2008). For this reason, cities with a more diverse economic structure can grow faster (Clark et al., 2003).

However, agglomeration diseconomies, such as higher transaction costs, can also occur (Richardson, 1995; Wheeler, 2003). As cities expand, the net benefits of urban areas might be overshadowed by congestion, pollution, labour shortage, increasing costs of non-mobile production factors, and bottlenecks in public goods, leading to decreased productivity (Glaeser, 1998; Neffke et al., 2011). Thus, transaction costs – including bargaining, contract-making, monitoring, enforcement, and protection from third-party search (Eggertsson, 1990; North, 1987) – may increase and limit the effectiveness of an economic system.

Literature has also shown the importance of external interactions for urban economic development, concluding that the role of local ties and physical proximity for clustering has been overestimated (Owen-Smith & Powell, 2004; Uzzi, 1997). Indeed, access to new knowledge does not only result from local interaction (the so-called 'local buzz') but is often acquired through strategic partnerships of inter-regional and international reach ('global pipelines') (Bathelt et al., 2004). Therefore, the interaction of firms with partners outside the city boundaries is necessary for economic development. Due to their 'compactness', cities are less self-sufficient than regions or countries as they depend on resources and connections to industrial sites and agricultural production beyond their borders.

Finally, various cooperation support mechanisms are present in cities, arising from the diversity of institutions and infrastructures (Lorenzen & Frederiksen, 2008). Support providers, such as cluster organisations, business incubators, trade associations, chambers of commerce, or innovation-focused government councils, compete with each other (Coletti, 2010). Therefore, these providers should have their niche and subsequent funds to support economic actors. Organising such cooperation is becoming a new urban public good (Boos et al., 2020).

In summary, recent research in urban studies has emphasised socio-economic interaction as a basis for understanding the constitution and growth of city economies and their growth (Glaeser, 1998, 2011; Hospers, 2003; Scott, 2001). The embeddedness in social networks, or strategic partnerships not geographically limited, appears more crucial than spatial proximity. This starting point for our search sets a theoretical framework to design a particular type of clusters in megapolises based on the distinction proposed by Kowalski and Marcinkowski (2014) between spontaneous or geographic clusters (Porter, 1998) and formalised cluster initiatives (Sölvell et al., 2003). In what follows, we will build upon the meta-organisational framework to outline a theoretical foundation for a new approach to cluster design adapted to the context of megapolises.

A meta-organisational framework for clustering

Research has been increasingly viewing clusters from an organisational perspective (Bell et al., 2009; Coletti, 2010; Laur et al., 2012). It implies organising business, government and academia efforts to launch, develop, and manage clusters, often referred to as cluster initiatives (Sölvell et al., 2003). Cluster initiatives establish cluster management organisations to fulfil management functions such as monitoring financial sustainability, members' outputs, and satisfaction (Schretlen et al., 2011).

Recent studies have suggested that such 'organised' clusters can be seen as meta-organisations or 'organisations of organisations' based on collective decision-making (Ahrne & Brunsson, 2008), resulting in higher collaboration across members. Meta-organisations rely not on contractual relationships but consensus (Berkowitz & Dumez, 2016) and provide a framework for collective action (Olson, 1965). This consensus-based relationship allows companies to collectively address problems that cannot be solved through contracts or market mechanisms (Gulati et al., 2012; Meyer & Höllerer, 2014). Literature has shown that 'organised' clusters and meta-organisations to a certain extent comply with the features of formal organisations such as membership, hierarchy (or a joint decision-making mechanism), rules, monitoring, and sanctions (Ahrne & Brunsson, 2008; Bell et al., 2009; Viachka, 2013).

Indeed, growing cluster membership points to the perceived advantages of being part of an 'organised' cluster (Graddy & Chen, 2006), such as the cluster management activities like initiation, development, and supervision of cooperation projects (Coletti, 2010). This membership represents a form of collective action where members share an understanding of a common issue, recognise the need for cooperation to solve it, and engage in joint activities. These elements imply developing 'protocols and shared rules' (Atherton & Johnston, 2008, p. 99) and providing 'a tacit sanction over non-fulfilment of agreed means of collaboration' (ibid. 2008, p. 103). Cluster governance is needed to ensure 'good' management, which is usually fulfilled by a board of cluster members and outside stakeholders. Cluster governance requires a clear definition of roles between management and governing bodies (Bell et al., 2009) and the degree of members' involvement in strategic planning (ESCA, 2022). A multi-level system of governance and management implies the presence of hierarchy as the basis for decision-making. Thus, some members are given special roles, such as representation in a cluster board, heading thematic groups, or managing projects. Along these lines, the meta-organisational framework can be a suitable lens for studying organised clusters having some formal organisation features.

Given the flexibility of the meta-organisational framework, it could be used to assemble the theoretical foundations for a particular type of clusters that correspond to the conditions of megapolises. As there are many actors, projects, and interests in the city, one of the cluster's roles could be their coordination. Such an approach is supported by Lupova-Henry et al. (2021), examining organised clusters from the 'meta-organisational' perspective. They suggest that these 'are not mere geographic areas but are coherent organisations which display joint decision making and are driven by common goals' (Lupova-Henry et al., 2021, p. 36). We will supplement these findings in the following subsection and look at super-clusters in megapolises from a meta-organisational perspective.

Urban super-clusters: blending the features of megapolises and meta-organisations

Building on the features of megapolises depicted earlier, we outline the distinctive characteristics of urban super-clusters, which differentiate them from traditional cluster initiatives, and apply a meta-organisational framework to urban super-cluster design. According to Scott (2001), the emergence of 'super-clusters of global city-regions' is linked with 'organisational bonds between different economic agents, which are frequently charged with multiple synergies' (Scott, 2001, p. 818). We suggest defining an urban super-cluster as a cluster organisation incorporating cluster initiatives and other associational forms, single entities, and individuals that can operate in different industries and are locally anchored but not bound contractually. A super-cluster does not replace traditional cluster organisations but provides members with a single platform for inter-sectoral, cross-cluster, and inter-regional interactions.

Urban super-cluster as a large-scale initiative hosting the entire sectors

As a rule, in a traditional cluster initiative, participants are limited to a hundred (Lindqvist et al., 2013). For example almost 60 per cent of EU-27 cluster organisations have less than 100 members, and only around 7 per cent have more than 400 (Franco et al., 2021). As clusters focus on facilitating collaboration among their members, interactions occur mainly within cluster boundaries. Thus, in large cities where multiple specialised cluster initiatives are present, potential cluster members are dispersed, and their collaboration is fragmented, making the agglomeration effects less significant. Thus, we suggest that, in large cities, it might be reasonable to involve all actors willing to cooperate under the umbrella of a super-cluster. This umbrella organisation could reduce fragmentation, supporting and enabling entire sectors to a cluster. For example the HealthCapital Berlin-Brandenburg cluster comprises over 20,000 members, including 500 major biomedical, pharmaceutical, and medical equipment producers; 130 hospitals; 25 universities; 18 R&D organisations; and 8 industrial parks. Easy admission of new participants led to a significant number of cluster members, resulting in a galore of supported joint projects. Ultimately, it helped the city's healthcare sector excel globally (Islankina et al., 2019). The meta-organisational approach allows for voluntary interpretations of membership (Lupova-Henry et al., 2021), ranging from formal participation (Ahrne & Brunsson, 2008) to collective identity and adherence to common goals (Glynn, 2008). Research and practice suggest that minimal membership requirements in a super-cluster and low entrance barriers would stimulate its expansion, which, however, depends on the effectiveness of cluster management.

Urban super-cluster as a cross-sectoral initiative fostering the emergence of new industries

Traditional clusters are usually guided by specialisation, whereas super-clusters have a greater potential to spread and reinforce the urbanisation effects (Lorenzen & Frederiksen, 2008). This potential refers to the importance of including new industries in a cluster, stimulating diversity, cross-sectoral combinations, and unrelated diversification. Given a varied taxonomy of meta-organisations (Gulati et al., 2012), the meta-organisational approach can support collective actions beyond industry boundaries (Garaudel, 2020). Indeed, Berkowitz et al. (2017) refer to 'cross-sectoral meta-organisations composed by multiple unrelated industries' (Berkowitz et al., 2017, p. 753). Members put in multisector efforts to achieve systemic progress in commonly shared issues like environmental sustainability. Such cross-sectoral meta-organisations are associated with flexibility, innovation, and mutual learning (Dewulf & Elbers, 2018) on the basis of the diversity of expertise (Berkowitz et al., 2020). The advantages of open membership for urban super-clusters allow the involvement of representatives from various industries. Each industry could participate either as individual entities or as a part of smaller sector-specific sub-clusters, making such an endeavour 'a cluster of clusters' (Johansson & Forslund, 2008). For example Hong Kong Science Park is an umbrella organisation for two clusters – Health@InnoHK (healthcare innovations) and AIR@InnoHK (artificial intelligence and robotics technologies). Their support is aimed at technology transfer in the priority areas of the urban economy, such as healthy ageing, robotics, and smart cities, which are highly innovative and interdisciplinary (Innovation and Technology Commission, 2022).

Urban super-cluster as an interactive initiative aiming at transaction costs reduction and open innovation

Conventionally, the increase in cluster membership is associated with higher transaction costs, which can impede the spread of knowledge and make a cluster initiative less manageable (Kogut & Zander, 1996). Thus, cluster organisations' role is to reduce those costs by building trust and promoting inter-firm collaboration (Huggins, 1998). This characteristic relies on various types of non-locational proximity – social, organisational, cognitive (Boschma et al., 2014) – reducing transaction costs (Lorenzen, 2009; Vang-Lauridsen & Chaminade, 2007). Socially and cognitively proximate cluster members more easily agree on the rules for their engagement, reducing uncertainties and facilitating joint activities (Atherton & Johnston, 2008). In urban super-clusters, these could be facilitated via digital collaboration platforms. The spread of ICT can 'reduce transaction costs of searching, evaluating and monitoring . . . and support a willingness among organisations to open up their innovation processes to the inflow and outflow of knowledge' (Remneland-Wikhamn & Knights, 2012, p. 279). The meta-organisational framework also links the reduction of transaction costs with facilitated communication (Hinds et al., 2002) and favours the use of ICT that allows for more significant externalisation of innovation (Srikanth & Puranam, 2010). For example the e-Cluster in Seoul is an online platform that aggregates information about the whole super-cluster and supports network interactions of participating mini-clusters, including joint project management, services, communication, and collective access to databases (KICOX, 2010).

Urban super-cluster as an open initiative profiting from outward linkages

The traditional view on clusters highlights the importance of local networking (Storper & Venables, 2004). Meanwhile, research suggests that innovation results from combining close and distant interactions (Owen-Smith & Powell, 2004). In the same way, the meta-organisational approach suggests the benefits of incorporating firms from other countries (Viachka, 2013). Thus, given its vast and diverse local membership, an urban super-cluster could help stimulate interactions with external partners and knowledge sources across the country and abroad. Such interaction is no less beneficial for the city and local businesses than stimulating internal collaboration. Like a soft hierarchy in meta-organisations (Ahrne & Brunsson, 2008), the hierarchy in local–global links of an urban super-cluster is not strict either (Andersson et al., 2004). For example the relationship between local firms and MNEs in the ICT cluster Zhongguancun (Beijing) is

> 'hierarchical and interdependent and evolutionary. Local firms' collaboration with MNCs provides them with vital technological and organisational training, which the local firms use strategically to develop their market networks and innovative capacity in the home market'
>
> (Zhou & Xin, 2003, p. 129)

Urban super-cluster as a public good, expanding mutual benefits

Clusters have been primarily associated with public goods due to shared know-how and infrastructure (Bekar & Lipsey, 2001) and trust-building (Andersson et al., 2004). Similarly, urban super-clusters could facilitate the provision of public goods, characterised by non-excludability and non-rivalry: that is cluster members cannot be excluded from applying for cluster services. Similarly, the involvement of one member does not make cluster services less available for others based on 'a collective consumption' premise (cf. Bekar & Lipsey, 2001). Digital platforms – falling into the category of digital public goods (UN Secretary-General for Digital Cooperation, 2020) – can be vehicles for the provision of public goods by urban super-clusters. According to the meta-organisational logic, such a platform can be seen as 'a system of assets available on a collaborative structure that allows different member organisations to efficiently derive value from it' (Berkowitz, 2018, p. 424). For example LSN XCHANGE – a digital collaboration platform in Life Science Nord cluster (Hamburg) – allows members to collectively and freely receive advisory services regarding regulatory issues (Islankina et al., 2019).

Methodology and case presentation

The previous section substantiated an urban super-cluster framework, which builds upon the meta-organisational logic and accounts for the features of megapolises. We will now explore the case of the Moscow Innovation Cluster through the lens of this framework to analyse whether these theoretical constructs are reflected in practice.

Methodology

Methodologically, our study is based on the approach of theory building from cases (Eisenhardt & Graebner, 2007) combined with natural experimentation (Lee, 1989). In this research, we used data on cluster members, its organisational structure (as collected from official sources), and data collected as a part of our consultancy for the Government of Moscow.

The theoretical construct of an urban super-cluster proposed in this chapter was elaborated from the empirical evidence of the Moscow Innovation Cluster the (MIC). The development of the MIC followed experimental logic due to testing an urban super-cluster framework designed explicitly for Moscow. Thus, the new cluster has been under our observation from its initial conceptualisation until now. In line with the natural experimentation approach, we believe that our theoretical propositions refer to objects and relations that cannot be observed directly (e.g. trust-building) and have logical consistency and explanatory force. Overall, in our research and consulting project, cluster theory was applied to data on the basis of the truthfulness of the theory. The results of our theorising were then put into controlled practice, which led to the formation of the MIC case. Finally, in this contribution, we analysed the MIC case and deduced a refined urban super-cluster construct with applying the meta-organisational framework.

Case presentation

As of the end of 2021, Moscow is the largest scientific and innovation hub in Russia, accounting for 35 per cent of domestic R&D expenditures and one third of the sector employment, 40 per cent of Web of Science publications, a quarter of national patent applications for inventions, and more than half (59 per cent) of all Russian high-tech start-ups (about 1,500). The economic structure of the city is highly diversified and comprises 42 traded industries (Abashkin et al., 2021), with the dominance of knowledge-intensive business services (21.91 per cent of all Russian sector employment) and creative industries (13.97 per cent) over manufacturing (3.95 per cent).

Given the large variety of specialised industries in Moscow, the city authorities decided to create a super-cluster that would encompass a range of industries rather than specialise in a single one and thus promote sectoral complementarities and foster innovation. The Moscow Innovation Cluster was founded in 2018–2019 (Figure 11.1), and it is managed by the MIC Foundation, established by and subordinate to the Government of Moscow. This foundation is governed by a supervisory board, comprising 14 members – the heads of

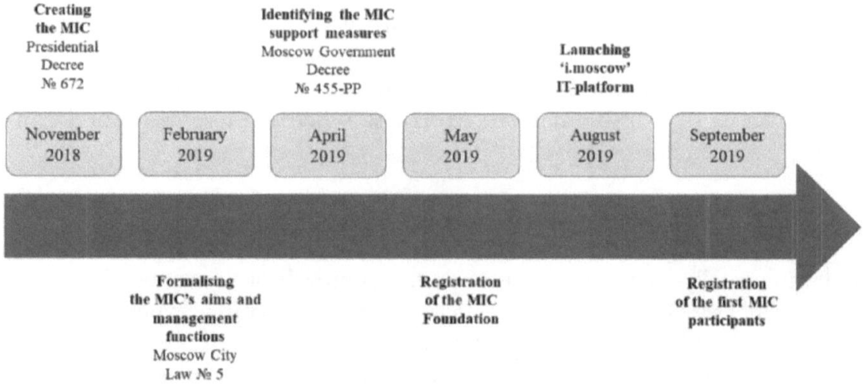

Figure 11.1 The MIC formation steps: 2018–2019

Source: authors

Figure 11.2 Tasks of the MIC

Source: authors

leading Russian R&D organisations and universities, state-owned corporations, national authorities, and innovation development agencies, all invited by the mayor of Moscow (the chairman).

Setting up innovative businesses and developing interdisciplinary product chains requires constant interaction between the R&D sector and industry. The cluster seeks to accelerate this cooperation and bring new goods and services to the market (Figure 11.2).

As the Government of Moscow aimed at increasing the cluster's scale, the requirements of potential participants are minimal. Potential members and partners are only required to have a legal entity status and be able to prove their sound financial situation (i.e. absence of bankruptcy). In addition, members are required to demonstrate their trustworthiness (i.e. absence of an 'unscrupulous supplier' status). The joining process is simplified and implies the registration on the 'i.moscow' website with e-signature for partners supplemented by a formal application for members.

The MIC unites R&D institutions (900+) and universities (280+), manufacturers and service providers (25,000+), and innovation infrastructure sites (1,500+), such as testing labs, co-working spaces, business incubators and accelerators and others. The super-cluster involves around 90 industries located in and outside Moscow. An organisation or an entrepreneur registered in any Russian region, except for the City of Moscow (Moscow Innovation Cluster, 2021a), can receive the status of MIC's partner. The number of regional partners exceeded 6,500 in July 2021, currently accounting for 30 per cent of the total cluster participation. The MIC's partners can benefit from various platform services (Table 11.1). The number of cluster participants (Moscow-based members and partners from 73 Russian regions altogether) has been continuously growing, as shown in Figure 11.3.

Apart from single-actor participation, the MIC hosts other cluster initiatives referred to as 'sub-clusters'. Organising in sub-clusters allows the MIC

Table 11.1 Availability of platform services to the MIC members and partners

Services	*Partners*	*Members*
Support measures navigator	Limited access	+
Support measures calculator	Limited access	+
Contract manufacturing exchange	+	+
Renting premises	+	+
Sub-clusters	Limited access	+
Investment packaging	-	+
Venture academy	-	-
Piloting	Limited access	+
Patent exchange	Limited access	+
Moscow accelerator	+	+
Technological contests	+	+
Factoring	+	+
Marketplace of goods and services	+	+
Map of innovative solutions	+	+

Source: Moscow Innovation Cluster, 2021a.

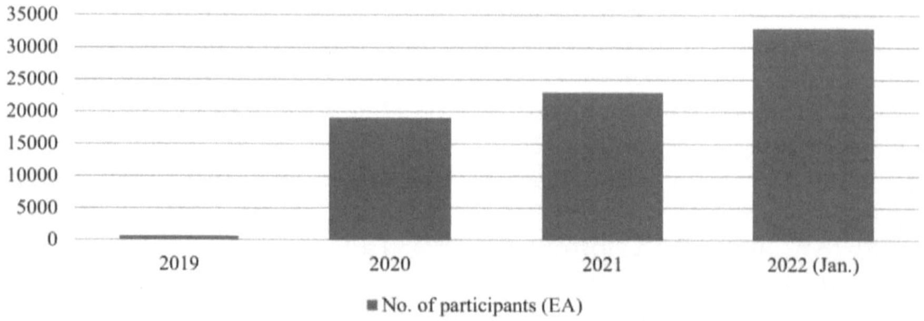

Figure 11.3 The dynamics of the MIC participation

Source: authors' calculations based on Moscow Innovation Cluster, 2021a

members to cooperate more personally and build trust while working on joint projects. A sub-cluster needs to be initiated by a MIC member, engage at least 30 other MIC members, and have a common goal and at least one innovation project between two and more members (Moscow Innovation Cluster, 2021b). Currently, there are ten sub-clusters involving from 32 to 78 members (Figure 11.4); some of them are mature and have been created long before the MIC's formation (e.g. 'Zelenograd', 'Troitsk', or Moscow Composite Cluster).

The 'i.moscow' digital platform has been created to enable self-organisation and cooperation among many heterogeneous actors. Through the MIC official website and social networks, cluster participants are informed about new projects, events, or calls for application and provided with detailed guidelines regarding public support and access to current statistics. The 'i.moscow' platform also features an electronic database of patents, a contract manufacturing exchange, a marketplace of goods and services, and technological contests (i.e. programmes for accelerated integration of innovative solutions of start-ups requested by large corporations).

Moreover, cluster participants have access to and can apply for public funding through the platform. There are two types of projects supported by the cluster financially: complex innovation projects to create new products or introduce new technologies and cooperative complex innovation projects. The former can be initiated by individual MIC members or by member collectives, while the latter is available to the members of MIC sub-clusters only. The applicants are entitled to financial support, up to 200 million RUB in a year (for up to 3 financial years). The number of innovation projects presented on the 'i.moscow' platform has increased along with its participation rate (Figure 11.5).

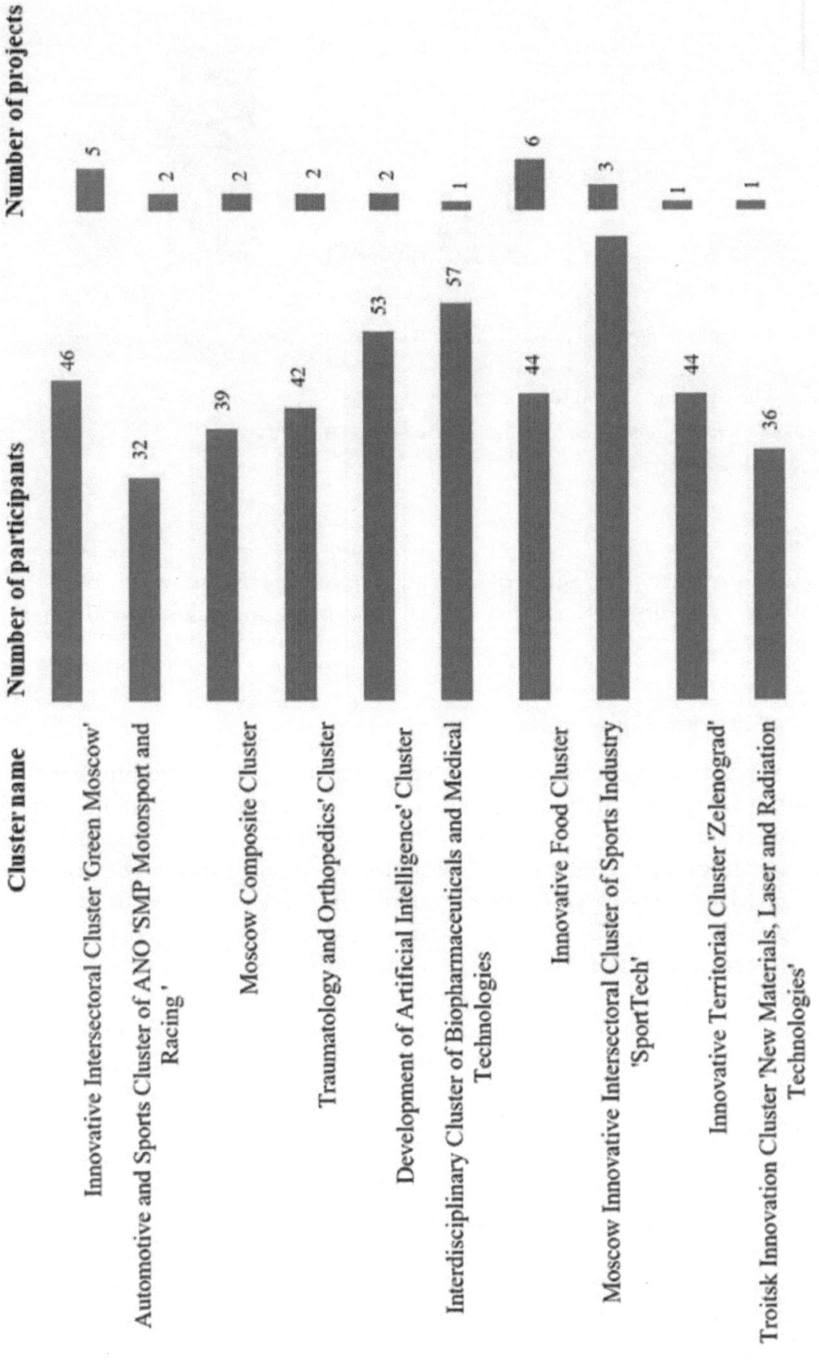

Figure 11.4 Sub-clusters of the MIC

Source: Moscow Innovation Cluster, 2021b

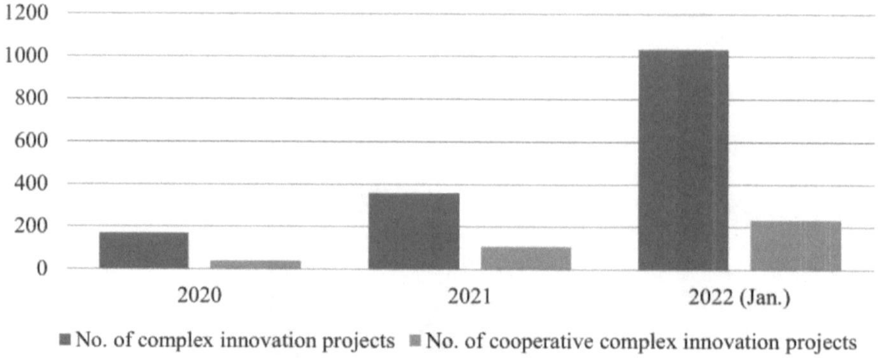

Figure 11.5 The dynamics of the MIC members' projects
Source: authors' elaborations based on Moscow Innovation Cluster, 2022

Findings

This section presents the results of our analysis of the Moscow Innovation Cluster along two dimensions: that of (1) an urban super-cluster and (2) a meta-organisation.

The MIC as an urban super-cluster

As an urban super-cluster, the MIC is characterised by (1) a large number of participants, (2) a variety of industries present in it, (3) the use of the digital platform to reduce transaction costs and promote open innovations, (4) openness to companies from other regions, and (5) provision of funding and public goods.

First, the MIC is the largest cluster initiative in Russia and probably one of the largest in the world. It is comparable in size with Zhongguancun in Beijing or HealthCapital in Berlin, the clusters that grasp entire sectors of urban economies. Indeed, the MIC's organisational logic seeks to capitalise on agglomeration externalities of the capital city by involving a large number of actors. As the Government of Moscow aimed at increasing the cluster's scale, the requirements to potential participants were minimal, and the process of joining was simplified.

Second, the MIC was intended to organise the vast and diverse innovation community to exploit new knowledge or recombine current mindsets in a new way. The cluster thus encompasses 90 industries and includes several sub-clusters. This organisational novelty seeks to compensate for the potential loss of personal communication that may result from the involvement of a large number of actors. Indeed, sub-clusters aim at engaging members in more trustworthy and unplanned cooperation to stimulate breakthrough innovations. For that purpose, sub-clusters are formed within cross-industrial and relatively new sectors (e.g. cybersport) driven by tailor-made financial incentives – the cooperative complex innovation projects.

In contrast to traditional clusters based on geographical proximity needed for collaboration, the MIC leveraged digitalisation to foster cooperation among multiple and varied stakeholders. The MIC's 'i.moscow' platform facilitates interaction between thousands of economic actors of various types and industries. The platform establishes uniform rules and requirements, thus minimising the risk of deception and helping speed up the search for partnerships. Further, the MIC participants can benefit from de-bureaucratisation since many business processes are automated, such as promotion, procurement, or application for support. For the MIC Foundation, the openness of data and structuring of information about cluster participants simplify monitoring.

Furthermore, the MIC is a Moscow-based cluster initiative; however, the opportunities for know-how exchange and the launch of cooperation projects have expanded beyond the city's borders. It hosts participants from other places as 'partners'. In contrast to a full member, a partner has limited access to super-cluster services but still benefits from joining. Indeed, as soon as cluster services became available to regional companies (May 2020), participants from 73 regions joined the MIC (August 2020). This element has broadened cluster 'pipelines' for bridging the gap between R&D centres, high-tech businesses, and universities concentrated in Moscow and industrial sites available in other regions at lower prices. Moreover, the MIC also seeks to internationalise: in September 2020, a cooperation agreement was signed between the MIC Foundation and the management organisation of the Zhongguancun super-cluster in Beijing (Moscow Innovation Cluster, 2021c).

Finally, the MIC has accumulated over 200 support measures available in the capital city on its digital platform. They are provided by the Government of Moscow, federal ministries, or development agencies, and some were launched exclusively for the MIC participants (e.g. a targeted subsidy to reimburse engineering expenditures). With its 'i.moscow' online platform, the cluster promotes and simplifies access to many funding and non-financial support for companies. These services help companies enter new markets, reduce the tax burden, access credits, develop new products, train personnel, and develop a research base (Moscow Innovation Cluster, 2021d). The MIC platform offers digital public goods. Registration on the platform and, consequently, participation in the cluster are open and free of charge for any member or partner. A constant expansion of the platform is in line with the logic of the public goods: the platform's efficiency increases with each new member at the same cost.

The MIC as a partial meta-organisation

Our case has demonstrated frequent collective actions at the micro-level – among members engaged in joint projects or sub-clusters. However, in the view of the MIC as 'an organisation of organisations', there has not been any common strategy, action plan, megaproject, or sectoral programme, which would mean the involvement of all cluster participants in regular discussions of the super-cluster issues.

The MIC is primarily a government-led cluster initiative. There is some hierarchy in the multi-level decision-making mechanism. The MIC Foundation deals with daily operational tasks, and the Supervisory Board deals with strategic considerations at twice-a-year sessions. However, cluster members have limited possibilities to affect any decisions regarding the MIC.

Membership (or participation in the MIC's terms) is voluntary. It allows for a variety of forms: local (Moscow-based actors) or external (actors from other regions), individual (entrepreneurs and organisations) or collective (sub-clusters), limited (partners) or full-fledged (members). Different forms of participation imply varying access to cluster services. As in meta-organisations, membership criteria and roles are defined to a certain extent, but participation in the MIC is far from being formal membership since it only implies creating a platform account.

The provision of funding is subject to regulation with rules and sanctions for violating the intended use of funds, usually in the form of paying the subsidy back. However, both apply only for financial support beneficiaries. General rules to define desirable behaviour or sanctions to punish opportunism are not elaborated for the MIC members.

Monitoring could be ascribed to an open and voluntary tracking of the overall MIC progress through the 'i.moscow' platform. However, the MIC Foundation does not use monitoring to ensure compliance with the cluster rules or evaluate the participants' performance, which is typical for organisations, meta-organisations, and traditional cluster initiatives.

Table 11.2 illustrates the features of meta-organisations, as emphasised in existing research, and supplements formal organisations' traditional attributes (Ahrne & Brunsson, 2005, 2008) and shows which of the MIC features are consistent with them.

Table 11.2 The MIC's compliance with meta-organisational features

Meta-organisational features	*Matching the MIC's features*
1. Membership not bound by contracts or employment	+
2. Decision-making based on consensus and not hierarchy	+/– (no consensus in the absence of collective action, hierarchy only in the multi-level decision-making between the MIC Foundation and Supervisory Board)
3. Voluntary self-regulation	+/– (regulation by the MIC Foundation only for funding applicants and beneficiaries)

Meta-organisational features	*Matching the MIC's features*
4. Strong dependence on members	–
5. Spread of confidence and trust among members	+/– (individual support for start-ups is the key task for the MIC Foundation so far)
6. Knowledge transfer, a collective learning	+/– (information flows go through the MIC Foundation, not circulating among the participants)
7. Enhancement of social responsibility	–
8. Low membership fees to attract members	+
9. Collective action	+/– (only in a form of joint projects)
10. System-level (common) goal	–
11. Information rather than products or services as an output	+
12. Combination of formal instruments and a flexible organisational structure for facilitating cooperation	+
13. Organising other organisations	+
14. Using outreach or nudging strategies to persuade new members to join	+

Source: *authors' elaboration based on Ahrne & Brunsson, 2005, 2008; Berkowitz, 2018; Berkowitz & Dumez, 2016; Gulati et al., 2012; Lupova-Henry et al., 2021.*

Discussion and conclusion

The growth of cities and strengthening of urban features call for an evolution of innovation-support mechanisms, including the cluster policy. Urban clusters have a great potential to spread and reinforce agglomeration effects. However, it requires solving a dilemma of cluster policy: whether to focus on a single industry or sector or many related industries.

Our research suggests a case-based theory for justifying a new cluster policy in megapolises. It involves five key features: (1) a large number of participants, (2) open membership for various industries, (3) the use of the digital platform to reduce transaction costs and promote open innovations, (4) openness to companies from other regions and participation of external partners, and (5) financial incentives for cooperation and offering public goods.

Along these lines, we suggest referring to urban clusters as super-clusters. This notion does not imply replacing traditional cluster initiatives but instead launching a common platform for their interaction. As we have seen from the case study, the MIC has all the features of an urban super-cluster. That is mainly due to the 'i.moscow' platform, which helps to promote and involve a significant number of varied members and partners, reduce transaction costs, match localised and external participants, and offer access to support measures and public goods. The MIC's digital platform became an interface facilitating the implementation of innovation promotion policies. It has been used for implementing support measures and providing new digital services such as business acceleration or technological contests, expanding external linkages. They ensure cooperation among business, science, and the city for scaling innovative entrepreneurship. They also cover growing industries (e.g. gaming), state-of-the-art technologies, smart production, sustainable development, and social innovations. The MIC has expanded a set of specific support measures for technology entrepreneurs, such as launching grants for individual and cooperative innovation projects. As a result, there has been an increase in the cluster's membership, industrial diversity, inter-regional partnerships, and sub-clustering.

Our analysis also demonstrates that the MIC is consistent with the key features of meta-organisations. However, there are also important dissimilarities such as the absence of collective decision-making, a common goal, reliance on consensus, and dependence on other members. Some of these differences are due to urban specifics, while others have other natures and would require additional action by the authorities. The future will show whether it is possible and appropriate to resolve them, given the size and diversity of cluster members. In our opinion, it might be relevant to focus on the key areas and projects identified together with the MIC's participants than unite and influence many stakeholders at once. This basic idea of cluster policy needs rethinking and can be addressed through the lens of urban super-clusters. It may also be promising to specify a meta-organisational model in relation to the features of megapolises and clarify the category of collective action in this context.

This study has some limitations, which open up new directions for further research. First, sampling could be extended as we considered only one cluster and one megapolis. Second, a quantitative method could be implemented to process data on the cluster members' activity supplemented by expert interviews. Third, further comparison of the MIC's industrial composition with the sectoral structure of Moscow is needed to agree on the extent to which heterogeneity is an ideal environment for inter-sectoral interactions. Overall, this study could inspire new contributions concerning the role of clusters and digital services in fostering innovation in megapolises. The chapter contains implications for policymakers regarding the potential of clusters in promoting innovations in large cities and for cluster managers regarding the design of support measures and business processes in cluster initiatives.

Acknowledgement

The chapter is based on the study funded by the Basic Research Program of the HSE University.

References

Abashkin, V., Gokhberg, L., Eferin, Y., Ivanova, E., Kutsenko, E., Nechaeva, E., & Tyurtchev, K. (2021). Atlas jekonomicheskoj specializacii regionov Rossii. *National Research University "Higher School of Economics"*. https://doi.org/10.17323/978-5-7598-2379-7

Ahrne, G., & Brunsson, N. (2005). Organizations and meta-organizations. *Scandinavian Journal of Management, 21*(4), 429–449. https://doi.org/10.1016/j.scaman.2005.09.005

Ahrne, G., & Brunsson, N. (2008). *Meta-organizations*. Edward Elgar Publishing. www.e-elgar.com/shop/gbp/meta-organizations-9781847209504.html

Andersson, T., Schwaag-Serger, S., Sorvik, J., & Hansson, E. W. (2004). *The cluster policies whitebook* (Vol. 49). IKED.

Atherton, A., & Johnston, A. (2008). Clusters formation from the "bottomup": A process perspective. In C. Karlsson (Ed.), *Handbook of research on cluster theory* (Vol. 1, pp. 93–113). Edward Elgar Publishing.

Bathelt, H., Malmberg, A., & Maskell, P. (2004). Clusters and knowledge: Local buzz, global pipelines and the process of knowledge creation. *Progress in Human Geography, 28*(1), 31–56. https://doi.org/10.1191/0309132504ph469oa

Beaudry, C., & Schiffauerova, A. (2009). Who's right, Marshall or Jacobs? The localization versus urbanization debate. *Research Policy, 38*(2), 318–337. https://doi.org/10.1016/j.respol.2008.11.010

Bekar, C., & Lipsey, R. G. (2001). Clusters and economic policy. *Canadian Journal of Policy Research, 3*(1), 62–70.

Bell, S. J., Tracey, P., & Heide, J. B. (2009). The organization of regional clusters. *Academy of Management Review, 34*(4), 623–642. https://doi.org/10.5465/amr.2009.44882930

Berkowitz, H. (2018). Meta-organizing firms' capabilities for sustainable innovation: A conceptual framework. *Journal of Cleaner Production, 175*, 420–430. https://doi.org/10.1016/j.jclepro.2017.12.028

Berkowitz, H., Bucheli, M., & Dumez, H. (2017). Collectively designing CSR through meta-organizations: A case study of the oil and gas industry. *Journal of Business Ethics, 143*(4), 753–769. https://doi.org/10.1007/s10551-016-3073-2

Berkowitz, H., Crowder, L. B., & Brooks, C. M. (2020). Organizational perspectives on sustainable ocean governance: A multi-stakeholder, meta-organization model of collective action. *Marine Policy, 118*, 104026. https://doi.org/10.1016/j.marpol.2020.104026

Berkowitz, H., & Dumez, H. (2016). The concept of meta-organization: Issues for management studies. *European Management Review, 13*(2), 149–156. https://doi.org/10.1111/emre.12076

Boos, V. O., Gokhberg L, Islankina, E., Ismagulova, S., Kutsenko, E., Streltsova, E., & Tyurchev, K. (2020). *HSE global cities innovation index: 2020*. Национальный исследовательский университет "Высшая школа экономики". www.elibrary.ru/item.asp?id=45677857

Boschma, R., Balland, P. A., & Vaan, M. (2014). The formation of economic networks: A proximity approach. In A. Torre & F. Wallet (Eds.), *Regional development and proximity relations* (pp. 243–266). Edward Elgar Publishing.

Clark, G. L., Gertler, M. S., & Feldman, M. P. (2003). *The Oxford handbook of economic geography*. Oxford University Press.

Coletti, M. (2010). Technology and industrial clusters: How different are they to manage? *Science and Public Policy, 37*(9), 679–688. https://doi.org/10.3152/030234210X12778118264413

Cooke, P. (1995). Regions, clusters and innovation networks reconsidered. In P. Cooke (Ed.), *The rise of the Rustbelt* (pp. 3–16). UCL Press.

Dewulf, A., & Elbers, W. (2018). Power in and over cross-sector partnerships: Actor strategies for shaping collective decisions. *Administrative Sciences, 8*(3), 43. https://doi.org/10.3390/admsci8030043

Dobbs, R., Smit, S., Remes, J., Manyika, J., Roxburgh, C., & Restrepo, A. (2011). Urban world: Mapping the economic power of cities. *McKinsey Global Institute, 62*. www.

mckinsey.com/~/media/mckinsey/featured%20insights/urbanization/urban%20world/mgi_urban_world_mapping_economic_power_of_cities_full_report.pdf

Eggertsson, T. (1990). *Economic behavior and institutions: Principles of neoinstitutional economics.* Cambridge University Press. https://doi.org/10.1017/CBO9780511609404

Eisenhardt, K. M., & Graebner, M. E. (2007). Theory building from cases: Opportunities and challenges. *Academy of Management Journal, 50*(1), 25–32. https://doi.org/10.5465/amj.2007.24160888

ESCA. (2022). *Cluster management excellence.* European Secretariat for Cluster Analysis. www.cluster-analysis.org/cluster-management-excellence

Feldman, M. P., & Audretsch, D. B. (1999). Innovation in cities: Science-based diversity, specialization and localized competition. *European Economic Review, 43*(2), 409–429. https://doi.org/10.1016/s0014-2921(98)00047-6

Florida, R., Adler, P., & Mellander, C. (2017). The city as innovation machine. *Regional Studies, 51*(1), 86–96. https://doi.org/10.1080/00343404.2016.1255324

Franco, S., Murciego, A., Salado, J. P., Sisti, E., & Wilson, J. (2021). *European cluster panorama: Leveraging clusters for resilient, green and digital regional economies.* Publications Office of the European Union. https://clustercollaboration.eu/sites/default/files/2021-12/European_Cluster_Panorama_Report_0.pdf

Garaudel, P. (2020). Exploring meta-organizations' diversity and agency: A meta-organizational perspective on global union federations. *Scandinavian Journal of Management, 36*(1), 101094. https://doi.org/10.1016/j.scaman.2020.101094

Glaeser, E. L. (1998). Are cities dying? *Journal of Economic Perspectives, 12*(2), 139–160. https://doi.org/10.1257/jep.12.2.139

Glaeser, E. L. (2011). *Triumph of the city: How urban spaces make us human.* Pan Macmillan.

Glynn, M. A. (2008). Beyond constraint: How institutions enable identities. In R. Greenwood, C. Oliver, T. B. Lawrence, & R. E. Meyer (Eds.), *The SAGE handbook of organizational institutionalism* (pp. 413–430). SAGE Publications Ltd. https://doi.org/10.4135/9781849200387

Graddy, E. A., & Chen, B. (2006). Influences on the size and scope of networks for social service delivery. *Journal of Public Administration Research and Theory, 16*(4), 533–552. https://doi.org/10.1093/jopart/muj005

Gulati, R., Wohlgezogen, F., & Zhelyazkov, P. (2012). The two facets of collaboration: Cooperation and coordination in strategic alliances. *Academy of Management Annals, 6*(1), 531–583. https://doi.org/10.5465/19416520.2012.691646

Hinds, P., Kiesler, S. B., & Kiesler, S. (2002). *Distributed work.* MIT Press.

Hospers, G.-J. (2003). Creative cities: Breeding places in the knowledge economy. *Knowledge, Technology & Policy, 16*(3), 143–162. https://doi.org/10.1007/s12130-003-1037-1

Huggins, R. (1998). Local business co-operation and training and enterprise councils: The development of inter-firm networks. *Regional Studies, 32*(9), 813–826. https://doi.org/10.1080/00343409850117979

Innovation and Technology Commission. (2022). *ITC–InnoHK clusters.* www.itc.gov.hk/en/technological_infrastructure/innohk_clusters.html

Islankina, E., Kutsenko, E., Filina, F., Pankevich, V., Popova, E., & Moiseieva, V. (2019). *Biomedical clusters worldwide: Success factors and best practices.* Национальный исследовательский университет "Высшая школа экономики". www.elibrary.ru/item.asp?id=45578751

Johansson, B., & Forslund, U. (2008). The analysis of location, colocation and urbanization economies. In C. Karlsson (Ed.), *Handbook of research on cluster theory* (Vol. 1, pp. 39–66). Edward Elgar Publishing Ltd.

Ketels, C. (2013). Recent research on competitiveness and clusters: What are the implications for regional policy? *Cambridge Journal of Regions, Economy and Society*, *6*(2), 269–284. https://doi.org/10.1093/cjres/rst008

KICOX. (2010). *The industrial complex cluster program of Korea. Clustercollaboration.eu.* Korea Industrial Complex Corporation Cluster. https://clustercollaboration.eu/sites/default/files/international_cooperation/the_industrial_complex_cluster_program_of_korea_2010.compressed.pdf

Kogut, B., & Zander, U. (1996). What firms do? Coordination, identity, and learning. *Organization Science*, 7(5), 502–518. https://doi.org/10.1287/orsc.7.5.502

Kowalski, A. M., & Marcinkowski, A. (2014). Clusters versus cluster initiatives, with focus on the ICT sector in Poland. *European Planning Studies*, *22*(1), 20–45. https://doi.org/10.1080/09654313.2012.731040

Lämmer-Gamp, T., Meier zu Kôcker, G., & Alslev Christensen, T. (2011). *Clusters are individuals: Creating economic growth through cluster policies for cluster management excellence.* Danish Ministry of Science, Innovation and Higher Education. https://books.google.be/books?id=kuxItwAACAAJ

Laur, I., Klofsten, M., & Bienkowska, D. (2012). Catching regional development dreams: A study of cluster initiatives as intermediaries. *European Planning Studies*, *20*(11), 1909–1921. https://doi.org/10.1080/09654313.2012.725161

Lee, A. S. (1989). Case studies as natural experiments. *Human Relations*, *42*(2), 117–137. https://doi.org/10.1177/001872678904200202

Lindqvist, G., Ketels, C., & Sölvell, Ö. (2013). *The cluster initiative greenbook 2.0.* Ivory Tower Publishers.

Lorenzen, M. (2009). Creativity in context: Content, cost, chance, and collection in the organization of the film industry. In A. C. Pratt & P. Jeffcutt (Eds.), *Creativity and innovation in the cultural economy* (pp. 93–118). Routledge.

Lorenzen, M., & Frederiksen, L. (2008). Why do cultural industries cluster? Localization, urbanization, products and projects. In P. Cooke & R. Lazzeretti (Eds.), *Creative cities, cultural clusters and local economic development* (pp. 155–179). Edward Elgar Publishing.

Lupova-Henry, E., Blili, S., & Dal Zotto, C. (2021). Designing organised clusters as social actors: A meta-organisational approach. *Journal of Organization Design*, *10*(1), 35–54. https://doi.org/10.1007/s41469-021-00092-5

Lupova-Henry, E., & Dotti, N. F. (this volume). Clusters as collective actors and agents of change for new sustainable path development. In E. Lupova-Henry & N. F. Dotti (Eds.), *Clusters and sustainable regional development: A meta-organisational approach.* Routledge.

Marshall, A. (1920). *Principles of Economics* (8th ed.). Macmillan.

McCann, P. (2008). Agglomeration economics. In C. Karlsson (Ed.), *Handbook of research on cluster theory* (Vol. 1, pp. 23–33). Edward Elgar Publishing.

Meyer, R. E., & Höllerer, M. A. (2014). Does institutional theory need redirecting? *Journal of Management Studies*, *51*(7), 1221–1233. https://doi.org/10.1111/joms.12089

Moscow Innovation Cluster. (2021a). *About the cluster–I.moscow.* Moscow Innovation Cluster (MIC). https://i.moscow/o-klastere

Moscow Innovation Cluster. (2021b). *Inter-sectoral clusters.- i.moscow.* Moscow Innovation Cluster (MIC). https://i.moscow/intersectoral_clusters/

Moscow Innovation Cluster. (2021c). *MIC-Zhongguancun Russian-Chinese technology competition–I.moscow.* Moscow Innovation Cluster (MIC). https://i.moscow/technology_competition

Moscow Innovation Cluster. (2021d). *Support measures.* Moscow Innovation Cluster (MIC). https://i.moscow/measure-supports

Moscow Innovation Cluster. (2022). *Projects and needs*. Moscow Innovation Cluster (MIC). https://i.moscow/proekty-i-potrebnosti

Neffke, F., Henning, M., Boschma, R., Lundquist, K.-J., & Olander, L.-O. (2011). The dynamics of agglomeration externalities along the life cycle of industries. *Regional Studies, 45*(1), 49–65. https://doi.org/10.1080/00343401003596307

North, D. C. (1987). Institutions, transaction costs and economic growth. *Economic Inquiry, 5*(3), 419–428. https://doi.org/10.1111/j.1465-7295.1987.tb00750.x

Olson, M. (1965). *The logic of collective action: Public goods and the theory of groups*. Harvard University Press.

Owen-Smith, J., & Powell, W. W. (2004). Knowledge networks as channels and conduits: The effects of spillovers in the Boston biotechnology community. *Organization Science, 15*, 2–21. https://doi.org/10.1287/orsc.1030.0054

Porter, M. E. (1998). Clusters and the new economics of competition. In A. J. Scott (Ed.), *Global city-regions: Trends, theory, policy* (pp. 139–157). Oxford University Press.

Remneland-Wikhamn, B., & Knights, D. (2012). Transaction cost economics and open innovation: Implications for theory and practice. *Creativity and Innovation Management, 21*(3), 277–289. https://doi.org/10.1111/j.1467-8691.2012.00639.x

Richardson, H. W. (1995). Economies and diseconomies of agglomeration. In *Urban agglomeration and economic growth* (pp. 123–155). Springer.

Schretlen, J.-H., Dervojeda, K., Jansen, W., & Schaffmeister, B. (2011). *Uncovering excellence in cluster management*. PricewaterhouseCooper. www.pwc.com/gx/en/psrc/pdf/cluster_management.pdf

Scott, A. J. (2001). Globalization and the rise of city-regions. *European Planning Studies, 9*(7), 813–826. https://doi.org/10.1080/09654310120079788

Sölvell, Ö., Ketels, C., & Lindqvist, G. (2003). *The cluster initiative greenbook*. Ivory Tower Publishers.

Srikanth, K., & Puranam, P. (2010). Integrating distributed work: Comparing task design, communication, and tacit coordination mechanisms. *Strategic Management Journal, 32*(8), 849–875. https://doi.org/10.1002/smj.908

Storper, M., & Venables, A. J. (2004). Buzz: Face-to-face contact and the urban economy. *Journal of Economic Geography, 4*(4), 351–370. https://doi.org/10.1093/jnlecg/lbh027

TCI Network. (2022). *Where the experts in clusters and innovation ecosystems interact, learn and get inspired*. www.tci-network.org/

Tyurchev, K. S. (2021). Management of innovative systems: From national to local level. *Public Administration Issues, 4*, 185–206. https://doi.org/10.17323/1999-5431-2021-0-4-185-206

United Nations. (2018). *The world's cities in 2018*. United Nations. https://digitallibrary.un.org/record/3799524

UN Secretary-General for Digital Cooperation. (2020). *Roadmap for digital cooperation [Report of the UN Secretary-General]*. UN Secretary-General for Digital Cooperation. www.un.org/techenvoy/sites/www.un.org.techenvoy/files/general/Roadmap_for_Digital_Cooperation_9June.pdf

Uzzi, B. (1997). Social structure and competition in interfirm networks: The paradox of embeddedness. *Administrative Science Quarterly, 42*, 35–67. https://doi.org/10.2307/2393808

van den Berg, L., & Braun, E. (2017). *Growth clusters in European metropolitan cities: A comparative analysis of cluster dynamics in the cities of Amsterdam, Eindhoven, Helsinki, Leipzig, Lyons, Manchester, Munich, Rotterdam and Vienna*. Routledge.

van den Berg, L., Braun, E., & van Winden, W. (2001). Growth clusters in European cities: An integral approach. *Urban Studies, 38*(1), 185–205. https://doi.org/10.1080/00420980124001

Vang-Lauridsen, J., & Chaminade, C. (2007). Global-local linkages, spillovers and cultural clusters: Theoretical and empirical insights from an exploratory study of Toronto's film cluster. *Industry & Innovation, 14*(4), Article 4. http://lup.lub.lu.se/record/950123

Viachka, A. (2013). *Comparing firms' associational strategies across sectors and locations: Cluster initiatives as meta-organizations.* Stockholm School of Economics.

Wheeler, C. H. (2003). Evidence on agglomeration economies, diseconomies, and growth. *Journal of Applied Econometrics, 18*(1), 79–104. https://doi.org/10.1002/jae.678

Zhou, Y., & Xin, T. (2003). An innovative region in China: Interaction between multinational corporations and local firms in a high-tech cluster in Beijing. *Economic Geography, 79*(2), 129–152. https://doi.org/10.1111/j.1944-8287.2003.tb00205.x

12 Meta-organisations and clusters in climate regimes

Abrar CHAUDHURY and Carolina STECCA DOUEK

Introduction

Tackling climate change is one of humanity's most pressing issues in the twenty-first century. Populations in developing countries that rely on sectors sensitive to climate change have been the ones most affected by rising temperatures, droughts, flooding, and extreme weather events (IPCC, 2014). The urgency for a coordinated global climate approach to limit global warming to below 2-degree Celsius, agreed under the 2015 Paris Agreement by 196 nations, has necessitated collective action from a range of public, private, civil, and community actors. These are expected to operate under a common climate regime and offer local solutions for their vulnerable populations. Understanding how different independent actors organise themselves and interact with others within a global effort is crucial to delivering appropriate climate action.

In order to study the independent activities of the global climate regime actors, this chapter applies the meta-organisation and clusters frameworks. The main objective of meta-organisations is to facilitate collective action through its members (Ahrne & Brunsson, 2005; Gulati et al., 2012; Spillman, 2018). Moreover, the meta-organisational framework is conducive to the governance of sustainable innovation (Berkowitz, 2018). However, meta-organisations' inherent characteristics as 'autonomous actors with autonomous actors as members' (Ahrne et al., 2016, p. 7), especially in global regimes, can limit their ability to drive collective action. Indeed, the meta-organisational challenges include loose organisation, competing interests, and members' independence as well as potential conflicts of interest among members, whose activities 'are also shaped by other structural factors and actors' (Chaudhury et al., 2016, p. 247). These factors limit meta-organisations' ability to manage a smooth transition based on unified objectives effectively.

This chapter argues that these challenges of collective action in meta-organisations can be alleviated if actors are organised in multiple clusters and sub-clusters within the meta-organisation. Traditionally, clusters are considered geographical agglomerations of organisations benefiting from proximity and continued social interactions to gain specialisation and competitive advantage over their non-cluster peers (McCann & Folta, 2011; Porter, 1998). Recent

DOI: 10.4324/9781003215066-16

research goes beyond the geographic advantage and explores the evolution of clusters and how clusters renew and reconfigure relations over time to develop new configurations and pathways (Harris, 2021; MacKinnon et al., 2019). We build on Harris (2021) to study emerging organisational clusters in the global climate regime. We show that actors in global climate regimes participate in multiple clusters bringing together capabilities, structures, and networks needed for action. At the same time, their interactions are shaped by shared goals of the meta-organisation and the broad scope of the climate challenge. Each cluster has its unique objectives and characteristics – for example focus on particular climate change-related themes or geography. The clusters further interact with other clusters and create dynamic action pathways for the cluster organisations to follow. We capture this dynamic configuration through a novel concept of 'cluster pathway', which helps explain the different approaches by cluster organisations to climate action and the varying outcomes. While these are initially created to address the requirements of the meta-organisation, they evolve independently beyond the meta-organisation and, in turn, adopt unique cluster pathways influencing the project design and implementation.

This chapter uses the case of the Green Climate Fund (GCF) to study global climate action within a meta-organisational framework. GCF was conceived in 2010 and became operational in 2015 under Article 11 of the United Nations Framework Convention on Climate Change (UNFCCC). Its mandate is to finance the transition of developing countries to low-carbon and climate-resilient pathways in alignment with the UN Paris Agreement goals. GCF is the largest dedicated public climate fund. It operates through intermediary organisations – accredited entities (AEs) – to finance climate projects in developing countries in line with their specific strategies (Green Climate Fund, 2021). The AEs in GCF are a deliberate introduction to develop local implementation capability, limit direct involvement by GCF in local activity, promote a transparent distribution of funding, and set up a mechanism of accountability and transparency. Currently, GCF has 113 AEs, including private or public, non-governmental, sub-national, national, regional, or international organisations. Each AE is an independent entity. They are very different from large multilateral development banks, national financial institutions, or local non-governmental organisations, with similar goals of accelerating climate action in developing countries.

Based on this financing operational model, we argue that GCF operates as a meta-organisation or an 'organisation of organisations' (Ahrne & Brunsson, 2005; Berkowitz & Dumez, 2016; Gulati et al., 2012) funding climate action through its constituent AE organisations. We further argue that the AEs, within the GCF meta-organisation structure and guidelines, operate as clusters of organisations (Porter, 1998) motivated by a common goal of transitioning developing countries to a sustainable low-carbon and climate-resilient pathway. Even though the AEs work towards a common transition goal under the GCF meta-organisation, we demonstrate that the GCF-funded projects are influenced by the different clusters the AEs are part of, leading to distinct development and implementation pathways. The 'cluster pathway' allows us to capture the differentiated approach and examine how GCF projects materialise across different geographies and through different actors. Early lessons from meta-organisation and 'cluster pathway' approach are beneficial for GCF, AEs, and developing countries to set up robust projects against the backdrop of constraints and opportunities that clusters offer, especially as GCF ramps up its financing in future.

Despite progress on the global climate science-policy dialogue, there is too little research on how clusters of climate finance organisations in a global system interact within a common meta-organisational framework and its implication for climate action. This chapter focuses on the ways that the AE organisations operate across multiple clusters and 'translate' and 'do the work' to support climate action locally. Specifically, it asks how the GCF-funded projects are impacted by the cluster pathway AEs follow. Viewing GCF as a meta-organisation allows for a systematic analysis of the structural features of the GCF meta-organisation and the AE clusters using established analytical methods. We offer fresh theoretical and methodological insights into how clusters operate and interact in global regimes to develop local solutions.

The rest of the chapter is organised as follows: first, we provide a theoretical frame for developing the novel 'cluster pathway' approach and its application in global regimes under the meta-organisation framework. It is followed by a brief overview of the methodology used and an analysis of the existing clusters operating under GCF in the global climate regime. It concludes with an exploration of the interactions between the clusters and the meta-organisation within the global climate regime. We contribute to the cluster and meta-organisation literature by demonstrating how actors develop capabilities and structures and networks, both through interactions within clusters and by building linkages across multiple clusters, creating distinct action pathways.

Theoretical background: meta-organisation and cluster pathways

This section provides the theoretical background for developing the cluster pathway approach under the meta-organisation frame applied to the GCF case. We posit meta-organisation and clusters as complementary lenses to view collective action in global climate change regimes. However, as discussed, meta-organisation's loose organisation, competing interests, and independence of its members may not translate into effective local action (Berkowitz & Dumez, 2016; Chaudhury et al., 2016). We demonstrate that a multi-actor and multi-level governance approach (Cash et al., 2006) encourages actors to organise themselves in multiple clusters and create 'cluster pathways', bringing together appropriate capabilities and networks to translate and operationalise shared goals of the meta-organisation. This approach is in line with research that has demonstrated the ability of the meta-organisational framework to help align multiple geographically dispersed clusters around a common sustainability goal (see Nadegger & Dobusch, this volume).

Complexity is a major challenge for actors working in sustainability transition, and no single entity can enable this transition (Chaudhury et al., 2017; Ferraro et al., 2015). Entities in this space have to operate beyond their organisational boundaries and capabilities and take an inter-organisational and network approach for collective action to interact with others that bring resources, knowledge, and skills for implementation (Bodin & Crona, 2009; Chaudhury et al., 2017; Porac et al., 1995; Powell et al., 1996; Ritter & Gemünden, 2003; Wasserman, 1994). However, collective action at a global scale, especially in climate change, is complex because the many actors' interests, motivations, and capabilities require alignment (Newell et al., 2012). For example global funding for climate action is skewed towards mitigation because impacts can be measured as opposed to adaptation funding that is harder to measure but is demanded by developing countries (Chaudhury, 2020). Getting many actors to collaborate globally requires robust frameworks and incentives that are not always obvious.

Unlike networks that focus on the broader relations of organisations, clusters offer a more profound perspective for studying climate action through the collective activities of the organisations in a particular field. Michael E. Porter defines clusters as 'concentrations of interconnected companies and institutions in a particular field' (Porter, 1998, p. 78). Traditional cluster studies focus on organisations operating in a particular geography or sector, such as the Silicon Valley ecosystem or the Detroit automobile sector. These bring different organisational actors together to create improved economic opportunity, benefit from economies of scale, and enable sectoral transformation and policy alignment (McCann & Folta, 2011; Porter, 1998). Many of these traditional clusters operate locally and benefit from the proximity of other organisations. With global climate regimes, we see the emergence of a novel cluster of organisations that interact under a commonly agreed agenda set by the meta-organisations and implement climate activities locally (Chaudhury et al., 2016). These organisations bring resources, knowledge, and skills for local climate action. However, they are not viewed as a cluster under traditional definitions because they operate in different geographies to meet global goals and national priorities.

Clusters, however, overtime can become specialised such that knowledge and networks become homogenous, which inhibits innovation and transformation (Menzel & Fornahl, 2009) required to tackle the climate challenge. The literature highlights the dynamic nature of clusters and their ability to renew and evolve to meet their objectives (Menzel & Fornahl, 2009). Moreover, through collective action and policy-led initiatives from the meta-organisations, clusters can create new or renew existing pathways (Martin & Martin, 2017; Miörner & Trippl, 2017). Path creation and new path development concept (Hassink et al., 2019) is defined as the 'emergence of new industries and economic activities in regions' (MacKinnon et al., 2019, p. 114). Harris (2021, p. 437) further introduces the concept of cluster institutional configuration, 'defined as the combination of shared goals, behaviours and relations between cluster actors involved in a cluster [to understand how] actors drive clusters through their evolutionary trajectories'. He argues that clusters do not emerge by random chance but from actors' agency. We build on the path development and cluster institutional configurations concepts to trace the role of clusters in climate regimes. However, we argue that because of the urgency of the climate challenge and the need for diverse capabilities, organisations build heterogeneous clusters through the evolution or renewal of clusters and participation in different clusters. We label this configuration as 'cluster pathway' – that is the participation of actors in multiple clusters to develop necessary capabilities and networks for climate action, shaped by the meta-organisation they are part of. Once established, these cluster pathways can influence climate action beyond the meta-organisation. However, this can also create tensions with the meta-organisation. We see clusters as overlapping and interconnected through a complex system of actors, structures, and networks. These clusters are also dynamic as new actors join, populations of organisations change, and power relations shift. Understanding this dynamic configuration of actors, spread across many clusters, is important to reveal how climate action diffuses locally and the variations to project design and implementation that occur.

Figure 12.1 shows our conception of the cluster pathway under the meta-organisation. The clusters and sub-clusters A (1,2), B (1,2), and C (1,2) emerge

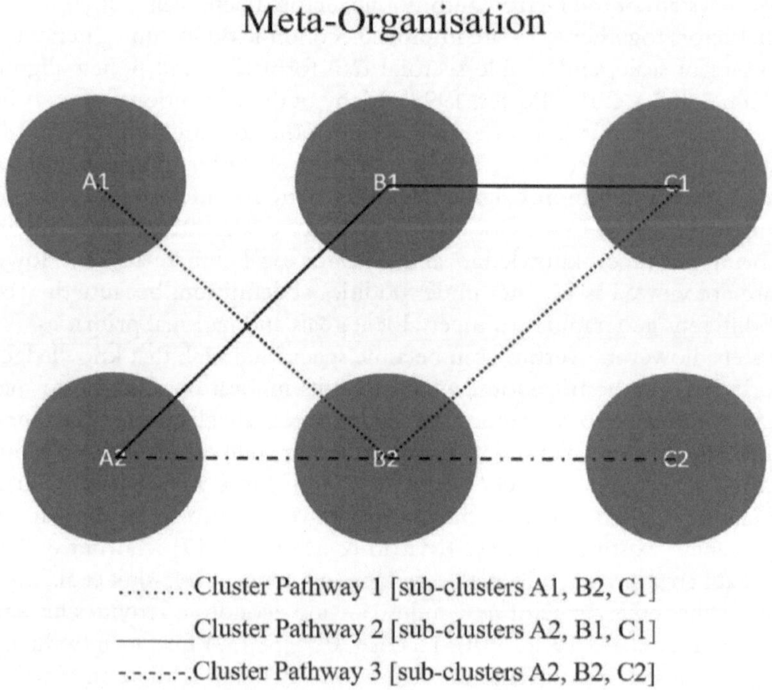

Figure 12.1 Cluster pathway under the meta-organisation

Source: authors

to comply with the meta-organisation's governance and operational requirements. Actors participate in multiple clusters to develop the appropriate capabilities, structures, and networks for action. We exemplify this with three cluster pathways, although there can be several permutations of pathways. In cluster pathway 1, actors are part of sub-clusters A1, B2, and C2, which are different from cluster pathway 2 represented through sub-clusters A2, B1, and C1. Each cluster has its individual properties and dynamics that, when combined with other clusters, give rise to distinct pathway characteristics that are important for actors to recognise and navigate for successful outcomes. Actors can also switch to other clusters to meet the meta-organisation's requirements. New clusters can form, and others may become redundant, which adds to the complexity of the pathway. Tracing and analysing cluster pathways are essential for effective outcomes and learning.

We thus view GCF as a meta-organisation and AEs and other entities that are part of its ecosystem as clusters that operate in distinct cluster pathways but are united by a global climate agenda. This view offers fresh insights into how GCF and AEs support countries' transitions to low-carbon and resilient pathways under the GCF meta-organisation. AEs sit between GCF and nation-states to deliver climate action. To bring the right organisational capabilities and networks to tackle the climate challenge, AEs form part of multiple clusters based on the organisational form, climate themes, and geographies in which they operate. This creates distinct 'cluster pathways' to reconcile the stringent and multiple requirements of GCF and the needs of the nation-states they serve. While the clusters originate from GCF, the pathways are curated by the AEs beyond the GCF meta-organisation to meet the funding and project requirements. These cluster pathways may benefit some AEs over others resulting in varying quality of approach and outcomes. For example international AEs can leverage funding actors in their networks without benefiting other cluster AEs. Also, the clusters are not static: new actors can join on the invitation of the AEs, or more AEs can be added by GCF. These dynamics can change the characteristics of the clusters and open new pathways or make existing ones redundant. The following section applies the cluster pathway framework to our GCF case study.

Case study: Green Climate Fund

GCF was set up as an independent public body to fund climate action in developing countries through financial resources provided by industrialised countries to compensate for their historical emissions. It takes a country ownership approach by requesting projects from countries to be presented through the AEs and building local implementation capacity. In reality, GCF acts as a meta-organisation and exerts significant influence over the AEs. It sets detailed guidelines and rules for deciding which entities are accredited and can access funding, the themes eligible for funding, the types of projects preferred, the geographies where projects are prioritised, and the financial structures through which funding is offered. GCF's stringent accreditation and funding rules cascade to the AEs, shaping their operation and project design. As of 15 November 2021, GCF had approved 190 projects with a direct funding outlay of USD 10.1 billion.

The GCF ecosystem goes beyond direct AE intermediaries. Following the country ownership principle, GCF requests each country seeking funding to develop a climate strategy in which local priorities, including sectors and projects, are highlighted. Moreover, every new GCF project must be approved by the National Designated Authority (NDA), the focal public entity in the country for GCF. To complement their capabilities, AEs can engage other executing entities (project developers, consultants, advisers, experts) in the design, planning, and implementation of the projects. Figure 12.2 depicts a simplified GCF funding approval process, demonstrating how these different organisations operate and interact under the GCF meta-organisation.

Additional entities can be part of the GCF meta-organisation. For instance these entities can be non-governmental and grassroots organisations advocating for specific climate priorities; local authorities having differing agendas from national ones; consulting companies filling the information gaps on climate impacts and scientific data; and specialised service providers providing reports with high-level detail, as demanded by GCF. Organisations involved in creating GCF projects sometimes do not interact with GCF directly; however, multiple interactions happen among entities, such as discussions about the local priorities the government wants to advance. At the same time, NDAs are also directly

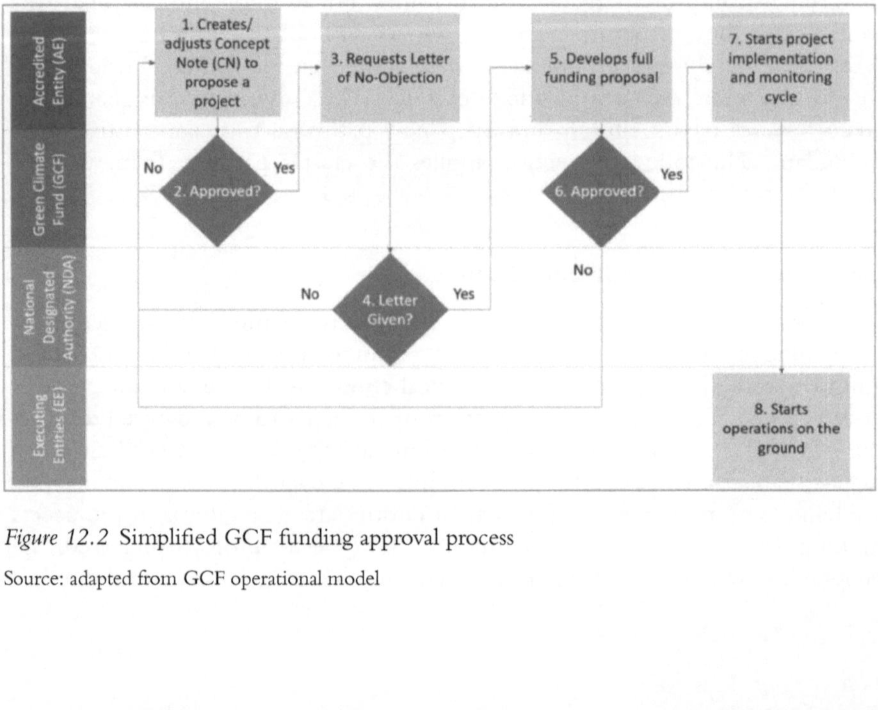

Figure 12.2 Simplified GCF funding approval process

Source: adapted from GCF operational model

influenced by GCF through the creation of a list of priority areas for investment. This structure not only yields significant control to AEs to influence local activities but also is a source of many challenges and debates.

Methods

This chapter applies a mixed-methods approach of qualitative and quantitative analysis (King et al., 1994; Silverman, 2013). The qualitative element comprised over 40 semi-structured interviews of approximately 60 minutes each with AEs, GCF team members, NDAs, and other executing entities supporting the project. These entities are based globally across Asia, Africa, Europe, North America, Latin America, and Australasia. Several expert interviews were also conducted with project developers outside the GCF ecosystem. The interviews focused on the motivation and activities of the AEs in GCF-funded project development and execution, their relation and interactions with GCF and other AEs, the influence of GCF on their operations, and their interactions with other organisations. Similarly, interviews with GCF team members looked at the role and relationship of GCF with AEs and their influence on these organisations. The interviews were supplemented with data from a detailed review of funded project proposals, GCF reports and guides, and published and grey literature on GCF and climate finance.

Analysis and discussion

Clusters in GCF meta-organisation

Based on the data from our interviews and literature review, within the GCF climate funding landscape, we see the emergence of three distinct clusters that we label as strategic, thematic, and geographic (see Table 12.1). These clusters shape and influence how projects are designed, funded, and implemented. Although AEs have a significant responsibility in these clusters, they are not the only actors forming them. AEs operate within the narrow sphere of the GCF meta-organisation influence and are the point of contact bringing these guidelines towards other cluster participants. These clusters, in return, can yield significant independent and collective power to shape climate activities globally and locally. These clusters are further explored with examples in this section.

While AEs may not formally identify themselves as being part of a specific cluster, their role and activities are cluster-based. Every AE, executing entity, and NDA within the GCF meta-organisation is part of one or more strategic, thematic, and geographic clusters – it will then interact within and through clusters to shape the final version of the GCF project it is involved with. Viewing these as clusters offers important insights into their collective influence and action. We discuss the different types of clusters and their interactions here.

Table 12.1 Comparison of clusters within GCF meta-organisation

	Strategic cluster	*Thematic cluster*	*Geographic cluster*
Sub-clusters	Direct access entities International access entities	Adaptation Mitigation Both	Priority regions (Small Island, Least Developed, and African states) Other developing countries
Member Organisations	Accredited entities, national designated authority, executing entities, consultants other project organisations	Accredited entities, thematic experts, thematic networks, academics	Accredited entities, national governments, national entities, interest groups, experts
Governing Structure	GCF Meta-organisation	Global climate regime	UN system, nation-states

Strategic cluster

Presently, GCF has 113 AEs comprising a broad cluster of private, public, non-governmental, sub-national, national, regional, and international bodies and range from large global financial institutions, multilateral organisations, government ministries, private banks to local NGOs, each bringing its own set of organisational expertise, operational structure, and networks for developing and implementing climate projects. At a strategic level, the AEs operate in two distinct clusters – 71 direct access entities (DAEs) and 42 international access entities (IAEs) based on their activities' organisational setup and geographical scope. The DAEs are sub-national, national, or regional organisations nominated by the country's NDAs and operating within a specific national geography or region. The IAEs represent United Nations agencies, global multilateral, bilateral, international financial institutions, and international NGOs that bring a wide range of global expertise and co-financing opportunities for projects that cross borders and thematic areas. The strategic cluster also includes multiple organisations invited by the AEs to participate in GCF-funded projects. The AEs curate this cluster, notably comprising consultants (for project development support), NDA (for project no-objection), executing entities (for project implementation), financial institutions (for co-financing opportunities), research institutions (for project analysis), civil society organisations (for on-ground project support), and other organisations (for allied support). AEs may take up all or some roles, with many working with multiple organisations in the GCF project cycle.

AEs in each cluster confront similar operational challenges. The DAEs, for instance, need to be nominated by developing country NDAs and have to work closely with national governments and local communities to develop projects. The IAEs, with their global scope and expertise, work across multiple geographies and themes, bring external resources to supplement the GCF funding, and have more technical capacity, on average, to propose more complex projects. The IAEs also collaborate and bring knowledge beyond the GCF sphere to support climate action, making them an attractive option for GCF to fund. For example the International Development Finance Club (IDFC), a group of 26 organisations, joined forces to implement the Paris Agreement agendas. Out of the 26 members, 10 are GCF's AEs. The DAEs, on the other hand, with their localised focus, lack such concrete collaboration and learning opportunities, although some are part of south-to-south and other local networks. It is interesting to note that, theoretically, part of the mandate of GCF's IAEs is to help increase the capacity of DAEs – which would suggest that stronger bonds between these two types of clusters need to be created. Nevertheless, based on interviews, it can be inferred that greater collaboration occurs within groups than between them. This finding reinforces the idea that, although these clusters are not geographic, significant commonalities generated by GCF's agenda-setting power create a cluster dynamic within them.

Thematic cluster

The AEs operate across two key thematic climate clusters of mitigation (reducing emissions) and adaptation (increasing resilience). Some AEs operate on both cross-cutting themes of mitigation and adaptation. Of the total approved funding, 14 per cent is dedicated to adaptation, 57 per cent to mitigation, and 29 per cent to cross-cutting projects. The GCF prioritises eight specific action themes (four each under mitigation and adaptation clusters): Mitigation – 1) energy generation and access; 2) transport; 3) buildings, cities, industries, and appliances; and 4) forest and land use. Adaptation – 1) health, food, and water security; 2) infrastructure and built environment; 3) livelihoods of people and communities; and 4) ecosystems and ecosystem services. It sets specific rules and guidelines for the thematic clusters. For mitigation, the focus is on CO_2 emissions reduction, and for adaptation, it is the number of lives benefited. Both the DAE and IAE clusters develop projects under these thematic clusters. However, expertise among the thematic mitigation and adaptation clusters is uneven. Mitigation with its global appeal in developed economies and a tangible metric of CO_2 equivalent have attracted significantly more private investment than adaptation (Chaudhury, 2020; CPI, 2019), which is also the case within GCF, despite the commitment to an equal funding split between the two themes. The IAE cluster brings significant external investments and expertise to mitigation, while adaptation efforts remain challenging for both clusters due to a lack of acceptable metrics. AEs within these clusters also interact in theme-based activities. For example separate thematic conferences are held for mitigation and adaptation, where AEs participate in a specific theme, with some overlapping participation by IAEs with their cross-cutting interests and capabilities.

Interestingly, an AE's focus on the thematic cluster (mitigation or adaptation) is usually associated with the work that the AE focused on prior to creating

GCF. Naturally, organisations that focus on generating renewable energy, for example, are more comfortable pursuing projects that can be classified as mitigation-only projects. On the other hand, organisations that focus on biodiversity conservation have historically promoted greater engagement of local populations in remote regions and tend to have a more adaptation-focused approach. This difference creates siloed expertise with limited opportunities for engagement across thematic clusters. The difficulty of accurately measuring the impact of adaptation-focused projects has also been a significant limitation for more AEs receiving funds for these.

Geographic cluster

Along with the focus on the thematic clusters, AEs develop projects in geographic clusters prioritised by GCF to support the most vulnerable countries under the guidance of the Paris Agreement. These prioritised geographic clusters comprise the Least Developed Countries (LDC), Small Island Developing States (SIDS), and the African States. GCF has committed to spending 50 per cent of the total adaptation funding for projects in these three geographic clusters. Countries within each geographic cluster share common climatic challenges, such as rising sea levels in the SIDs or high poverty rates in LDCs. Their populations have a low capacity to adapt to the growing threats of climate change (Adger et al., 2003). AEs within the three geographic clusters interact beyond the GCF domain and have active representation at international negotiations to generate a collective demand for action. Accordingly, the AEs actively develop projects in these prioritised geographic clusters and benefit from simplified approval procedures and enhanced support in accessing financial resources dedicated by GCF.

Cluster pathways: how do cluster characteristics shape projects?

The AE is part of each GCF project's strategic, thematic, and geographic cluster. Each cluster with its distinct characteristics and priorities shapes how the project is conceived, funded, organised, and implemented, which creates a distinct cluster pathway. Its characteristics are, in turn, shaped by those of the individual clusters. Evaluating projects without considering the influence of the different clusters on the project would offer an incomplete picture. For example a DAE may develop an adaptation project for an LDC country, working with the NDA and other ministries, distinct from an IAE developing an adaptation project in SIDS co-financed by its resources. As a result, AE projects progressing through different cluster pathways are influenced by the strength of the strategic AEs, participation of other organisations, debates around thematic goals for climate action, and priorities within geographic clusters. Further, the same AE can be part of a different cluster pathway – for instance if it moves from an adaptation to a mitigation project in a different country. This difference in cluster pathways can be instrumental in how the project progresses.

Figure 12.3 highlights the process through which projects are created and how different clusters influence the project characteristics. It illustrates four different projects led by AEs that follow standard GCF investment guidelines and are shaped by national contexts, as represented by the two grey columns on each side of the figure. Despite a common global agenda, the intrinsic characteristics of the cluster pathway, however, influence the project's final design. Every AE belongs to three dimensions of clusters: strategic, thematic, and geographic. Take, for example, AE 1 in Figure 12.3. That AE is an IAE (bottom-left part of the circle), focused on adaption (upper-part of the circle) and operating in a priority region (bottom-right part of the circle). These characteristics will influence the final shape of Project 1. The four projects have different shapes and colours to represent the variations in final projects generated by the influences of the clusters to that an AE belongs. We can analyse the thematic cluster differences to understand better how final projects may differ. If an AE specialises in mitigation or only has the capabilities to create such projects, it is unlikely to get involved with adaptation, even where this is the country's priority.

The same idea can be reflected from another point of view. Each organisation that is part of GCF's ecosystem will be a part of different clusters. The way these organisations interact inside each cluster and with the adjacent clusters will impact the final project design and outcomes.

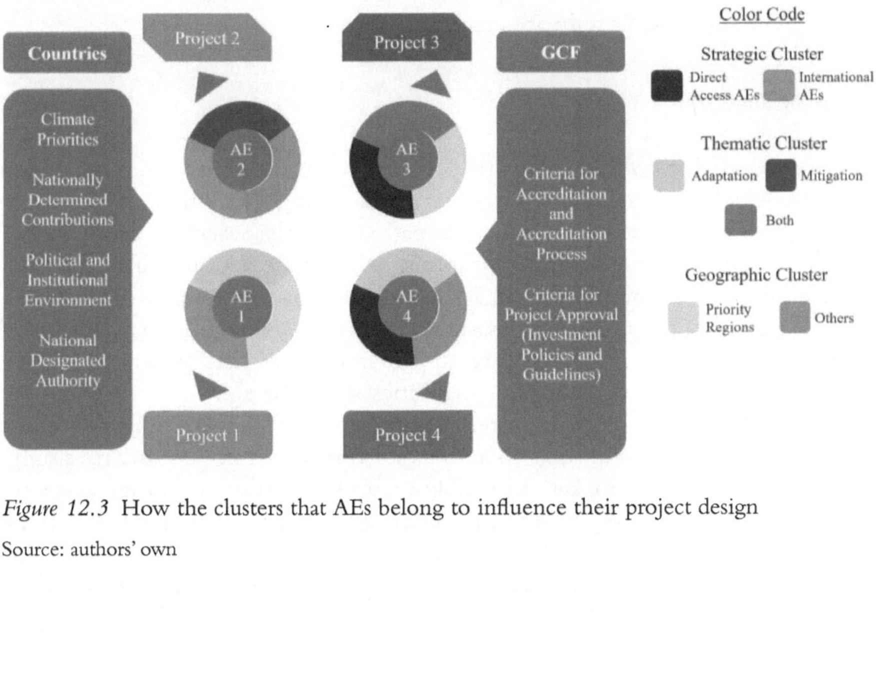

Figure 12.3 How the clusters that AEs belong to influence their project design

Source: authors' own

Discussion

The analysis of the GCF meta-organisation and the cluster pathways offers insights into the influence of GCF on the AEs and the cascading impact on the role of AEs in facilitating climate action in developing countries. Simultaneously, analysing AEs positioning in the three clusters – strategic, thematic, and geographic – offers a deeper understanding of its capabilities and networks, and, consequently, project design, implementation pathways, as well as the unique opportunities and challenges these bring to the project cycles.

How cluster pathways and meta-organisation can shed light on the creation of impactful climate projects

GCF is an organisation that, from its inception, was structured as a meta-organisation. Although it attempts to influence the complex web of organisations it is connected to, GCF has a limited say in the types of projects created by the AEs. Under the country ownership principle, countries' projects are driven by their priorities and needs. Naturally, different priorities between GCF and other actors in its network may lead to conflicts of interest and less efficient outcomes than would otherwise be desirable.

The concept of cluster pathways helps us understand why specific sectors or geographies still do not have projects financed by GCF. It can also help GCF and other organisations committed to combating climate change understand where and what capabilities are needed and the capacity-building activities that must be developed to unlock additional investment and engagement. From this perspective, cluster pathways use GCF as a micro-representation of the broader global climate debate and offer insight into how to increase institutional mobilisation in the fight against climate change.

A case for diversity

Climate change is a complex issue that requires coordinated action on a global scale. No single organisation is capable of managing everything. Creating a meta-organisation offers an important path to catalyse action by bringing disparate actors under a common umbrella. As climate action is initiated and delivered by AEs in countries, if all AEs are similar or have similar capabilities, then the power of the meta-organisation and its clusters decreases significantly.

The more GCF is capable of attracting organisations that belong to different clusters, the larger the pool of capabilities it will be able to leverage when funding new projects. Furthermore, it is more likely that existing organisations will have the needed tools to address local issues. A better understanding of clusters' functioning makes it possible to understand which other types of organisations need to be recruited by GCF as AEs or whether new clusters are needed. It also offers insight into which organisations may be better positioned to either directly implement a specific type of project or support other organisations trying to do so. For example virtually all adaptation projects are being implemented by non-private organisations (either governments, multilateral organisations, or NGOs). Although this is partially attributable to technical barriers and the difficulty of measuring the impact of adaptation projects, it also shows which types of entities are missing from GCF's network and where links should be established in the existing cluster organisation. Ultimately, new strong heterogeneous clusters can emerge with the right capabilities and networks to meet the climate agenda. Helping to bring capacity to players with other characteristics will strengthen GCF's network as a whole.

Improving cooperation and networks

We observed significant cooperation within clusters but not across them through our research. For instance several DAEs reported seeking support from other DAEs in the accreditation process. However, there was no formal mechanism for such information sharing, leading to repetition of the same difficulties experienced by others with accreditation. Most AEs reported that GCF does not formally seek and capture the learning opportunities for AEs.

On the other hand, many IAEs reported frequent collaboration with other IAEs outside the GCF regime. These collaborations allowed them to support other international organisations seeking accreditation, bring more robust expertise in project design, develop strong proposals through shared learning, and use their co-financing strength to attract GCF funding. All these elements have resulted in IAEs securing over 80 per cent of the total GCF funding, despite being 37 per cent of the total. Just 4 IAEs have more projects than all the combined projects of 71 DAEs. What has been less clear, although equally relevant, is how the interactions between the two strategic clusters (DAEs vs IAEs) are taking place. Organically, little collaboration has emerged from these groups, with more intra-group collaboration and capacity-strengthening taking place inside each group.

Although GCF has tried to promote cooperation, it is important to foster other types of informal mechanisms to enhance collaboration. By applying the tool of cluster pathways to GCF, it is possible to identify the overlaps between clusters to find new ways of bolstering capabilities and cooperation. For example this could be done by identifying which DAEs and IAEs are working exclusively on adaptation issues in specific geographies and then encouraging them to co-apply. Using these curated networks to foster collaboration could accelerate the pace at which AEs acquire knowledge and develop stronger projects in geographies that need it most.

Finally, using the existing cluster network to disseminate knowledge, best practices, and lessons learned can also help equip AEs to implement more projects with the greatest impact. Leveraging these sub-networks, such as the International Development Finance Club in the case of IAEs, can help coordinate action towards common goals without demanding that GCF becomes even more stringent with its requirements. Taking GCF from the centre of the cluster network and viewing it as one of the nodes could lessen the additional bureaucracy to get projects off the ground. It is also important to strengthen information sharing among existing clusters instead of information flowing through the GCF meta-organisation.

Conclusion

GCF was created as an entity with a meta-organisation model in mind. Its focus on increasing country ownership and fostering local capacities has shaped the model towards giving significant responsibilities to AEs. By doing so, GCF has generated incentives to create non-geographic clusters. These clusters are not solely made of AEs but comprise a broad set of organisations involved in approving and implementing GCF projects. These clusters, in return, create dynamic pathways to build capabilities that are now strongly influencing project design and implementation.

Through semi-structured interview research, we concluded that three types of clusters emerged within the GCF entities ecosystems – strategic, thematic, and geographic. Entities in the strategic cluster can be divided between DAEs and IAEs, based on the institution's focus (local or global). In this case, it was possible to observe significant cooperation within clusters but little collaboration between them – although this is one of GCF's key objectives. Entities in the thematic clusters focus on adaptation, mitigation, or both types of projects. Difficulties measuring causality and lack of information have hindered additional private sector engagement with adaptation projects and limited GCF disbursements in this area. Finally, organisations in the geographic clusters tend to cooperate closely to bring additional attention to the specific requirements in those regions. However, local barriers have limited more exponential investments and transformational projects locally.

This chapter shows that the interactions within and between clusters in GCF shape capabilities and networks and, in turn, strongly influence project design. The 'cluster pathway' approach offers fresh insight into how the global ecosystem is maturing in the fight against climate change through clusters shaped by the meta-organisation. It highlights the need to rigorously study clusters in global regimes and the type of informal networks that can be leveraged to accelerate the transition to a low-carbon and climate-resilient economy.

Finally, this chapter contributes to the broader literature of clusters and meta-organisations. It does so by demonstrating that some of the weaknesses of meta-organisations in organising collective action can potentially be overcome by adding additional flexibility to the system. Allowing member organisations to self-organise into sub-clusters around their common goals and follow their unique pathways to developing more impactful projects can allow natural sub-networks to emerge. This contribution may help fill some of the gaps left by the loose structures and conflicting interests in meta-organisations.

References

Adger, W. N., Huq, S., Brown, K., Conway, D., & Hulme, M. (2003). Adaptation to climate change in the developing world. *Progress in Development Studies, 3*(3), 179–195.

Ahrne, G., & Brunsson, N. (2005). Organizations and meta-organizations. *Scandinavian Journal of Management, 21*(4), 429–449. https://doi.org/10.1016/j.scaman.2005.09.005

Ahrne, G., Brunsson, N., & Kerwer, D. (2016). The paradox of organizing states: A meta-organization perspective on international organizations. *Journal of International Organizations Studies*, 7(1), 5–24.

Berkowitz, H. (2018). Meta-organizing firms' capabilities for sustainable innovation: A conceptual framework. *Journal of Cleaner Production, 175*, 420–430. https://doi.org/10.1016/j.jclepro.2017.12.028

Berkowitz, H., & Dumez, H. (2016). The concept of meta-organization: Issues for management studies. *European Management Review, 13*(2), 149–156. https://doi.org/10.1111/emre.12076

Bodin, Ö., & Crona, B. I. (2009). The role of social networks in natural resource governance: What relational patterns make a difference? *Global Environmental Change, 19*(3), 366–374. https://doi.org/10.1016/j.gloenvcha.2009.05.002

Cash, D., Adger, N., Berkes, F., Garden, P., Lebel, L., Olsson, P., & Young, O. (2006). Scale and cross-scale dynamics: Governance and information in a multilevel world. *Ecology and Society, 11*(2). https://doi.org/doi:citeulike-article-id:1049380

Chaudhury, A. S. (2020). Role of intermediaries in shaping climate finance in developing countries: Lessons from the green climate fund. *Sustainability, 12*(14), 5507. https://doi.org/10.3390/su12145507

Chaudhury, A. S., Thornton, T. F., Helfgott, A., & Sova, C. (2017). Applying the robust adaptation planning (RAP) framework to Ghana's agricultural climate change adaptation regime. *Sustainability Science*. https://doi.org/10.1007/s11625-017-0462-0

Chaudhury, A. S., Ventresca, M. J., Thornton, T. F., Helfgott, A., Sova, C., Baral, P., Rasheed, T., & Ligthart, J. (2016). Emerging meta-organisations and adaptation to global climate change: Evidence from implementing adaptation in Nepal, Pakistan and Ghana. *Global Environmental Change, 38*, 243–257. https://doi.org/10.1016/j.gloenvcha.2016.03.011

CPI. (2019). *Global landscape of climate finance 2019* (CPI Report). Climate Policy Initiative. www.climatepolicyinitiative.org/wp-content/uploads/2019/11/2019-Global-Landscape-of-Climate-Finance.pdf

Ferraro, F., Etzion, D., & Gehman, J. (2015). Tackling grand challenges pragmatically: Robust action revisited. *Organization Studies*. https://doi.org/10.1177/0170840614563742

Green Climate Fund. (2021). *GCF: Financing climate action*. Green Climate Fund. www.greenclimate.fund/sites/default/files/document/20211026-financing-climate-october-2021.pdf

Gulati, R., Puranam, P., & Tushman, M. (2012). Meta-organization design: Rethinking design in interorganizational and community contexts. *Strategic Management Journal, 33*(6), 571–586. https://doi.org/10.1002/smj.1975

Harris, J. L. (2021). Rethinking cluster evolution: Actors, institutional configurations, and new path development. *Progress in Human Geography, 45*(3), 436–454.

Hassink, R., Isaksen, A., & Trippl, M. (2019). Towards a comprehensive understanding of new regional industrial path development. *Regional Studies, 53*(11), 1636–1645. https://doi.org/10.1080/00343404.2019.1566704

IPCC. (2014). *Summary for policymakers: Climate change 2014: Impacts, adaptation, and vulnerability. Part A: Global and sectoral aspects. Contribution of working group II to the fifth assessment report of the intergovernmental panel on climate change*. Intergovernmental Panel on Climate Change. https://epic.awi.de/id/eprint/37530/1/IPCC_AR5_SYR_Final.pdf

King, G., Keohane, R. O., & Verba, S. (1994). *Designing social inquiry: Scientific inference in qualitative research*. Princeton University Press.

MacKinnon, D., Dawley, S., Pike, A., & Cumbers, A. (2019). Rethinking path creation: A geographical political economy approach. *Economic Geography*, *95*(2), 113–135.

Martin, H., & Martin, R. (2017). Policy capacities for new regional industrial path development: The case of new media and biogas in southern Sweden. *Environment and Planning C: Politics and Space*, *35*(3), 518–536. https://doi.org/10.1177/0263774x16665845

McCann, B. T., & Folta, T. B. (2011). Performance differentials within geographic clusters. *Journal of Business Venturing*, *26*(1), 104–123.

Menzel, M.-P., & Fornahl, D. (2009). Cluster life cycles: Dimensions and rationales of cluster evolution. *Industrial and Corporate Change*, *19*(1), 205–238. https://doi.org/10.1093/icc/dtp036

Miörner, J., & Trippl, M. (2017). Paving the way for new regional industrial paths: Actors and modes of change in Scania's games industry. *European Planning Studies*, *25*(3), 481–497.

Nadegger, M., & Dobusch, L. (this volume). Meta-organisations as drivers for sustainability across tourism clusters in the Alps: A case study of "Alpine Pearls". In E. Lupova-Henry & N. F. Dotti (Eds.), *Designing and managing clusters for sustainability*. Routledge.

Newell, P., Pattberg, P., & Schroeder, H. (2012). Multiactor governance and the environment. *Annual Review of Environment and Resources*, *37*(1), 365–387. https://doi.org/10.1146/annurev-environ-020911-094659

Porac, J. F., Thomas, H., Wilson, F., Paton, D., & Kanfer, A. (1995). Rivalry and the industry model of Scottish knitwear producers. *Administrative Science Quarterly*, *40*(2), 203–227. https://doi.org/10.2307/2393636

Porter, M. E. (1998, November 1). Clusters and the new economics of competition. *Harvard Business Review*. https://hbr.org/1998/11/clusters-and-the-new-economics-of-competition

Powell, W. W., Koput, K. W., & Smith-Doerr, L. (1996). Interorganizational collaboration and the locus of innovation: Networks of learning in biotechnology. *Administrative Science Quarterly*, 116–145.

Ritter, T., & Gemünden, H. G. (2003). Interorganizational relationships and networks: An overview. *Journal of Business Research*, *56*(9), 691–697.

Silverman, D. (2013). *Doing qualitative research: A practical handbook*. SAGE Publications Ltd.

Spillman, L. (2018). Meta-organization matters. *Journal of Management Inquiry*, *27*(1), 16–20. https://doi.org/10.1177/1056492616688856

Wasserman, S. (1994). *Social network analysis: Methods and applications*. Cambridge University Press.

Part 4

Conclusions

13 Conclusions

Evgeniya LUPOVA-HENRY and
Nicola Francesco DOTTI

Clusters as meta-organisations

This edited volume has aimed to conceptualise the role of 'organised' clusters in regional transitions towards sustainability by proposing the meta-organisational perspective. Given clusters' often-considerable weight in the regional economies, their contribution to sustainable (or unsustainable) regional development can be significant. To date, literature has primarily analysed regional clustering within the framework of sustainability transitions as a way to uncover the pre-existing industrial base and explain industry formation as a path-dependent process (Hansen & Coenen, 2015). However, recent research suggests that 'organised' clusters may have agency and the necessary competencies to act deliberately and change regional ecosystems (Lupova-Henry et al., 2021).

Clusters, traditionally defined as geographic concentrations of firms in a particular field (Porter, 1998), are increasingly seen as 'organised' entities rather than merely 'territories' or 'geographical areas'. Indeed, introducing the concept of 'clusters', its uptake in the policymaking circles, and the subsequent rise of the cluster policies have changed the nature of clustering. From 'spontaneous' geographical agglomerations of firms, clusters have become 'organised' entities with formal organisations' attributes (cf. Ahrne & Brunsson, 2011). As such, clusters can be seen as deliberate collective actors within their environments, which have the potential to drive the transformation in their regions or nations.

The contributions to this volume have drawn upon the 'meta-organisational' perspective (Ahrne & Brunsson, 2005; Gulati et al., 2012) to conceptualise the role of clusters as organised collective agents. This perspective suggests that 'organised' clusters can be seen as 'organisations of organisations' (see also Ahrne & Brunsson, 2011). Such clusters can be defined as territorially anchored groups of independent organisations engaging in joint decision-making, pursuing system-level goals and capable of purposive collective action (Lupova-Henry et al., 2021). This perspective recognises the importance of the contextual setting for the evolution of a cluster but, at the same time, attributes agency to clusters implying a two-way relationship between an 'organised' cluster and its environment.

DOI: 10.4324/9781003215066-18

The meta-organisational perspective on clusters brings about a new set of questions at the intersection of the organisation and management fields; policy and governance research; and economic geography, regional, and cluster studies. This volume thus brought together researchers from diverse fields and disciplines to address these questions and bring insight into the role of clusters as collective agents in regional sustainability transitions. The volume has a global overview with cases from Europe and beyond.

Our contribution

This volume's contributions have brought several insights into the relationships between meta-organising and clustering in the framework of sustainability transitions. In Part 1, the contributions conceptualise clusters as responsible actors in sustainability transitions and develop adequate methodological approaches to study clusters through the meta-organisational lens. Part 2 focused on empirical cases that 'zoom into' the process of meta-organising clusters and examine how it drives individual members to transition towards sustainability. Part 3 'zooms out' and inscribes meta-organisations and clusters in a broader context to discuss their influence on and interactions with their environments.

Each chapter within this volume contributes to various literature streams, including sustainability transition literature, clean technologies, social sustainability, and global climate regimes. In this concluding chapter to the volume, we will seek to summarise our key learnings from these contributions. We see two main insights of the meta-organisational perspective on clusters that can be relevant in the framework of regional sustainability transitions: embracing ambiguity and incorporating complexity.

Embracing the ambiguity of complex organisation forms

First, the meta-organisational perspective on clusters allows for embracing the ambiguity inherent in complex organisation forms. By 'ambiguity', we refer to the fact that clusters, seen as meta-organisations, can be understood in at least two ways. First, they can be seen as networks of actors that interact within the meta-organisational framework but remain independent and pursue their own goals. Thus, on the one hand, clusters can provide 'niches' – or protective spaces – allowing divergent behaviours and sustainable innovations to survive before competing in the mainstream regional economic ecosystem. Contributions by Viachka and Duprat (see Chapter 5 in this volume); Saniossian, Beaucourt, Lecocq (see Chapter 6 in this volume); Cappellano and Calavita (see Chapter 7 in this volume); and Viachka (see Chapter 8 in this volume) provide insights into the inner workings of 'organised' clusters and the ways these create conditions conducive to the emergence of sustainable innovations.

Second, meta-organised clusters are actors within their broader environments where members' independent actions will build up to constitute collective agency by a cluster as a meta-organisation. From this point of view, clusters can act as 'ecosystem builders' to shape the regional economic development paths facilitating the adoption of (sustainable) innovations, thus, ultimately supporting sustainable development. Berkowitz and Gadille (Chapter 4 in this volume) set the theoretical grounds for clusters' 'responsible actorhood' with empirical evidence further developed in Part 3. Bor and O'Shea (Chapter 9 in this volume) and Nadegger and Dobusch (Chapter 10 in this volume) investigated the interactions between internal and exogenous dynamics of clusters, while Kutsenko, Ismagulova, and Ivanova (see Chapter 11 in this volume) and Chaudhury and Stecca Douek (Chapter 12 in this volume) place clusters and meta-organisations in broader contexts. The whole Part 3 discussed the ways meta-organisations may leverage collective action to foster sustainability transitions in their broader environments.

While human nature seeks to disentangle, classify, and organise, this ambiguity of the meta-organisational context is something we need to embrace. A cluster, as a meta-organisation, is not easily decomposable into the elements constituting it. Moreover, trying to do so, we may lose the broader view of how collective action is born, and collective actorhood is enacted.

Incorporating complexity in sustainability transitions

This volume's contributions have shown that the meta-organisational perspective on clusters can help incorporate the complexity that is inherent in sustainability transitions. While a 'traditional' view on clusters as competitiveness drivers expects these to follow the 'specialisation' and 'growth' imperatives, the meta-organisational view shifts the perspective towards collective agency and actorhood that can be directed towards a different set of goals. This shift allows broadening both the scope of clusters' activity – not being limited to a narrow industrial code or geographical area – and the types of actors involved. While most literature discussing 'organised' clusters focuses on the role of 'cluster secretariats', the meta-organisational perspective embraces the complexity of collective action. It suggests that a multitude of actors within and outside the cluster contribute to shaping the cluster direction.

Indeed, clusters' ability to (re-)shape regional development paths and steer them towards sustainability may stem from their acting on the boundaries of multiple fields and interacting with actors pursuing different objectives with heterogenous rules. This, however, increases the complexity of clusters' organisational design and may require reconciling multiple perspectives in the absence of a strong hierarchy, as presented in the first part of the volume. Empirical contributions in Parts 2 and 3 have demonstrated the importance of organisational flexibility, allowing members to gather in sub-groups around common sub-goals or sub-projects. Such an approach is necessary for addressing sustainability issues, which is a complex task cutting across different industries and sectors of activity. Indeed, the meta-organisational perspective is valuable specifically for understanding the role of organised clusters in sustainability. As sustainability transitions require large-scale and cross-sectoral changes, clusters have to broaden their scope to involve a variety of actors from multiple interconnected sectors. Thus, holding to the industrial specialisation premise that has been one of the main elements in the 'traditional' understanding of clusters may no longer be sensible.

To sum up, the chapters within this volume contribute to theory by further developing the meta-organisational perspective on clusters and shifting our perception of clusters – from 'geographical areas' to collective agents. This shift aims to correct some potentially risky conceptualisations. Indeed, 'organised' clusters can no longer be seen as purely 'spontaneous' agglomerations of firms and should be perceived as 'organised' entities having the attributes of formal organisations, such as membership and joint decision-making (Ahrne & Brunsson, 2011). This conceptualisation opens the opportunity to conceive them as purposeful entities – that is actors interacting with and shaping their environment to survive.

Future research avenues

The meta-organisational perspective in cluster studies paves the way for a new conceptualisation of clusters as deliberate collective actors. It provides the 'vocabulary' to address the realities of 'organised' clustering. Seeing clusters as deliberate collective actors within their environments can enable them to become the driving force of the transformation in their regions or nations. Moreover, viewing 'organised' clusters as deliberate actors suggests that these can potentially be held responsible for their action or non-action. Thus, seeing 'organised' clusters as deliberate collective actors might be one of the ways to enable them to make more conscious choices, empower them to become the drivers of change, and, at the same time, hold them responsible for their collective decisions.

While the interest in the role of clusters in sustainability has been growing in the literature (cf. De Chiara, 2016; Sedita & Blasi, 2021), the present volume is the first foray into the meta-organisational perspective on clusters and their role in sustainability transitions. The contributions to this volume have brought several insights and opened up many avenues for future research. Specifically, the critical determinants of cluster agency could be further elaborated on through large-scale empirical studies with cross-national and -regional comparisons. These comparisons would bring insight into the influence of 'socio-material entanglements' and their inter-connections with clusters' ability to act collectively towards sustainability transitions. Finally, future research can further explore the role of visions and discourses in clusters' agency by leveraging streams of research such as transition management (e.g. Loorbach et al., 2017) or the 'visioning for sustainability' literature (Broman & Robèrt, 2017; Holmberg & Robèrt, 2000; Quist, 2013; Quist et al., 2011; Vergragt & Quist, 2011). These approaches have received attention in academic and practitioner circles as valuable tools for developing desirable future visions and strategies towards sustainable development.

References

Ahrne, G., & Brunsson, N. (2005). Organizations and meta-organizations. *Scandinavian Journal of Management, 21*(4), 429–449. https://doi.org/10.1016/j.scaman.2005.09.005

Ahrne, G., & Brunsson, N. (2011). Organization outside organizations: The significance of partial organization. *Organization, 18*(1), 83–104. https://doi.org/10.1177/1350508410376256

Berkowitz, H., & Gadille, M. (this volume). Meta-organizing clusters as agents of transformative change through "responsible actorhood". In E. Lupova-Henry & N. F. Dotti (Eds.), *Clusters and sustainable regional development: A meta-organisational approach*. Routledge.

Bor, S., & O'Shea, G. (this volume). The roles of meta-organisations in transitions: Evidence from food packaging transition. In E. Lupova-Henry & N. F. Dotti (Eds.), *Clusters and sustainable regional development: A meta-organisational approach*. Routledge.

Broman, G. I., & Robèrt, K.-H. (2017). A framework for strategic sustainable development. *Journal of Cleaner Production, 140*, 17–31. https://doi.org/10.1016/j.jclepro.2015.10.121

Cappellano, F., & Calavita, N. (this volume). Are North American clusters transitioning to clean technologies? In E. Lupova-Henry & N. F. Dotti (Eds.), *Designing and managing clusters for sustainability*. Routledge.

Chaudhury, A. S., & Stecca Douek, C. (this volume). Meta-organisations and clusters in climate regimes. In E. Lupova-Henry & N. F. Dotti (Eds.), *Designing and managing clusters for sustainability*. Routledge.

De Chiara, A. (2016). *Implementing sustainability strategies in networks and clusters: Principles, tools, and new research outcomes*. Springer.

Gulati, R., Wohlgezogen, F., & Zhelyazkov, P. (2012). The two facets of collaboration: Cooperation and coordination in strategic alliances. *Academy of Management Annals, 6*(1), 531–583. https://doi.org/10.5465/19416520.2012.691646

Hansen, T., & Coenen, L. (2015). The geography of sustainability transitions: Review, synthesis and reflections on an emergent research field. *Environmental Innovation and Societal Transitions, 17*, 92–109. https://doi.org/10.1016/j.eist.2014.11.001

Holmberg, J., & Robèrt, K.-H. (2000). Backcasting: A framework for strategic planning. *International Journal of Sustainable Development & World Ecology*, 7(4), 291–308. https://doi.org/10.1080/13504500009470049

Kutsenko, E., Ismagulova, S., & Ivanova, E. (this volume). Urban super-cluster as a novel approach to clustering in megapolises: The case of Moscow innovation cluster. In E. Lupova-Henry & N. F. Dotti (Eds.), *Designing and managing clusters for sustainability*. Routledge.

Loorbach, D., Frantzeskaki, N., & Avelino, F. (2017). Sustainability transitions research: Transforming science and practice for societal change. *Annual Review of Environment and Resources, 42*(1), 599–626. https://doi.org/10.1146/annurev-environ-102014-021340

Lupova-Henry, E., Blili, S., & Dal Zotto, C. (2021). Clusters as institutional entrepreneurs: Lessons from Russia. *Journal of Innovation and Entrepreneurship, 10*(1), 7. https://doi.org/10.1186/s13731-021-00149-5

Nadegger, M., & Dobusch, L. (this volume). Meta-organisations as drivers for sustainability across tourism clusters in the Alps: A case study of "Alpine Pearls". In E. Lupova-Henry & N. F. Dotti (Eds.), *Designing and managing clusters for sustainability*. Routledge.

Porter, M. E. (1998). Clusters and the new economics of competition. In A. J. Scott (Ed.), *Global city-regions: Trends, theory, policy* (pp. 139–157). Oxford University Press.

Quist, J. N. (2013). Backcasting and scenarios for sustainable technology development. In J. Kauffman & K.-M. Lee (Eds.), *Handbook of sustainable engineering* (pp. 749–771). Springer Netherlands. https://doi.org/10.1007/978-1-4020-8939-8_52

Quist, J. N., Thissen, W., & Vergragt, P. J. (2011). The impact and spin-off of participatory backcasting: From vision to niche. *Technological Forecasting and Social Change*, *78*(5), 883–897. https://doi.org/10.1016/j.techfore.2011.01.011

Saniossian, J., Beaucourt, C., & Lecocq, X. (this volume). Managing social and sustainability issues in a territory through multi-stakeholder meta-organizations. In Lupova-Henry & N. F. Dotti (Eds.), *Clusters and sustainable regional development: A meta-organisational approach*. Routledge.

Sedita, S. R., & Blasi, S. (2021). *Rethinking clusters: Place-based value creation in sustainability transitions*. Springer Nature.

Vergragt, P. J., & Quist, J. (2011). Backcasting for sustainability: Introduction to the special issue. *Technological Forecasting and Social Change*, *78*(5), 747–755. https://doi.org/10.1016/j.techfore.2011.03.010

Viachka, A. (this volume). Clean technology clusters: Meta-organising firms for sustainability. In E. Lupova-Henry & N. F. Dotti (Eds.), *Designing and managing clusters for sustainability*. Routledge.

Viachka, A., & Duprat, L. (this volume). We are all in this together: The significance of meta-organisations for cluster policy. In E. Lupova-Henry & N. F. Dotti (Eds.), *Designing and managing clusters for sustainability*. Routledge.

Index

Note: Page numbers in *italics* indicate a figure and page numbers in **bold** indicate a table on the corresponding page.